SUCCESS
IN MULTI-LEVEL
MARKETING

SUCCESS IN MULTI-LEVEL MARKETING

Gini Graham Scott, Ph.D.

PRENTICE HALL
Englewood Cliffs, New Jersey 07632

Prentice-Hall International (UK) Limited, *London*
Prentice-Hall of Australia Pty. Limited, *Sydney*
Prentice-Hall Canada, Inc., *Toronto*
Prentice-Hall Hispanoamericana, S.A., *Mexico*
Prentice-Hall of India Private Limited, *New Delhi*
Prentice-Hall of Japan, Inc., *Tokyo*
Simon & Schuster Asia Pte. Ltd., *Singapore*
Editora Prentice-Hall do Brasil, Ltda., *Rio de Janeiro*

© 1992 *by*

PRENTICE-HALL, Inc.

Englewood Cliffs, NJ

10 9 8 7 6 5 4 3

Library of Congress Cataloging-in-Publication Data

ISBN 0-13-656315-5

PRENTICE HALL
Business Information & Publishing Division
Englewood Cliffs, NJ 07632
Simon & Schuster, A Paramount Communications Company

Printed in the United States of America

TAMI HOAG

THE BOY

DUTTON

DUTTON
An imprint of Penguin Random House LLC
penguinrandomhouse.com

Previously published in Dutton hardcover, trade paperback, and mass market editions
First Dutton value trade paperback printing: January 2024

Copyright © 2018 by Indelible Ink, Inc.
Penguin supports copyright. Copyright fuels creativity, encourages diverse voices, promotes
free speech, and creates a vibrant culture. Thank you for buying an authorized edition of this
book and for complying with copyright laws by not reproducing, scanning, or distributing
any part of it in any form without permission. You are supporting writers and allowing
Penguin to continue to publish books for every reader.

DUTTON and the D colophon are registered trademarks of Penguin Random House LLC.

THE LIBRARY OF CONGRESS HAS CATALOGUED THE
HARDCOVER EDITION OF THIS BOOK AS FOLLOWS:
Names: Hoag, Tami, author.
Title: The boy : a novel / Tami Hoag.
Description: First edition. | New York : Dutton, [2018] |
Identifiers: LCCN 2018050539 (print) | LCCN 2018052358 (ebook) |
ISBN9781101985403 (ebook) | ISBN 9781101985397 (hardcover)
Subjects: | BISAC: FICTION / Suspense. | FICTION / Mystery & Detective / Police
Procedural. | GSAFD: Suspense fiction. | Mystery fiction.
Classification: LCC PS3558.O333 (ebook) | LCC PS3558.O333 B69 2018 (print) |
DDC 813/.54—dc23
LC record available at https://lccn.loc.gov/2018050539

Printed in the United States of America
1st Printing

BOOK DESIGN BY TIFFANY ESTREICHER

ISBN: 9780593475225

HOW THIS BOOK CAN HELP YOU SUCCEED IN MLM

Multi-level marketing (MLM)—also referred to as network marketing, personal selling, and word-of-mouth marketing—offers unlimited opportunities for those with the right product—and the right selling techniques, combined with perseverance, persistence, and—yes—a bit of being in the right place at the right time. It also offers great flexibility and freedom: You can devote as much or as little time to selling as you want, ranging from a full-time commitment to a few hours a week. And the rewards are proportionate: Those giving it their all can reap the multi-thousand-dollar checks and million-dollar-a-year incomes, while many part-timers average several thousand dollars a month.

You can make of MLM what you will—and another big plus is you can usually start with very little investment—less than $100 in many companies for an introductory sales kit and some product samples—in return for the possibility of making a large income—and doing it as the independent head of your own company.

Today the appeal of MLM seems to be on the rise once again: MLM is a $35 billion industry in sales worldwide with sales of about $9–10 billion annually in the U.S., according to Debbi Ballard, president of the International Multi-Level Consultants, using figures drawn from estimates developed by the Multi-Level Marketing International Associates.[1]

For many, MLM offers a supportive, community-type way of doing business as part of a network, which provides not only money, but friendship, good feelings, and support by positive, motivated, success-oriented people.

The computer and communications revolution has also contributed to MLM's rapid growth today, because these make possible MLM sales networks circling the globe and using instant communications to spread the word. The computer has made it possible to track commissions easily under all sorts of marketing systems, which provide levels of overrides for large groups of people who are part of an ever-growing sales teams.

Success in Multi-Level Marketing is designed to help you become successful in this growing, dynamic industry, no matter what your level of participation and no matter what type of product or service you are selling. It is designed so you can draw from this book what you want to use for your particular program, based on how much time and effort you have to devote to achieving your goals.

If you want to go through the book chapter by chapter, it's designed to be a comprehensive step-by-step guide to mastery in MLM. Or if you prefer, you can pick and choose the chapters that apply most for you. You can also use this as an aid for training your distributors, because the more you help the people in your sales group succeed, the more you do too!

---

[1] Based on these figures, MLM is a major segment of the direct selling industry, whose total figures are $50 billion worldwide and $12 to 15 billion in the U.S.

TABLE OF CONTENTS

Part I

CREATING THE RIGHT ATTITUDE FOR SUCCESS

Chapter 1

HOW TO USE MLM IN YOUR DIRECT SALES PROGRAM

There are four types of direct sales programs that you can pursue:

1. A direct sales company with a network of sales representatives to show the product line,
2. A party plan program with counselors and advisors,
3. A multi-level network or personal marketing company with independent distributors, or
4. Your own entrepreneurial venture.

How does multi-level marketing (MLM) differ from these? And what are its advantages? This chapter will discuss each of these avenues briefly, compare them to other forms of marketing, and then describe the way in which MLM selling works and how it can be an even bigger money-making advantage with the right program and sales techniques.

But, first, let's take a look at how MLM began—and how it has developed into a billion-dollar-a-year industry.

HOW MLM BECAME THE SUCCESSFUL
FORM OF SELLING IT IS

The tradition of MLM selling is actually very old, since it draws on a number of principles of sales and organization that have proved to be very successful. It incorporates the principles of direct selling, which go back to preindustrial times, when a person with a product to sell simply contacted friends and neighbors or set up shop in a temporary market, a bazaar in a public square, or even by the side of a road. Also, it depends on the principles of spreading ideas through personal and social networks, which have tremendous power in changing attitudes and transforming society. Consider how Judaism and Christianity have spread from one person to another within a growing community.

MLM draws on the time-tested principle of the pyramidal organization. For example, military organizations, school systems, and corporations have all flourished using this kind of structure.

MLM emphasizes the power of personal contact and persuasion in selling, where the salesperson becomes much more than just a clerk who rings up sales—someone who may be a teacher, counselor, guide, information broker, helper, and bringer of new ideas as well. The itinerant salesman who traveled from town to town in a small cart during the 1800s in America is part of this personal contact/direct sales tradition.

Later, with the industrial revolution, people in direct sales not only sold their own products but, increasingly, represented larger companies and received a commission on sales. And then, in the 1940s, direct selling took a new twist with the emergence of the first multi-level marketing companies—Nutrilite Systems and Stanley Home Products. The difference was that now, salespeople not only got a commission on the products they sold directly, but they also got a bonus or override for recruiting other people to sell the product. The commission structure applied to more than one level—

hence the term multi-level, which was first used then to refer to this type of selling, though as noted, the development of multi-level structures is very much older.

In the 1950s, Amway and Shaklee contributed a genius for marketing and organization building to the MLM industry, and as a result each developed a massive sales network to market household and health products, respectively. Today, both companies have about 1 million distributors each, and together have about $2 billion in sales. The main strategy used by distributors for these companies includes home meetings, personal demonstrations, and larger business opportunity meetings and rallies. Although the distributors do sell a large number of products at retail, a major concern is recruiting prospects to become part of the sales network, too.

Using a slightly different approach that features party plan demonstrations by a network of well-trained consultants, Mary Kay launched what was to become a multimillion-dollar skin care and cosmetics empire in the 1950s. In this kind of sales program, the distributor works with a host or hostess to set up a sales demonstration and party. Although the distributor may hope to interest some customers in becoming distributors and putting on sales parties, too, the focus is initially on retail sales.

For a time there was some question about the legality of the MLM sales plans, and Amway ended up battling the U.S. government for about a decade. But in a 1979 decision, Amway's multi-level plan got a clean bill of health. Since then, the floodgates have opened, and thousands of new MLM companies have emerged, including some that have become well known, including Forever Living, Herbalife, and Neo-Life, with over 50,000 distributors each.

The key to this legitimacy is that these companies are using the multi-level structure to *retail* products *of value,* which do have a *retail market* for *customers* who want to buy them; they are not just creating sales structures to recruit people who want to make money, where the value of the product or the customer base for it is questionable. In any event, as these MLM and direct sales companies have grown, they have assumed all sorts of forms and adopted all sorts of names, so that the distinctions between which is multi-level or not have become fuzzy indeed. This is the case because some companies that describe themselves as direct sales, party plan, or by other names really do have multi-level structures where distributors do recruit other distributors.

Technically, any company for which a distributor engages in this recruiting might be considered an MLM company—although many companies use other terms or deny the MLM connection because the term *multi-level* has recently gotten mixed up with pyramid schemes, chain letters, and assorted dubious recruiting schemes. For example, the Mary Kay company presents itself as a direct sales or party plan company and claims it is not an MLM company because its marketing plan only goes down two levels. And other firms with plans that pay commissions down several levels describe themselves as "network" or "personal" marketing companies to emphasize the personal interaction that occurs between the distributor, customers, and other distributors in the network.

In fact, the marketing plans of all these companies vary extensively, whatever name they use. But what these companies do share in common is the freedom the distributor has to market the product or service according to his or her personal style. Whether the distributor is called a sales representative for a direct sales company, a sales associate for a party plan company, or a distributor for a multi-level company—and whatever the commission—the basic principle is the same. The individual has considerable latitude in deciding the best way to sell a product or service, subject to company guidelines, and can use a great deal of creativity in using marketing and promotion techniques.

In fact, in MLM and party plan companies, the individual is an independent contractor, essentially a small entrepreneur, who is creating his or her own business with the products of the company he or she represents. And whereas a sales representative for a direct sales company is typically limited to a specific territory, the party plan or MLM distributor can sell wherever he or she wants.

Sales reps and distributors also vary in the amount of time they commit to marketing a product or service. Some do it part time; some full time. Some represent one company; some more than one. Many operate out of their own homes; others set up small offices or distribution centers. Some emphasize sales through personal contact and variously employ one-on-one presentations, sales parties, or opportunity meetings. Others rely much more on mail order or telemarketing techniques. The techniques are almost as varied as the people who practice them.

And the names people are called vary widely, too, depending on the kind of company they represent and the role they play. For example, people may be called counselors, advisors, sales associates, sales representatives, distributors, or any number of other names. But for simplicity I use the terms direct salesperson, sales associate, MLMer, or distributor interchangeably to refer to anyone involved in multi-level direct sales.

HOW THIS BOOK IS ORGANIZED

This book is designed to be a step-by-step guide and to offer an array of success strategies from which you can choose.

Part I begins with a basic introduction to what MLM is and how MLM marketing differs from other types of selling including other types of direct sales techniques. Many people still aren't clear about what a multi-level company is and how it differs from other direct sales companies.

Part I also focuses on how to prepare to sell after you have chosen the company you will represent. It emphasizes the importance of knowing your product, your company, and your marketing plan, and obtaining the sales literature you need.

You'll discover the kind of attitude you need for success in marketing, because this is where success begins—with your outlook and approach. This section also emphasizes the importance of goal setting and persistence to achieve what you want.

Part II covers the diversified techniques for getting customers and distributors. Although some people in direct sales may be interested only in getting customers, others primarily in recruiting and building a sales organization, this book discusses both topics concurrently, since many distributors do both at the same time and both are equally important.

In Part III the techniques for creating and maintaining a successful sales organization are discussed.

Next, Part IV covers some special events that can be useful in making sales and building your organization.

MARKETING DIRECT SALES

The three major categories of marketing are retailing, mail order or direct mail, and direct sales, all of which can be structured to provide for MLM selling.

Retailing: The most common form of marketing today. You go to a store and buy something at retail. In turn, the retailer gets products from one of three sources: a wholesaler or distributor, a sales representative who takes orders for the manufacturer, or directly from the manufacturer.

Mail Order or Direct Mail: In mail order, you purchase something from an ad (usually in a magazine or newspaper, sometimes on TV), which directs you to mail in your payment. In direct mail, you receive a flyer or catalog in the mail and again purchase by mail.

Direct Sales: In direct sales, a representative from the company contacts you personally. This person may be an outside employee for the company, a commissioned salesperson, or an independent entrepreneur distributing the products for one or more companies. He or she may call you on the phone, use a telemarketing system, go door to door, sell to you from a booth at a trade show or consumer fair, organize a sales party for you, or otherwise sell direct.

Types of Direct Sales Programs

There are three major types of direct sales programs, though often there is much overlap in fitting particular programs into these categories. The best rule of thumb is to categorize the company by its primary focus.

Traditional Direct Sales Program: In this program, the person in direct sales works for the company as a sales representative and is usually assigned a limited territory in which to sell the company's products. The individual is usually closely supervised by the company and may even have specific hours to work in the field. He or she may sometimes be supplied leads by the company, too, and can variously call on individuals, organizations, stores, or companies. Normally, the salesperson will only seek to sell to customers and will not aim to recruit others to market the line. However, if the company is large enough, it will have a sales management structure, with sales managers assigned to oversee several salespeople in an area and perhaps some regional or national managers to oversee the local managers. All of these managers will get overrides on the salespeople they supervise and possibly a salary.

Party Plan: In this situation, the salesperson is frequently called a counselor, consultant, advisor, or sales associate, and usually sells by putting on a sales party. He, or more usually she, can sell items such as dishes (Tupperware), cosmetics (Avon and Mary Kay), or more recently, sensual adult products. In some party plan programs, the sales associates are hired directly by the company; in others, the distributor can recruit—usually from among the more interested customers who attend a party. Typically, the sales associate organizes a sales party by finding a willing host or hostess who invites some friends, neighbors, or business associates. Once the party is arranged, the sales associate does the presentation, sells products at the party, and commonly gives the host or hostess a commission, or at least some free gifts or extra discounts. Then, later, the associate will commonly follow up with customers to see if they need more products, might be interested in hosting their own party, or even would like to represent the company.

Entrepreneurial Venture: This kind of program is basically a create-it-yourself opportunity. You buy some product wholesale from a manufacturer or work out arrangements to secure a service wholesale. Then you sell it via direct sales yourself, however you want—to friends, to business associates, at flea markets, for conventions, and so on. You aren't a distributor for another company, since you are marketing these products under your own name, and you have no guidelines from the company to follow on how to market its goods. Essentially, you are free to do as you want.

Multi-Level Marketing

Multi-level marketing (or however it is called—MLM, network marketing, personal marketing, personal selling, etc.) actually draws on other types of marketing since an MLM company is one with a certain kind of marketing and compensation plan involving several levels of group organization and commission payment, and it can use any type of selling methods (such as traditional direct sales, party plan, or mail order). Although any sales method can be adapted to this plan, until recently multi-level marketing has primarily involved direct personal sales. But now more and more MLM distributors are using direct mail, mail order, and TV or cable plugs to promote sales.

The key difference between MLM and other forms of sales is that the multi-level distributor is not only seeking to sell to customers retail, but also is looking for distributors to sell the product or service to others. The multi-level distributor then trains these distributors to find and train others and not only gets a sales commission, bonus, or override when the distributors in his or her sales group make sales, too.

Another distinguishing characteristic of MLM·is that the salesperson, usually called a distributor, sales associate, or consultant, is an independent contractor who may sell anywhere, although he or she is usually subject to company guidelines regarding advertising and the manner in which the product can be sold. (For example, even though the distributor can sell anywhere in the country, certain kinds of places—such as retail stores and trade shows— may be off limits.)

In the past decade, companies have coined all sorts of names to refer to multi-level programs, such as "network marketing" and "personal marketing" because of some concerns over the association of MLM with illegal pyramid schemes, though most recently the trend has reverted to using the term MLM. In any case, there seems to be no real difference between the companies using these names. The main reason for using them seems to be the controversial image surrounding MLM. Many members of the general public still confuse MLM with pyramid schemes and chain letters, and many shady operators are still trying to legitimize illegal pyramids and letters by calling them MLM opportunities. But a wave of prosecutions during the late 1980s appears to have cleared out the worst offenders, so that increasingly, legitimate companies using a multi-level structure are going back to the more descriptive term—multi-level or MLM. But whatever the term used—personal sales, network marketing, word-of-mouth marketing, and so on, they all refer basically to the same thing—MLM.

THE BASICS OF MULTI-LEVEL MARKETING

Multi-level programs have enjoyed a continuing upsurge since the 1980s because MLM offers the possibility of high earnings through the principle of multiplication of effort. You create an organization to market the product or service, and your earnings are based on what the members of your team earn as well as on your own efforts. In turn, when you select a good program and promote it effectively, you can develop an extremely large sales organization, for you help your immediate team members develop their own teams, and their organizations become part of your group.

This organizational building process means that you build your success on the success of others, and you play a crucial role in helping your distributors succeed by teaching them what to do. In short, a key principle of MLM is that you succeed by helping others succeed, too.

Another reason MLM has enjoyed growing popularity is that you are not just selling a product to a customer and going on to make more sales. Instead, you are sharing the product and business opportunity with the distributors you sponsor, and you are teaching them to do the same, so you create a warm, supportive organization to market the product.

You might think of MLM this way: it involves creating a marketing network by sharing a product or service with a few people; then they share it with a few people; then they share it, and so on; until soon there is an ever-growing network of people involved in distributing the product. And the larger your own network grows and the more product your network sells, the more you earn.

HOW MUCH YOU CAN EXPECT TO EARN IN MLM

Currently, some MLM superstars are making $50,000, $100,000, even $200,000 a month in big companies like Amway, Shaklee, and Neo-Life, just as top performers attain big earnings in any industry. And some have become millionaires many times over.

But it is important to realize that making this kind of money takes perseverance, usually full-time effort for a year or more, plus a measure of luck. Also, these top earners represent only a tiny percentage of the millions of MLM distributors.

More generally, people in MLM pursue this as a sideline, spending a few hours a week in order to earn a few hundred or thousand dollars extra a month. According to many MLM experts, it takes about six months to a year for the average person to earn about $1,000 to $2,000 a month working about five to six hours a week. For example, in the early 1980s, when *Multi-Level Marketing News* (no longer published) did a study of its readers, who were probably more active than the average multi-level distributor, it found that the average respondent made about $11,000 a year marketing the products of about four different companies (about $15,000 in today's economy). And today this same pattern prevails for most distributors—it is a part-time supplement to their other job activities.

However, the specific earning picture varies greatly from program to program, since growth patterns differ widely. So to get a better picture of what is typical, ask about what the average and the most active distributors earn in your own program. At the same time, realize that these general industry and specific company averages are only guidelines, for, ultimately, how much you earn is up to you, since you are an independent contractor, your own boss, which means you can work as hard or as little as you want, and wherever you want since there are no territories. But if you want to do well, be prepared for hard work—just as you have to work hard to be successful in almost anything.

From time to time you may run into programs offering to make it very easy for you to do very well by doing very little. For example, in the 1980s, there was a sudden flowering of all sorts of we'll-do-it-for-you programs—usually called national sponsoring programs, clubs, or recruiting services, which offered to do all the work for distributors in return for a membership fee. But in reality, these programs were glorified pyramid schemes that didn't work because they soon ran out of enough new persons to make the program pay off for any but the few on the top. So the point is that MLM, like any form of selling, takes hard work. It's not a guarantee for success.

HOW YOUR INCOME AND
ORGANIZATION GROW IN MLM

In traditional sales programs, income is based on one's personal sales. You get a commission for whatever you sell. But in MLM, your income depends on several factors, besides what you yourself sell—the size of your group, how much product your group purchases and sells, and the size of your commission at each level in your organization. Although some MLM companies distinguish between different types of earnings—such as commissions for your direct sales and bonuses or overrides when people in your sales group sell something—to make the topic easier to talk about, I use these terms interchangeably and usually call everything commissions.

You have to work out the figures yourself for each program, since every marketing plan differs in various respects: the number of levels, the commission rate at each level, the amount of product consumers and distributors are likely to buy, the minimum purchase requirement, if any, to get a commission, and so on.

But the basic principle of building an MLM organization and making it grow and pay off is the same. It works like this.

First, there's just *you* marketing the product. Initially, you may be buying at wholesale and selling some product at retail, which is one way to earn money as well as introduce people to the product who might later become part of your sales team.

But a key principle in MLM is then to start building your organization by locating others to sell the product as soon as you can. You don't want to forget the importance of finding customers and selling the product, because about 90 percent of the people who show any interest in your program will be primarily or only interested in being a customer, not in going into business, and your commissions in a legitimate MLM company come only from product or service sales—not from just recruiting. But then, once you do locate these prospective enthusiastic salespeople, teach them not only to sell the product but to find others to be distributors too. That's how you build an MLM sales team and get your team members to build their own teams, so your organization and your profits from products grow.

The MLM Principle of Multiplication

In typical MLM presentations, you'll hear about the basic theory underlying MLM, which is that your organization grows geometrically through the principle of multiplication. For example, suppose you know two persons, and they know two persons, and they know two, and so on. If this growth pattern continues, your team will look like this if it grows to four levels:

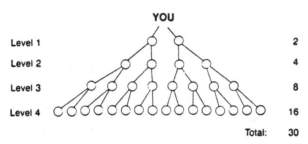

YOU	
Level 1	2
Level 2	4
Level 3	8
Level 4	16
Total:	30

You only knew 2 persons but you have gotten 30 into your organization.

Now suppose you and each of your team members recruited an average of three distributors each. Your growth pattern to the fourth level would look like this:

You
3
9
27
81
―――
120

Now when you add one more person, the growth of your group will theoretically multiply like this:

You	You	You
4	5	6
16	25	36
64	125	216
256	625	1,296
340	780	1,554

Then, by adding your average commission earnings for each person in your organization, you can see what you potentially might earn, at least theoretically. As we shall see, the actual growth of the MLM organization and your earnings are much less precise, though this model does help understand the basic principle of MLM growth. For example, suppose you get an average monthly commission of $10 per person. Your total monthly commission based on the size of your organization might look something like this:

$$120 \text{ persons} \times \$10 = \$ \ 1{,}200$$
$$340 \text{ persons} \times \$10 = \$ \ 3{,}400$$
$$780 \text{ persons} \times \$10 = \$ \ 7{,}800$$
$$1{,}554 \text{ persons} \times \$10 = \$15{,}540$$

Then, if you are able to build an even larger organization, your income potential can increase that much more. Significantly, though—and this is one reason MLM has become so popular—you don't have to sign up the world to build a large group. In fact, you shouldn't. You should focus on working with a few individuals and training them to build a group, too. But they have to be the right people—those who will put the necessary effort into building an organization. You may have to sponsor a dozen, two dozen, three dozen persons to find them. But when you do, the key principle of MLM is to concentrate on helping those few select persons be successful.

In short, an MLM sales program works best when you *build deep, not wide.* If you build wide, you end up spending too much time recruiting new people yourself, and you won't have the time to help your direct recruits learn how to sponsor and teach others. *So the key is to work with a few people and teach them to do what you do.* Then, your organization grows. (If you are going to be explaining MLM to others, you can use Charts 1.1 and 1.2 to help you do this.)

But, in reality, you will have numerous persons in your organization who will perform very differently. For example, you might have one hotshot who brings in ten recruits, another who brings in three, several who do nothing at all, and

**CHART 1.1: HOW YOU MULTIPLY YOUR EFFORTS
IN MULTI-LEVEL**

You and Your Recruits
Share the Program with
an Average of Two Persons

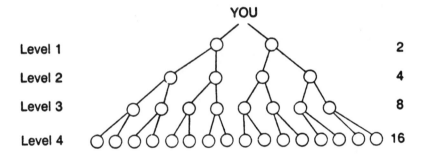

You and Your Recruits
Share the Program with
an Average of Three Persons

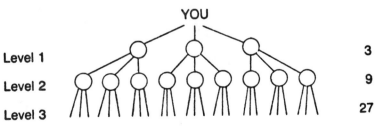

CHART 1.2: BUILDING AN ORGANIZATION—WHAT HAPPENS IF YOU EACH BRING IN AN AVERAGE OF:

	2 PERSONS	3 PERSONS	4 PERSONS	5 PERSONS	6 PERSONS
	YOU	YOU	YOU	YOU	YOU
Level 1	2	3	4	5	6
Level 2	4	9	16	25	36
Level 3	8	27	64	125	216
Level 4	16	81	256	625	1,296
Level 5	32	273	1,024	3,125	7,776
Total	62	393	1,364	3,905	9,330

some who average about four to six each. And they, in turn, will have persons who perform differently. Plus, if your company is set up that way, many people who are really customers only (or almost exclusively) will be on the books as distributors, although in practice they are really just buying and not selling at all. In fact, nine out of ten people under most distributors are not interested in selling at all. Thus, your organization is more likely to look something like this:

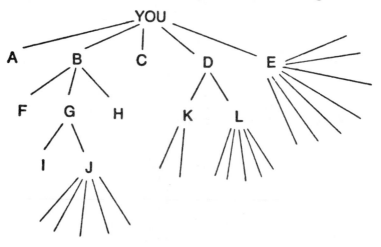

BUT IS MLM A PYRAMID?

Frequently, you'll hear people compare multi-level selling to a pyramid, and certainly, the diagrams just presented· show a pyramid structure. But when people say MLM is a pyramid, they are referring to the illegal pyramid and chain letter schemes that have been repeatedly exposed for the scams they are.

It is important to recognize the crucial differences, so you can point these out to people who make these objections and understand them yourself so you can avoid such schemes yourself and are reassured that the company you represent is perfectly legitimate.

First, multi-level marketing is a legitimate way of moving merchandise. As long as a multi-level company adheres to key guidelines, which your own company may tell you about—such as only paying commissions on products and not sales, permitting product returns of products in good condition within a certain period of purchase for salespeople who drop out, and don't put undue pressure on salespeople to stock up on large quantities of product to increase earnings—a multi-level program is perfectly legal. In fact, some of the biggest companies today are involved in multi-level marketing—either by marketing products themselves with a multi-level sales plan or by supplying products to MLM companies. For example, some of the big corporate names which have been involved in recent years include Beatrice Foods (supplies foods to an MLM company) and Kodak Films (some film products are distributed multi-level). Also, celebrity names have been involved in endorsing MLM products, such as Dick Gregory, who endorsed a Bahaman diet program.

A key difference between an MLM program and an illegal pyramid is that multi-level marketing actually moves a valuable product or service, and all payouts are made for sales of that product or service, not for recruitment. By contrast, an illegal pyramid usually offers no product with any real value, and it operates on the principle of making payments for recruiting others. Even though some kind of product or service may be offered, this usually just serves as a front, since this is not a really valuable product worth the money paid (e.g., a few sheets of paper that claim to be a report on success secrets for $10). So, generally, only money moves through the network created by a pyramid, and no one gets any valuable product in return for the money that is paid.

Two other major differences are that in MLM, consumers do want to purchase the product or service, and then do not have to become distributors to make a purchase. Also, distributors do not have to buy the product to market it, although most do. By contrast, in the pyramid, everyone must join the network to participate.

The differences are also obvious in the results of participation. In a legitimate MLM program, everyone benefits, because consumers get valuable products and services, while those selling them reap rewards for their marketing efforts—and these rewards can be very great because of the team-building multiplication effect. By contrast, a pyramid is a get-rich-quick scheme in which only a few people benefit—the first to get involved. When the inevitable saturation occurs, the people on the bottom of the pyramid run out of new prospects to join the organization and lose money.

In short, like other forms of sales, multi-level marketing provides the basis for building a long-term business which offers a valuable product and good service, while a pyramid scheme produces a few winners and a lot of losers who get hurt because nothing is purchased and only money is passed along. You can see these differences summarized in Chart 1.3.

THE ADVANTAGES OF A MULTI-LEVEL BUSINESS

Direct sales and multi-level businesses have been growing at a rate of about 30 percent annually since the 1980s because these operations have a number of major

CHART 1.3: THE DIFFERENCES BETWEEN MLM AND THE PYRAMID

MULTI-LEVEL MARKETING	THE PYRAMID
A completely legal form of business.	An illegal rip-off scheme.
Based on the principle of sponsoring and teaching others, to help them succeed in an ongoing business.	Based on the principle of getting in first or very early, so one can sign up others and encourage them to do the same.
Involves moving valuable products or services from the producer to the consumer.	Involves moving money from someone on the bottom of the pyramid to someone on top. (Occasionally a product may be offered, but it is usually of little value, and the product is incidental to the emphasis on recruiting people to sign up and give money to someone else.)
Consumers can purchase products and services without getting involved in the marketing program; conversely, those marketing the program do not have to purchase products to market them (though it helps).	Everyone has to join the pyramid to participate; and no valuable products are offered to the consumer. Some pyramid programs do have products, but they are not sold retail, just moved among recruits, and generally no one actually uses the products.
A recognized form of business as long as the company adheres to applicable state laws; in turn, multi-level distributors and companies gain assorted tax benefits from the government.	A get-rich scheme that is regarded as a fraud by the government; participants are thus subject to various fines and punishments.
Those who join the program later can make more than those who joined before them based on their efforts, since there are always new consumers and potential distributors for the program.	Those who join the program later usually make much less and eventually lose money, because, after a while, the market becomes saturated or the scheme is exposed for what it is.

21

advantages for the person who wants to start a business. Most of these advantages exist in any form of direct sales while some are true of MLM businesses in particular. These key MLM advantages are summarized as follows:

1. *If you are already using the product as a consumer, you get extra savings as a distributor or sales rep,* because you can purchase the product at wholesale.

2. *You get to use and sell a better quality product at a lower price.* Since the direct sales or MLM company has a team of independent businesspersons marketing and promoting the product, it doesn't have to do as much advertising and promoting itself. As a result, it can spend that money on the product itself or on the commissions it pays to those in the field.

3. *You are in business for yourself and have the freedom and tax advantages that go with this.* You can choose your own hours and decide how much time you want to devote to the business. Also, you can use the business as a tax shelter to reduce your taxes on your income because your business makes many things you have deductible—such as the part of your home and equipment used in your business. In turn, such deductions can be quite valuable. For example, if you are in a 25 percent tax bracket, you are spending about three months of the year working for the government just to pay taxes. But by having your own business, you can get back some or most of this, so you are spending these months working for yourself.

4. *You can go into an MLM business for very little money—usually less than $100.* And, in return, the income potential can be quite high. By contrast, in most businesses, the start-up costs are tremendous, while the risks are high. Back in the early 1980s, *Multi-Level Marketing News* did a

survey of typical costs involved in launching a small retail business and found the costs ranged from $7,000 to $30,000 at the low end (to start a travel agency, $7,000 to $24,000; a barbershop, $15,000 to $25,000; a plant store, $11,000 to $24,000) to $50,000 or $100,000 or even more for other kinds of businesses. Add about 40 percent to translate into today's prices. (For example, it costs $60,000 to $100,000 to start a camera shop, $50,000 to $60,000 for a hardware store, $50,000 to $100,000 for a medium-sized restaurant.) Then, if you look at the failure rate, you'll see that 60 to 80 percent fail within five years, according to statistics from the Small Business Administration.

The franchise boom, which started in the late 1940s, occurred because franchising offered a way to reduce the failure rate, by providing franchise holders with a proven formula for success and training. And franchising has proved to be an extremely successful way to step into a growing business of your own. However, you still need high levels of capital. (For example, a McDonald's franchise costs over $100,000.) But in a good MLM company, you get both the training and the opportunity to use the company name for a minimal investment.

5. *There is little overhead, because you can run an MLM business from your home.*

6. *You are not required to stock any inventory, though you should have some inventory on hand, if only for samples.* In most sales businesses, you have to have an extensive inventory, and if something doesn't sell, you're stuck with it. But in most MLM companies today, distributors can deal direct with the company. So you just need enough product to supply your retail customers and new distributors who need samples. Then, they can order direct from the company, and the company computer will

credit you with a commission for any sales made by people in your organization.

7. *You have no territorial restrictions in MLM companies.* With no restrictions, you can sell the product anywhere. In most sales positions and in a franchise you are limited to a certain area.

8. *In MLM companies, you can expand your earnings based on what others in your group do.* In traditional retail, direct sales, and franchise operations, you are limited to what you or your own store sell. But in MLM your earning potential can expand exponentially, because you can build a large, growing organization that makes money for you.

9. *You offer personal service to customers, and today, that's a real plus.* In this age of discount house, department store, and catalog showroom shopping, customers can easily feel like just a number; and typically, store clerks don't know much about the product—just what it says on the box. But you can provide personal service. Moreover, yours is one of the few businesses today that can offer to bring the product to the customer.

10. *An MLM business is ideal for a couple or a family since it can be based in the home, and working together can bring everyone closer together, too.*

11. *The business provides an opportunity for fun, travel, new friends, and positive learning experiences*—and you can probably think of other advantages.

So, with all these advantages, it's not surprising MLM is one of the fastest-growing forms of business today.

BUT IS MULTI-LEVEL MARKETING SELLING?

Some people try to claim multi-level marketing isn't selling and describe it as "sharing," since an essential part of it is sharing, teaching, and sponsoring, and "selling" has acquired some negative connotations in our culture. People associate selling with fast-buck operators, with high-pressure salesmen, with sales hype that turns a product message into pure puffery, and with the act of convincing someone to buy something he or she does not need or want, or can't afford. But these kinds of scams and manipulatives are simply abuses, and selling is a perfectly respectable, honorable calling.

In fact, the most successful salespeople know that effective selling involves responding to real needs and real desires by providing a valuable service or supplying a product that answers those needs and wants. Such sales-people are true judges. For example, top sales and market-ing executives like John Sculley of Apple Computers clear over $2 million in compensation today.

Thus, there is nothing wrong with being in sales, and no reason to make MLM sound as if it isn't sales when telling people about it. Of course it is selling. An essential part of it is sharing, teaching, and sponsoring. But in the end, a product or service is sold, too.

Sometimes, MLM people try to recruit others by claim-ing that they aren't involved in selling, because many persons feel they can't sell anything, regardless of their opinion of the selling profession. They believe it takes a special kind of per-son to sell something, and when they hear about any kind of marketing, they think, "Oh, no, I can't do that. I don't know how to sell." Or they think, "I don't feel right about selling something to my friends."

But these people are wrong on two counts:

1. We are all salespeople to some degree. *We* are always selling ourselves, even if we do not think so. When we apply for a job, we have to sell ourselves to our prospective em-ployer. When we hire people, we have to sell them on the advantages of working for us or our company. And even when we meet people, we are in effect *selling* them on the fact that we are a nice person to know. And they are selling us the same thing. Similarly, if we ask someone to do something for

us, go with us somewhere, go out on a date, listen to a new idea, whatever—all that is selling of some form. Our action may not involve directly moving a product or service, but we are selling someone on something—on us, on participating in some activity, on feeling a certain way.

2. When people think about selling, they are often thinking about the negative, high-pressure aspects of selling a product no one wants. But another way to think of selling is to view it as a means of giving information and sharing an opportunity that will bring someone a valuable benefit.

Thus, this form of marketing definitely involves selling but involves sharing, teaching, and sponsoring, too. Selling is just the final step. After sharing the message, you persuade or sell people on the benefits of the program. Then, you sponsor and teach them how to share the message and sell others. And there's nothing wrong with doing this—we sell ourselves to others all the time.

You may want to emphasize the sharing and teaching aspects of marketing to a person who initially resists the idea of selling when you present your program as a business opportunity. But, yes, MLM is selling—and that's perfectly fine.

Chapter 2

GETTING PREPARED: TIPS ON THOROUGHLY UNDERSTANDING YOUR PRODUCT AND COMPANY

Once you have chosen the products and company you want to represent and are convinced they are good, the next step is getting prepared.

The key is to know your product and your company thoroughly. Also, in seeking people for your sales team, you need to be completely knowledgeable about the company's marketing plan. Then, whether you are selling to customers or potential prospects for new distributors, you want to know how to give a solid, professional presentation and answer any questions that are likely to come up. Plus, you want to obtain the necessary sales literature to buttress what you say.

Learn as much as you can in the beginning to get started on the right foot. Then, keep learning all you can as you go along. The more knowledgeable you are, the more professional your presentation, the more effective you will be.

To get this information, read all you can about the product and the company. Sit down with your MLM sponsor or sales leader and ask him or her to go into the program in depth. Also, go to at least one, or preferably more, product demonstrations or opportunity meetings, so you feel solid about the program. These activities are valuable, too, because they will connect you with others marketing the product and will help you feel more motivated, excited, and inspired to get out and market it.

There are three main areas where you should be prepared to give information and have the necessary sales literature to back you up. These are (1) product information, (2) company information, and for recruiting a sales group, (3) marketing plan information.

KNOWING YOUR PRODUCT

You must know much more about the product than if you were just a user, and you must be able to translate this knowledge into a brief product description that makes the product appeal to what the potential customer wants and needs.

To be convincing and persuasive, you must fully understand and stress three main points about the product: (1) its major selling *features*, (2) the *benefits* of purchasing the product because it has these features, and (3) the advantages of this product over the competition.

You should know this information for each product in the line and be able to talk about the features, benefits, and competitive advantages of the product line, brand name, or company, as a whole. If you can draw on your own experience of using the products in making these points, this certainly helps.

But whether you use the products or not, learn about their unique features and how these benefit the user so you can make your sales presentation accordingly. These features include product characteristics such as:

- the nature of the product and what it does (for example, tastes better, looks better, works better)
- the price of the product (for example, it has a lower cost)

- the quality of the materials used (such as it is of higher quality)
- the service offered with the product (for example, the customer will receive better maintenance or special training in using the product)

Once you know product features, think about how these product features translate into user benefits. For example, a diet product has the *feature* of having fewer calories and less fat. But the selling *benefit* is that the reduced calories and fat will take off pounds which will make you thinner and healthier and improve your appearance.

Also, acquire any backup technical knowledge needed to enable you to explain why the product works as it does or has other features and benefits. This information is particularly important if you are marketing a line of high-technology products, food, diet programs, or drug products, where people are likely to ask questions. When they do start probing, it's not good enough to say, "I started using this product, and I lost five pounds and never felt better." This may satisfy some people. But you have to be able to explain about the ingredients, for example, if someone wants more detailed information.

Finally, become familiar with the competition. Try out some of your competitor's products to learn how they are similar and different and to see how their features and benefits compare. Perhaps sit in on one of your competitor's product demonstrations or opportunity meetings to see what their distributors say.

Sometimes, your company or sponsor may be reluctant for you to investigate the competition, because they are afraid you may get recruited away. However, if your product is good or better and you are really committed to it, that shouldn't happen. Also, when you know about the competition, this enables you to say that you have made an informed choice in deciding to promote your product or service, which helps to give you credibility when you market it. At the same time, this gives you more assurance because you have made your choice based on a full knowledge of the field, and you can knowledgeably tell others about the differences.

Even if there are relatively few product differences, you may have other valid reasons for selecting that product (such as liking the company better or getting more local support). When you are informed, you can most effectively pitch these advantages, because you know what your product offers relative to the competition.

KNOWING YOUR COMPANY

Besides knowing about its products, you should also be knowledgeable about the organization and management of any company you represent. You should have gained some of this information when you were deciding what products or services to market, and now you should make yourself even more familiar with the company so you can convincingly talk about it to others.

You can get much of this information from company literature, but if you truly get serious about the product line, a visit to company headquarters might be in order. Meet the management personally and look over their offices. Take a tour through their factory. You'll feel more solid about the company, and you will convey this confidence to your customers and to anyone on your sales team.

Some of the key areas to investigate include:

- Who are the company officers? What kind of professional background do they have? What is their track record in other business ventures, if any?
- How long has the company been in business?
- What is the company's sales volume? How fast is its sales volume growing?
- How many distributors does the company have now?
- How fast is its distributor network growing?
- How prepared is the company to handle growth?

- How open is the company to making information available about itself and its officers?
- Is the company a member of professional or trade associations in its field? Is it listed with local business agencies, such as the Chamber of Commerce and Better Business Bureau? And if so, what is its record?
- Has the company filed the necessary business and legal documents to do business in the states where it is operating?
- How has the company arranged to handle its computer records? (Some use a computer service; some keep track of computer records internally.) Does the company have a good record for paying out commissions accurately and on time?

KNOWING YOUR MARKETING PLAN

If you are seeking others to join your sales network, be fully familiar with your company's marketing plan, so you can convincingly present the business opportunity. First, study the descriptive material offered by your company, and review additional materials prepared by your sponsor or others working with you in marketing the product line. Know what the commissions and bonuses are on sales by you and others in your sales network, and know if your company has purchase volumes, minimum requirements, breakaway bonuses, or other special payment incentives.

Then work out some scenarios to show what you and your sales group are likely to make, given certain assumptions about your success in recruiting new active distributors and the amount of product moved by each distributor. Sometimes your sales group leader or sponsor may already have developed some projections, but you may have to work out these scenarios yourself.

Due to current postal regulations and various state laws, companies are not permitted to create extended projections, since the authorities have ruled it is misleading to suggest hypothetical earnings. Companies can only show the basic structure of the plan and how these might translate into earnings for a few representative levels. Or they may publish the average earnings of an average distributor. However, if you are dynamic and promote the product line successfully, you will make much more than the conservative estimates and projections now used by MLM companies to comply with the laws.

So think about the possibilities, and write out or review these projections to gain a firmer sense of how you will make money with your product and how much you can make. To avoid any legal problems, don't mail these extended projections to prospective recruits. But you can use them to go over the program with people on a one-on-one basis. Still, be sure to emphasize that any projections are only hypothetical, not necessarily what any particular person will earn.

Some key points to know about your marketing plan include the following:

- What is the commission for direct sales? What are the commissions, bonuses, or overrides at each level?

- What kind of purchase volumes or minimums are necessary each month to get a bonus? to remain an active distributor?

- How many first-line distributors are necessary to get a commission from your group's efforts? (Some companies may require a certain number of people at your first level or require you to recruit one new person a month, sometimes up to a certain number or group size for you to get these performance bonuses.)

- How large must your organization be before you qualify for extra commissions or leadership bonuses? How much volume must your sales organizations do before the company pays out extra commissions or leadership bonuses?

- How much commission money is the company paying out to its sales force, assuming it pays out commissions to active distributors on all levels?

You may be able to find some of these answers from company literature or from your group leader or sponsor. If not, try to work out the answers yourself. Some answers may not be that easy to find, since some marketing plans are extremely complex and hard to decipher, so you may need a computer to understand what is being paid out to whom. But do what you can to get the full picture.

This way, you not only can give a more knowledgeable, convincing presentation, but you have a better idea of what to do to achieve a certain income goal. (For example, to make $3,000 a month, you realize you need about three hundred distributors in your sales group doing a volume of about $100 a month each.) Also, you better understand how to work with your organization because you know how the payouts for sales are distributed.

Since companies distribute the percentages paid out in commissions and bonuses in very different ways, these differences suggest different ways to proceed. For example, if you are marketing products for a company with a simple 7 percent down five levels plan, the earnings picture is relatively straightforward, and the earnings potential of each distributor for you is about the same. But if your company offers 1 percent on the first level, 33 percent on the second level, and 12 percent, 6 percent, and 3 percent respectively on the third, fourth, and fifth levels, as one company has, this encourages distributors to put new recruits under their first-level sign-ups.

It is also important to understand the marketing plan fully, so you can field questions like: How does the company make money? If the company seems to be paying out too much, people tend to get suspicious, and the company may be on shaky ground eventually, too.

Remember, when a company with a network or MLM sales program is new, it will only be paying out about 25 percent of its compensation plan, since its first distributors are only starting to build their organizations. But as the company grows and its distributor ranks fill out, it starts to pay out more—probably 50 percent by the end of its first six months to a year, and then perhaps 75 to 80 percent or so after that.

Since most distributor networks do not fill out completely, the company will generally never make full payouts.

In any event, the company's marketing plan should be realistic, and you should be able to show others how this is so. So work out the percentages to indicate how much your company pays under various conditions, or get this information from your group leader or sponsor. Normally, companies pay out about 35 to 60 percent to their sales force, and if the company appears to be paying any more or less, you should be able to explain this.

Finally, be able to answer questions about how the company's marketing plan complies with local and federal laws that affect multi-level marketing. You want to be able to assure people knowledgeably that the plan is reasonable and legitimate.

OBTAINING SALES LITERATURE

Make sure you have the necessary sales literature to back you up. Most good companies provide good quality literature, including full-color brochures. Or if you are launching your own product line, write your own. It is important to have this kind of material if you want to present your product or service in a good light and show that the company behind it is a successful, quality organization, too.

When a company is first starting, there may be some delays in getting this literature, and you may want to improvise by developing your own material or getting some distributor-produced literature from your group leader or sponsor if the company permits this (though be careful to conform to company guidelines when you get creative). Normally, though, the company will produce its own basic literature supply and will not allow distributors to produce their own material—unless approved by the company—to avoid misstatements and inappropriate claims.

Chapter 3

STAYING ON THE PATH TO SUCCESS: THE IMPORTANCE OF PERSISTENCE

To be successful, you must persist. The going may not always be easy, but you need to reaffirm your goals continually, repeat personal affirmations, accept the obstacles that come as challenges and learning experiences, and move on.

Now and then you may read of someone's instant success. Say someone wins the lottery or a contest entry is drawn giving that person millions. But mostly, success doesn't come as a fluke. Instead, in the ordinary course of things, you must be prepared for some solid hard work to achieve your ends.

So don't let skeptics discourage you. Many may just be lazy and unmotivated themselves, and they see your possible success as a threat to their own lack of goals, or they feel badly because when someone does well, that's a reminder they are not doing so. In the beginning, some of the worst skeptics may be friends and relatives who are used to seeing you as a certain kind of person. So they may not be ready, able, or willing to see you in the new role you want for yourself. Or they may not be interested in changing their own way of life and may feel your relationship with them is threatened if you change.

ASSOCIATE WITH SUCCESS-ORIENTED PEOPLE

It's crucial to associate with people who believe as you do. In *The Joy of Reaching the Top,* Dr. Dan Ford describes how persons tend continually to fall or rise to their own level wherever they may be. He met three men in Chicago who were going to move to Los Angeles. One was earning $100 a week as a dishwasher, another, about $200 a week as a factory worker, and a third, $1,000 a week as a salesman. When he saw them three months later in Los Angeles, they were doing and making about the same thing. The point of his story is that people tend to get into ruts and stay comfortable doing what they have done before, because change is uncomfortable. Likewise, there are many people who just talk or dream about what they would like to do but never do anything to make it happen.

Thus, when you are headed for the top, you must be willing to change to get there, and that may mean having to leave some individuals behind. You can offer them the opportunity to join you. But if they don't want to change, that's their privilege; you can't make them. And you may need to disconnect from them if they don't, because remaining close to these persons can hold you back because their contrary attitude toward yours can be discouraging or cause you to lose your motivation. Then, too, if they are critical of what you want to do, that can be even worse, since they may undermine your own confidence.

So to be successful, associate with successful people. Even if you are not quite where you want to be yet, join groups and participate in activities with those who are successful or want to be.

And when you do experience other's success, appreciate it, savor it, learn from it, and don't let feelings of envy or jealousy get you down because you feel you aren't doing enough yourself. Remember, you are on your own path: you have your own timetable for success, so you shouldn't let anyone else's success diminish yours. Moreover, remind yourself that most of these people worked hard to get where they are and are working just as hard to stay there. So they deserve the rewards of their hard work. Moreover, recognize that you will soon be in this position too if you follow their example.

Thus, stick around these people and use them as models. Talk to them about how they made it. Learn from them. Observe how they dress. Notice how they talk. And be aware that most of them are upbeat, positive, active, go-for-it individuals. Also, ask for their suggestions on other people you can contact who might help you, too. Successful people can help you succeed if you let them.

Conversely, avoid being around negative persons as much as you can. You may not be able to do so entirely. There may be a crank at work who complains all the time. Your mother may call you frequently to tell you about the latest problems of the relatives. Your seatmate on a plane or a guest at a party may start pouring out his or her troubles to you.

But as much as possible, cut down on your negative contacts or turn them into positive ones. For example, when the complainer at work starts to complain, you can rightly say you have another important task to do. You can tell your mother you don't want to hear about all the problems— instead, you'd like to hear about the good things that happened to family members. Or tell your complaining seatmate politely that you'd like to relax. And if someone at a party revels in the negative, you can graciously move away.

In short, to stay upbeat and positive, stay around upbeat, positive persons, who leave you feeling motivated, self-confident, and good.

TECHNIQUES TO KEEP YOURSELF MOTIVATED

When you're working toward success, keeping yourself continually motivated is necessary so you will keep on working enthusiastically toward your goal. Some strategies to use include the following.

Give Yourself Material Rewards.   Set yourself a goal, and when you achieve it, give yourself a reward. Or if you feel down, reward yourself to experience a lift. Even something small can have a motivating effect. Symbolically, you're telling yourself "I'm worth it" or "I can do it."

Put Up Pictures or Photographs of Objects You Want. Make a want book or want list. Then, look at this book or list from time to time, and visualize yourself getting the desired objects and using them. These objects can be very useful reminders to keep you going to achieve your goal. Also, thinking about what you want helps to plant the vision of having it in your subconscious.

Compete with Yourself.   Many successful people set their own personal goals and don't worry about what others are doing. The advantage of this approach is that you work on realizing your own potential and are not held back by a concern with what everyone else is doing. Remember, everyone has his or her own plan or purpose, and to be successful, you should focus on achieving your own goals.

Review the Success of Others.   Read the biographies of successful men and women. Notice the obstacles they had to overcome and the techniques they used to attain success. You will be able to identify with the experiences of many of these people, and their efforts to gain their goal will inspire you to work toward your own. Also, their stories will give you models to emulate and ideas you can apply in your own efforts toward success. While supersuccessful salespeople might serve as one model (such as the insurance man who made the million-dollar-a-year roundtable or the distributor who made $100,000 on his last month's check), the models you choose can come from any field where they are a success. So artists, writers, financiers, public leaders, top-flight teachers—just about anyone who has gained the top in anything—can be a source of inspiration to you.

Motivate Yourself by Motivating Others.   People who teach or lead others know this principle works. They may not feel like teaching or leading that day, but they must do it. Then, as they perform in that role, the excitement and enthusiasm of others wears off on them, and soon they are feeling motivated again. So, find ways to motivate others to perform, and you'll find these efforts are self-motivating, too.

Start now! Don't wait. The sooner you act, the sooner you'll reach your success goals. And if you procrastinate, you may find one excuse after another so as not to begin: "I'm not ready," "I need more information," "I have to think about things for a while."

Sometimes, of course, it is necessary to weigh alternatives and make decisions. But watch that these concerns don't become excuses that interfere with action, because you'll never be as ready as you would like to be or have as much information as you want. In addition, you can always weigh more alternatives.

However, you can learn more and improve your decision-making abilities as you act and just like actors find, when you start acting, any stage fright you feel before doing so goes away. So if you need to do so, take some time to make a reasoned decision about what to do. But then, act! Go for it! You may be nervous. You may make some mistakes. But we learn through acting, and the nervousness goes away. So make a decision and do it now! Or affirm you have become the person you want to become.

Doing so can help you succeed because it accomplishes two things. First, you remind yourself of your goals and so remotivate yourself to achieve. Second, by seeing yourself as having already achieved these goals, you put that thought into your subconscious or reinforce thoughts about this that are already there. Then, since your subconscious has power to actualize what is deeply etched in thought, your thoughts will eventually be manifested in action, if you think them long and hard enough.

Whatever your success goals, concentrate on their coming to pass. To affirm them, write them down and review them—at least twice a day—and when you do, say them over and over to yourself. Get relaxed, close your eyes, and visualize yourself as you want to be. Visualize having attained what you want. And most important, imagine that your success is happening now! You have achieved it and are experiencing and living it now! This way you imagine and affirm your success the way you want it to be.

Two ideal times to do this are in the morning when you wake up and at night before you go to bed. These are normally quiet times when you can be alone, and at these times, your subconscious is particularly receptive, for you can put aside the cares of the day and relax.

In fact, you can make this a very special time to reinforce the reality you are creating with your mind. For example, you might go to a special place or sit in a special chair when you imagine your success. Perhaps to create a more intense, contemplative mood, you might light a candle or turn on some soft music. Then, whatever setting you create, devote five to ten minutes to making affirmations actively and seeing your goal accomplished.

Also, you might try making affirmations with members of your sales team, since the group effort will provide further reinforcement for each of you, as well as bring you closer together to create a better functioning team. One way to do these group affirmations is to set aside a small part of a group meeting for this purpose. Then ask everyone to relax, close their eyes, and imagine having attained a personal goal.

Another way to use affirmations, if you are artistically inclined, is to draw some pictures of yourself achieving the goal you want. Or you might create a collage from magazine photos. Then, as you draw or look at these pictures later, the images will reinforce your conviction you are going to achieve your goal.

Some Examples of Affirmations:

I draw success, abundance, and good things to me.

I surround myself with wonderful, beautiful, successful people.

My life is filled with complete abundance. I have everything I want or need.

I am living the full life I want. I have a wonderful family, a beautiful home, the car I have always wanted, and I can travel whenever and wherever I want.

I have a winning, persuasive personality, and when I eagerly tell people about my business, they are eager to participate, too.

I am strong, powerful, and have absolute control over my life. I have attained my goal of making $100,000 a year in running my own business.

THINGS TO DO TO FEEL POSITIVE

There are a number of specific actions you can take to help you feel up again. Since different actions work for different people, use the ones that feel most suitable for you.

- *Put up positive reminders around your house, and walk around the house to look at them so you feel better.* For example, you might make up some posters that say something like this:

**WINNERS NEVER QUIT . . .
AND QUITTERS NEVER WIN**

**WHEN YOU'RE DOWN YOU'RE NOT OUT,
UNLESS YOU THINK YOU ARE**

**THERE ARE NO FAILURES . . .
JUST TEMPORARY DEFEATS**

- *Review your affirmations or goals.* Visualize yourself attaining them now.
- *Take a break from whatever you are doing,* and do something you usually like to do (for example, play tennis, go to a movie, call a friend).

- *Read an inspiring book* (such as a book on how some-one became successful).
- *Participate in an exercise designed to make you feel positive.* Here are two possibilities:
  - *A Meditation Exercise.* Sit down in a comfortable position; then visualize a column of positive energy flowing into your feet and up your legs to the bottom of your spine. Then, see it flowing up your spine. At the same time, visualize a second column of positive energy flowing in through your forehead and down your head and neck to the top of your spine. Then, this energy starts swirling around your spine and goes down. Notice the two columns of energy swirling about—one swirling up your spine, the other down, until they meet in the center to form a positive, vibrating ball of energy. Experience that feeling for several minutes, and then, feeling infused by this energy, open your eyes, get up, and direct your energy into any activity you want to engage in now.
  - *A Physical Exercise.* Stand up with your feet solidly on the ground. Then rapidly lift your right arm (or left arm if you are left handed) up and down, and each time your arm comes down, say with conviction, "I am positive . . . I am positive . . . I am positive." Or say, "I feel joy . . . I feel joy . . . I feel joy." Or something like that.

Chapter 4

SETTING YOUR
GOALS FOR SUCCESS

To succeed, you need a clear picture of where you are going and what you need to do to get there. Napoleon Hill, who specialized in studying success, has stated that "a definite purpose is the starting point of all achievement," and that's true in any kind of marketing. *You have to know what you want and how you're going to get it.*

Additionally, you must do more than just imagine it in general terms.

- Form a very specific, clear picture of what you want.
- Determine what you need to get there.
- Develop a plan of action.
- Obtain the tools, techniques, or personnel you need to put that plan in action.
- Set the date for achieving it.
- Begin at once.

You should be flexible, so you can modify the plan as needed. But always keep your purpose in mind.

Napoleon Hill has six basic principles of goal setting which can be readily applied to success in marketing your own product. Here's how his six basic steps apply:

1. *Fix in your mind your definite purpose or goal.* This way you have something concrete to work for. Also, determine your higher purpose, overall direction, or reason for being which provides an underlying rationale for wanting to achieve your goals. This way you can better put your goals in perspective. Also, knowing your purpose helps you keep on the path to achieving your goals. For example, higher purpose might be something like, "I want to be able to contribute to the betterment of society," or "I want to be able to express my creative abilities." Your major goal then becomes a means to achieving this higher end.

2. *Determine what you are willing to give up to achieve your goal.* Everything in life has its price, and achieving success does too. You may have to take time from your friends and family, take courses to learn key techniques, give up activities you enjoy to have time to work on your goal. Whatever it takes, you must be willing to pay the price, and you must be clear what this price is for you.

3. *Establish a definite date when you want to achieve your goal.* If necessary, give yourself more time, but establish a date now. This sparks you with a sense of urgency. You're not just dreaming about some far-off idea. You know you have to go after it now.

4. *Create a definite plan to go after your major purpose, and begin at once, even if you don't feel ready.* Your plan should list the specific steps you expect to take and when. Your goal may be long term—for example: "I want to have a sales volume of $50,000 and be earning $5,000 a month by January 1992." But you must figure out how to develop the necessary sales organization and keep your people motivated to produce the product volume you need to achieve those earnings.

5. *Write out a clear statement of what you want and your plan for achieving it.* You should put all of the steps of your plan in writing, such as in the planning guide described in the next section. Also, include in your plan some way to measure your progress to see how well you are doing as you go along.

6. *Read your written statement aloud in the morning and before you go to bed, and as you say it, see yourself in possession of that goal.* This way you remind yourself of your goal and experience yourself having achieved it, so your goal and your hope of achieving it seem real. As Emile Coué once said: "What the mind can conceive, the mind can achieve." So imagine repeatedly what you want to make it real, and your active imagination will attract to you what you need.

CREATING YOUR ACTION PLAN
TO ACHIEVE YOUR GOALS

The way to turn these basic principles into action in marketing is to create a detailed sales plan with the numbers worked out so you have a best estimate of how much you need to do to make your goals become a reality, whether you are selling these products yourself or building a sales group to work with you. The following four steps will help you create this plan.

1. *Determine your major purpose or goal, if you're not sure yet, by writing down all your goals; then establish your priorities.* Start by brainstorming. Let your creative processes go, and write down whatever comes. List where you want to live, the kind of car you want, and the amount of money you would like to make. Also, be very clear why you want that much money. The amount should be related to the life-style you want to live, so you can see that you need to make that much money.

When you brainstorm, don't feel restricted by your current situation, since you can change this. What you have done in the past has created your present situation. By the same token, your actions now can change what happens in the future.

The more concrete you make your future goals, the more likely you can realize them. Thus, when you list where you want to live or the kind of car you want, be specific.

Visualize how the house looks, notice the kind of furniture in it, and see yourself living there. Imagine the car in the driveway; be aware of its color. And so on. Some people use illustrations or cutout magazine pictures to make their goals especially vivid and concrete.

Then, rate your goals in terms of priorities to pick your most important goal. Or if two or more goals seem related, group them together to form an overall goal. For example, you can link your house, car, boat, and fur coat together as part of the new $100,000-a-year life-style you envision. Or if you want a $100,000 retirement vacation, that's fine, too. Just be clear about what you want.

2. *Set a tentative date to realize this goal and go backward from there to determine what you need to do to achieve this goal.* For example, if you are selling the product direct yourself, ask yourself such questions as: How many products do I need to sell personally to achieve a sales volume of $25,000 a month? How many products do I need to sell personally *each* week to meet this goal? How many customers must I contact *each week* to sell this many products? How many *per day?*

Or, if you are creating a sales network to market a product, ask yourself questions like the following: What kind of product volume do I need to earn $100,000? How many people do I need in my organization to get this kind of volume? How much on the average can I expect people to sell and what will my commission be on these sales? How many people do I need to recruit to get this many active people in my organization? How many people do I need to contact in order to get this many recruits?

You have to estimate about how many contacts will become active distributors and how much volume these active people will produce on the average. Start with an educated guess at first, and as you gain experience, modify the formula.

For example, in most businesses, the rule of thumb, widely quoted by people in sales is that 1 out of 3 persons contacted will be interested, and 1 out of 3 who come to a meeting will get more involved. Then perhaps one-fifth to one-third of these become active. So you may need as many as 27 to 45 contacts to get one active salesperson. Or you may need to make more or fewer contacts in your own situation. As you start making contacts and getting people interested, keep track of the response and make adjustments accordingly.

3. *If you are creating a sales team, work out the numbers to illustrate the relationship between the number of active persons in your group, their average product volume, the effort needed to recruit them, and the time needed to build up your organization to a desired level.* And if you find these numbers are too great, perhaps scale down your goals, extend your time frame for accomplishing them, or step up the amount of effort you intend to invest.

For example, suppose you answer these questions as follows:

Amount of product volume needed to earn $50,000 a year = 500,000

Number of active persons needed to produce the volume = 1,000

Number of persons I or others on my team need to sign up to gain 1,000 active people = 5,000

Number of interested persons I and my team members need to talk to to get 5,000 sign-ups = 15,000

Number of persons I and my team members need to contact personally to obtain 15,000 interested people = 45,000

Number of persons I and my team members need to contact personally for each active person = 45(45,000/ 1,000)

Length of time needed to contact 45 persons = two weeks

Length of time needed to build up an organization with 1,000 or more people, assuming I and my active

distributors get 1 new active person every two weeks
(45 contacts) = twenty-two weeks.

You can see how these assumptions translate into recruiting patterns for a sales group that has several levels in
Chart 4.1.

Many involved in sales group building use a shorthand
formula that suggests an organization will double every few
weeks, assuming a regular recruiting pattern. For example,
the following kind of table is found in many books and pam-
phlets about the multi-level marketing approach, with the
main difference being in the length of time needed for recruitment, or this doubling to occur (i.e., one new person a
week, every two weeks, every month). For example, say
the same assumption used in Chart 4.1 is used, that on the
average, each person in the organization will recruit one
new active recruit every two weeks. The following pattern
will result:

Week	1–2 =	1
Week	3–4 =	2
Week	5–6 =	4
Week	7–8 =	8
Week	9–10 =	16
Week	11–12 =	32
Week	13–14 =	64
Week	15–16 =	128
Week	17–18 =	256
Week	19–20 =	512
Week	21–22 =	1,024

However, this pure doubling model is not quite accurate, because as you'll notice in Chart 4.1, your organization more than doubles for the first few weeks. But, then
growth slows down somewhat in subsequent weeks, since
the people on the bottom level of your organization (level

CHART 4.1: RATE OF GROWTH IN A SALES NETWORK, ASSUMING YOU AND YOUR ACTIVE DISTRIBUTORS EACH RECRUIT ONE NEW ACTIVE DISTRIBUTOR EVERY TWO WEEKS

WEEKS	YOU RECRUIT	CUMULATIVE TOTAL LEVEL 1	LEVEL 1 PERSONS RECRUIT	CUMULATIVE TOTAL LEVEL 2	LEVEL 2 PERSONS RECRUIT	CUMULATIVE TOTAL LEVEL 3	LEVEL 3 PERSONS RECRUIT	CUMULATIVE TOTAL LEVEL 4	LEVEL 4 PERSONS RECRUIT	CUMULATIVE TOTAL LEVEL 5	TOTAL PERSONS WHOLE GROUP
1-2	1	1	—	—	—	—	—	—	—	—	1
3-4	1	2	1	1	—	—	—	—	—	—	3
5-6	1	3	2	3	1	1	—	—	—	—	7
7-8	1	4	3	6	3	4	1	1	—	—	15
9-10	1	5	4	10	6	10	4	5	1	1	31
11-12	1	6	5	15	10	20	10	15	5	6	62
13-14	1	7	6	21	15	35	20	35	15	21	119
15-16	1	8	7	28	21	56	35	70	35	56	218
17-18	1	9	8	36	28	84	56	126	70	126	381
19-20	1	10	9	45	36	120	84	210	126	252	637
21-22	1	11	10	55	45	165	120	330	210	462	1023
23-24	1	12	11	66	55	220	165	495	330	792	1585

five in the example) do not recruit additional people into your group, and you don't have any people on this level in your first few weeks.

Should your basic assumptions hold, you could be right on target in about 22 weeks, or just under five months. But, regardless of your assumptions, you will find that things won't happen exactly as you plan. You may find that you need more than 45 contacts over a 2-week period to get your one serious person. And others in your organization may have that experience, too. Or you may find that members of your organization become less motivated as time goes on. Conversely, you may have a really dynamic group and meet your organizational goals more quickly. Thus, you must continually revise your plans as you gain more experience and feedback on what works and how.

4. *Turn your overall numbers about product volume and the number of those you want to recruit into smaller, manageable chunks you can work with on a daily, weekly, and monthly basis.*

Your yearly plan gives you the big picture. But when you break it down into daily, weekly, or monthly goals, you have a clearer, more understandable target to shoot for, so you know better where you are *going* now, as well as where you *are*. Then, you can readily assess your progress as you go along and decide if your goals are realistic. If not, you can modify them.

You will still need to move the same amount of product personally or have the same number of people in your sales team to achieve your daily, weekly, or monthly targets as you do to reach your yearly goals. But breaking these time periods down to smaller ones makes it easier to understand exactly what you must do immediately to make your sales target.

For example, if your earnings goal is $50,000 a year, that's about $4,000 a month in earnings or $40,000 a month in product volume, assuming a 1-to-10 earnings-to-product-volume ratio. That means you must personally

move $40,000 in product a month, or, if you have 100 ac-
tive salespeople in your organization, each one must move
an average $400 in product a month for you to gain these
earnings. Now, that's an easier goal to work for than
$480,000 in volume a year.

Similarly, when you break that monthly goal down to
a weekly product-volume amount (say, $10,000 personal or
$100 for each person in your group), that's an even more
immediate goal.

CALCULATING YOUR SUCCESS IN
ACHIEVING YOUR GOALS

Whether you are setting yearly, monthly, weekly, or
daily goals or are figuring out your success in achieving
your goals, you need to use certain basic procedures. If you
are building a sales team as well as figuring in your own
sales, the process becomes even more complex. The following section will help you work out these different sources of
earnings potential.

Ask two questions to determine how much you have to
produce yourself or how many persons you need in your
sales group to produce this amount:

1. How much product must I or my group move to earn
   a commission of _____ for a (year, month, week)?
   To figure this out, take the average ratio of product
   volume to commission earnings and multiply this
   by the commission you want to earn. For example, if
   the ratio is 10 to 1, you need to move $30,000 worth
   of product to earn $3,000 in commissions. The for-
   mula for this procedure is as follows:

$$\begin{array}{ccc}
\text{Product Volume/} & \text{Desired} & \text{Product Volume} \\
\text{Commissions Ratio} \times \text{Commission} = & \text{Required} \\
(10) & (\$3{,}000) & (\$30{,}000)
\end{array}$$

2. If I am working with a sales team, how many people do I need in my group to move this much product? To figure this out, divide the desired total product volume by the average product volume of your active salespeople or distributors. Obviously, the higher each individual's product volume, the fewer persons you need. For example, if you need to gain a product volume of $30,000 in your total organization and each active distributor moves about $150 in product each month, you need 200 active persons in your organization.

$$\frac{\text{Total Product Volume Desired (\$30,000)}}{\text{Average Product Volume of Active Distributors (\$150)}}$$

$$= \text{Number of Distributors (200 needed)}$$

Next, if you are building a sales team, figure out how much time you need to get that many people in your group. To do this, determine how long it takes you on the average to recruit your active leaders, and assume they will each do about the same as you do to figure out your own success rate over time, break down the sponsoring process into three phases:

- *The initial contact phase,* when you make calls, place ads, and respond to them
- *The presentation phase,* when you make presentations or take interested prospects to meetings
- *The training phase,* when you assist your new distributors to become active themselves

To determine your average time to recruit and train each active distributor, determine approximately how many people you contact in each phase and how much time you spend with them.

The process is not as awesome as it sounds. You can keep simple records using the forms on the following pages, and these will tell you how you are doing each month.

But, first, here is an illustration of how this process might work in practice. Assume that say every third person you contact about joining your sales team is interested in going to a meeting, and out of every three people who go to a meeting, one signs up. Then, about a fifth of these become active. That means (1) you must contact three persons to get one interested person, (2) you must work with three interested persons to get one to sign up, and (3) you must get five to sign up to get one active distributor.

These figures, in turn, translate into contacting 9 persons to get one to sign up (3 times 3), and you must contact 45 persons to get an active distributor (3 times 3 times 5). If the contacts are already interested, you need to work with only 15 of them to get 1 active distributor (3 times 5).

Then, you need to attach hours to the average amount of time you spend with each person you deal with in each phase. For example, say you spend an average of 5 minutes on the phone or in casual conversation with each person you contact about setting up an appointment; an average of 1 hour for each presentation (including any travel and setup time); and an average of 4 hours training each new distributor. Your time to get that one active distributor would be about 39 hours, as follows:

```
Initial contacts: 45 @ 5 minutes each      =  4 hours
Presentations: 15 @ 1 hour each            = 15 hours
Training new distributor: 5 @ 4 hours each = 20 hours
                                    Total  = 39 hours
```

Now, assuming you are involved in marketing your product or service on a part-time basis, spending about 20 hours a week, on this you will average one new active distributor every two weeks. And if you make the same assumptions about your active distributors, they will do the same.

As noted earlier, these assumptions are only that, because those in your sales group may be more or less active than you are, and their level of activity may change over time, just as yours may. So you need to revise your figures and projections accordingly.

The charts in this chapter are designed to give you a general picture of how you are doing. But remember, your results are only as good as your assumptions and data. Be ready to change your assumptions as you gather more information about your performance.

DESIGNING YOUR WEEKLY PLAN OF ACTION

To establish your weekly plans, look at your overall goals and monthly program, and break down these figures into what you need to do each week.

Planning for Direct Retail Sales

To develop your plans for marketing a product directly, you need to determine the number of sales calls and presentations required to make so many sales. And you have to figure out how much time you need to do this, whatever your method of selling.

For instance, suppose that you are doing party plan selling and are seeking prospects who will put on a sales party for you. Also, suppose that you have to make about ten initial contacts to get three persons who want to have a personal presentation; you must give three presentations to get one person who would like to arrange a party. Now if you attach times and results to this, you may find that it takes you about one hour to make the first contacts by phone, another three hours to make presentations to interested people to get one commitment, and perhaps another three hours to work with the host to make the arrangements for actually putting on the party. That means, on the average, you are spending about seven hours to arrange and put on each party. If your average sales party produces about $300 in sales and nets you a commission of $140, that's about $20 an hour.

As you recruit others to do the same thing, you will increase your earnings through overrides on the sales made by those in your sales organization. But, normally, you will start by direct selling yourself—so you should know on the average how much you can expect to earn and how much time you must invest to earn this.

Charts 4.2–4.6 will help you to keep track of this.

Planning for Building a Sales Network

To figure out your earnings from your sales network, you must break down your activities to include the time you spend in recruitment and training activities. Using the previous example about building a group, suppose you need to contact about 100 persons a month or 45 every two weeks and make presentations to those who are interested, to get one active distributor. Also, suppose you need to work with your currently active distributors to motivate them and teach them to do the same.

Thus, on a weekly basis, you need to make about 20 contacts and invite about a third of these to meetings, and your distributors must do this, too.

Now, suppose it takes you about two hours to make calls or otherwise contact people who are interested in meeting with you to learn more. Then, you have to allow about one hour per meeting. So, you know you have to spend about ten hours per week in prospecting (two hours to set up meetings and eight hours for the meetings with the estimated five or six people who will be interested which includes a few extra hours for travel or setup time). At the same time, you have to spend about two hours working with your active first-level distributors—say you have five—so allocate another ten hours for that.

Once you have set up such a plan, over the week, observe how well your plan is working. Are you contacting about as many persons as planned in the time allotted? On the average, are you getting the positive response you expect? If you are selling direct, approximately what percentage of those

CHART 4.2: DAILY CONTACT SHEET AND TIME LOG FOR DIRECT RETAIL SALES

MONTH ———————

WEEK # ———————— DATE ————————

DAY OF WEEK	NEW PEOPLE CONTACTED ABOUT PRODUCTS OR SALES PARTY		PRESENTATIONS TO INTERESTED PEOPLE		SALES PARTY ARRANGEMENTS		NUMBER OF PEOPLE MAKING PURCHASES AND AMOUNT OF SALES		
	NUMBER CONTACTED	TIME SPENT	NUMBER CONTACTED	TIME SPENT	NUMBER AT PARTY	TIME SPENT	NUMBER	GROSS SALES	COMMISSION
Monday									
Tuesday									
Wednesday									
Thursday									
Friday									
Saturday									
Sunday									
Total									

CHART 4.3: MONTHLY SUMMARY OF PEOPLE CONTACTED, TIME SPENT, AND MONEY EARNED IN MAKING DIRECT RETAIL SALES

MONTH _____

WEEK	NEW PEOPLE CONTACTED ABOUT PRODUCTS OR SALES PARTY		PRESENTATIONS TO INTERESTED PEOPLE		SALES PARTY ARRANGEMENTS		NUMBER OF PEOPLE MAKING PURCHASES AND AMOUNT OF SALES		
	NUMBER CONTACTED	TIME SPENT	NUMBER CONTACTED	TIME SPENT	NUMBER AT PARTY	TIME SPENT	NUMBER	GROSS SALES	COMMISSION
Week 1									
Week 2									
Week 3									
Week 4									
Week 5									
Monthly Total									

CHART 4.4: NUMBER OF CONTACTS TO SET UP
A SALES PARTY AND AVERAGE EARNINGS

Data Taken from Monthly Summary for _____

1. Average Number of New Persons Contacted to Get One
   Interested Person:

   $$\frac{\text{Number of Persons Contacted}}{\text{Number of Persons Indicating Interest}} = \underline{\hspace{2cm}}$$

2. Average Number of Interested Persons Needed to Arrange
   One Sales Party:

   $$\frac{\text{Number of Persons Indicating Interest}}{\text{Number of Persons Agreeing to Host a Party}} = \underline{\hspace{2cm}}$$

3. Average Number of Persons at Party:

   $$\frac{\text{Number of Persons at Parties}}{\text{Number of Parties Given}} = \underline{\hspace{2cm}}$$

4. Average Amount Sold per Party:

   $$\frac{\text{Total Amount Sold}}{\text{Number of Parties Given}} = \underline{\hspace{2cm}}$$

5. Average Commission Earnings on Sales
   per Party:

   Average Amount Sold per Party × Commission $= \underline{\hspace{2cm}}$

Example: Monthly Totals from Monthly Summary of Persons
   Contacted and Time Spent

Number of New Persons Contacted = 36
Number Interested in Hearing More = 12
Number Agreeing to Host a Party = 4
Number at Parties = 48
Number Making a Purchase = 24

1. $\dfrac{\text{Number Contacted}}{\text{Number Interested}} = \dfrac{36}{12} = 3$

2. $\dfrac{\text{Number Interested}}{\text{Number Hosting Party}} = \dfrac{12}{4} = 3$

3. $\dfrac{\text{Number at Party}}{\text{Number Parties Given}} = \dfrac{48}{4} = 12$

4. $\dfrac{\text{Total Amount Sold}}{\text{Number Parties Given}} = \dfrac{\$1200}{4} = \$300$

5. Amount Sold × Commission = $\$300 \times 0.45 = \$135$

CHART 4.5: AVERAGE TIME AND EARNINGS IN PUTTING ON SALES PARTIES

Data Taken from Monthly Summary for _____

1. Average Time Spent Contacting New Persons:

$$\frac{\text{Total Time Contacting New Persons}}{\text{Number of New Persons Contacted}} = \underline{\hspace{2cm}}$$

2. Average Time Spent Giving Presentations to Interested Persons:

$$\frac{\text{Total Time Giving Presentations}}{\text{Number of Interested Persons}} = \underline{\hspace{2cm}}$$

3. Average Time Spent Arranging and Giving Party:

$$\frac{\text{Total Time Arranging and Giving Parties}}{\text{Number of Parties Given}} = \underline{\hspace{2cm}}$$

4. Average Time Spent in All Activities Involved in Putting on Parties:

$$\frac{\text{Total Time Contacting, Presenting, and Putting on Parties}}{\text{Number of Parties Given}} = \underline{\hspace{2cm}}$$

5. Average Amount of Earnings per Hour Spent:

$$\frac{\text{Average Commission Earnings per Party}}{\text{Average Time Spent per Party}} = \underline{\hspace{2cm}}$$

---

who you contact are becoming customers, and how much are they buying? Or if you are working on developing a group, what percentage of those you contact are signing in and becoming active? Is this as you estimated?

Then, as necessary, modify your projections or change your activities. For example, if your projections are on target, but you want to increase the number of customers or the number of new salespeople signing up, then increase the time you spend contacting and meeting new persons. Or if people aren't responding as enthusiastically as you expected, increase the amount of time you spend selling or recruiting—or perhaps improve your sales and recruiting techniques.

CHART 4.6: EXAMPLE OF AVERAGE TIME AND EARNINGS IN
PUTTING ON SALES PARTIES

Total Time Contacting New Persons = 4 hours
Total Time Giving Presentations = 12 hours
Total Time Arranging and Putting on Parties = 12 hours
Total Time Contacting, Presenting,
  and Putting on Parties = 28 hours
Average Earnings per Party = $140

1. $\dfrac{\text{Time Contacting Persons}}{\text{Number Contacted}} = \dfrac{4\ hr}{40} = \dfrac{240\ min}{40} = 6\ min$

2. $\dfrac{\text{Time Giving Presentations}}{\text{Number Interested}} = \dfrac{12\ hr}{12} = 1\ hr$

3. $\dfrac{\text{Time Arranging and Putting on Parties}}{\text{Number of Parties}} = \dfrac{12\ hr}{4} = 3\ hr$

4. $\dfrac{\text{Time Contacting, Presenting, and Putting on Parties}}{\text{Number of Parties}} = \dfrac{28\ hr}{4} = 7\ hr$

5. $\dfrac{\text{Average Earnings per Party}}{\text{Average Number of Hours Spent per Party}} = \dfrac{\$140}{7\ hr} = \$20\ \text{per hr}$

Similarly, assess the amount of time you need to spend with your customers or distributors. Do they need more help and therefore more of your time? Or are your people fine as they are? Find out what they need and plan your time accordingly. Then, advise your salespeople to do the same with their own distributors. You can use Charts 4.7–4.12 for keeping track.

WORKING OUT YOUR DAILY SCHEDULE

Use your weekly plans as a guide to set your schedule for each day. Say you are concerned with personal sales only and you know you have to spend about 7 hours for each sales party you organize. If you want to put on two parties a week, that means spending about 14 hours a week or about 3 hours a day (2 parties × 7 hours each = 14 hours a week or 2 hours a day if you do some work everyday; about 3 hours a

CHART 4.7: DAILY CONTACT SHEET AND TIME LOG FOR BUILDING A SALES ORGANIZATION

MONTH _____

WEEK # _____ DATE _____

DAY OF WEEK	NEW PERSONS CONTACTED ABOUT SALES GROUP		PRESENTATIONS TO INTERESTED PERSONS		TRAINING NEW DISTRIBUTORS		NUMBER OF SIGN-UPS BECOMING ACTIVE DISTRIBUTORS
	NUMBER CONTACTED	TIME SPENT	NUMBER INTERESTED	TIME SPENT	NUMBER SIGN-UPS	TIME SPENT	
Monday							
Tuesday							
Wednesday							
Thursday							
Friday							
Saturday							
Sunday							
Total							

CHART 4.8: MONTHLY SUMMARY OF PERSONS CONTACTED AND TIME SPENT IN BUILDING A SALES ORGANIZATION

MONTH _____

WEEK # _____   DATE _____

WEEK	NEW PERSONS CONTACTED ABOUT SALES GROUP		PRESENTATIONS TO INTERESTED PERSONS		TRAINING NEW DISTRIBUTORS		NUMBER OF SIGN-UPS BECOMING ACTIVE DISTRIBUTORS
	NUMBER CONTACTED	TIME SPENT	NUMBER INTERESTED	TIME SPENT	NUMBER SIGN-UPS	TIME SPENT	
Week 1							
Week 2							
Week 3							
Week 4							
Week 5							
Monthly Total							

CHART 4.9: NUMBER OF CONTACTS TO OBTAIN ACTIVE
DISTRIBUTORS FOR SALES ORGANIZATION

Data Taken from Monthly Summary for _____

1. Average Number of New Persons Contacted to Get One
   Interested Person

   $$\frac{\text{Number of Persons Contacted}}{\text{Number of Persons Indicating Interest}} = \text{_____}$$

2. Average Number of Interested Persons Needed to Get One
   Sign-up

   $$\frac{\text{Number of Persons Indicating Interest}}{\text{Number of Persons Signing Up}} = \text{_____}$$

3. Average Number of Sign-ups Needed to Get One Active
   Distributor

   $$\frac{\text{Number of Persons Signing Up}}{\text{Number of Active Distributors}} = \text{_____}$$

4. Average Number of Contacts Needed to Obtain One Active
   Distributor

   $$\frac{\text{Number of Persons Contacted}}{\text{Number of Active Distributors}} = \text{_____}$$

   Or multiply the results of #1 × #2 × #3 = _____

---

day if you put in just five days). Or if you are selling a big-ticket item directly, you can likewise plan how much time you need to spend on the average for each sale.

Similarly, if you are building a sales network, plan how much time to devote to that. For example, suppose you know that to attain your goal of one active distributor every two weeks, you have to spend ten hours a week prospecting and ten hours a week working with your active distributors. If you work five days a week, that averages out to approximately two hours a day prospecting and two hours a day working with active distributors. You can vary the exact amount per day, but to achieve your long-term goals, you know you must spend about four hours working each day.

Thus, at the beginning of each week, whatever your particular marketing approach, sketch out your overall

CHART 4.10: EXAMPLE OF NUMBER OF CONTACTS TO OBTAIN
ACTIVE DISTRIBUTORS FOR SALES ORGANIZATION

Example: Monthly Totals from Monthly Summary of Persons
Contacted and Time Spent

Number of New Persons Contacted = 45
Number Interested in a Meeting = 15
Number Signing Up = 5
Number of Sign-ups Becoming Active Distributors = 1

1. $\dfrac{\text{Number Contacted}}{\text{Number Interested}} = \dfrac{45}{15} = 3$

2. $\dfrac{\text{Number Interested}}{\text{Number Signing Up}} = \dfrac{15}{5} = 3$

3. $\dfrac{\text{Number Signing Up}}{\text{Number Active}} = \dfrac{5}{1} = 5$

4. $\dfrac{\text{Number Contacted}}{\text{Number Active}} = \dfrac{45}{1} = 45$

Or $\#1 \times \#2 \times \#3 = 3 \times 3 \times 5 = 45$

CHART 4.11: AVERAGE TIME SPENT TO OBTAIN ACTIVE
DISTRIBUTORS FOR SALES ORGANIZATION

Data Taken from Monthly Summary for _____

1. Average Time Spent Contacting New Persons
$\dfrac{\text{Total Time Contacting New Persons}}{\text{Number of New Persons Contacted}} =$ _____

2. Average Time Spent Giving Presentations to Interested Persons
$\dfrac{\text{Total Time Giving Presentations}}{\text{Number of Interested Persons}} =$ _____

3. Average Time Spent Training New Distributors Signing Up
$\dfrac{\text{Total Time Training New Distributors}}{\text{Number of New Distributors}} =$ _____

4. Average Time Spent in All Activities with Each Person
$\dfrac{\text{Total Time Contacting, Presenting, Training}}{\text{Number of New People Contacted}} =$ _____

CHART 4.12: EXAMPLE OF AVERAGE TIME SPENT TO OBTAIN ACTIVE DISTRIBUTORS FOR SALES ORGANIZATION

Example: Monthly Totals from Monthly Summary of Persons Contacted and Time Spent

Total Time Contacting New Persons = 3.75 hours
Total Time Giving Presentations = 15 hours
Total Time Training New Distributors = 20 hours
Total Time Contacting, Presenting, Training = 38.75 hours

1. $\dfrac{\text{Time Contacting Persons}}{\text{Number Contacted}} = \dfrac{3.75 \text{ hr}}{45} = \dfrac{225 \text{ min}}{45} = 5 \text{ min}$

2. $\dfrac{\text{Time Giving Presentations}}{\text{Number Interested}} = \dfrac{15 \text{ hr}}{15} = 1 \text{ hr}$

3. $\dfrac{\text{Time Training Distributors}}{\text{Number New Distributors}} = \dfrac{20 \text{ hr}}{5} = 4 \text{ hr}$

4. $\dfrac{\substack{\text{Time Contacting, Presenting,} \\ \text{Training Each Distributor}}}{\substack{\text{Number of New Persons} \\ \text{Contacted}}} = \dfrac{38.75 \text{ hr}}{45} = \dfrac{2{,}325 \text{ min}}{45} = 52 \text{ min}$

schedule. Then, at the end of your workday or before you go to bed each night, write out your "to-do list" for the following day, and indicate your priorities by numbering each item from one (very important) to five (not very important). Also, note the estimated time you need to perform each task, and roughly schedule when you plan to do what, in addition to your scheduled appointments.

If you can't do everything, accomplish the most important activities first, and transfer what you haven't done to a subsequent day, or perhaps drop an item entirely. As you complete each activity, check it off.

This daily planning system is not only ideal for keeping you organized and on target; you also can use it as a record for tax purposes to show how much time you have spent on various business activities.

ASSESSING YOUR PROGRESS

You should review your progress and as needed modify your goals or efforts to achieve them on an ongoing basis. Minireviews are fine on a daily or weekly basis. Ideally, plan a more comprehensive review once a month.

What Key Factors Should I Look at in Making My Review?

When you make your review, two key factors to consider are (1) time spent and (2) results. Find out how much *time* you are spending for what *results*. Ask yourself the following questions, using the charts just described (Charts 4.13 and 4.14).

My Progress in Direct Retail Sales

- On the average, how many prospects do I need to contact to make a sale or set up a sales party?
- In general, how much time am I spending for each sale I make or each sales party I put on?

My Progress in Building a Sales Group

- On the average, how many contacts do I need and how many distributors do I need to sign up to find an active distributor?
- How much time am I spending on the various phases of the recruiting-sponsoring process—making initial contacts and making presentations or taking prospects to meetings?
- How much time am I devoting to training my distributors?
- Overall, how much time do I need to sponsor and train one active distributor?

CHART 4.13: ESTIMATING YOUR OWN RATE OF ORGANIZATIONAL GROWTH
(ASSUMING YOU AND YOUR ACTIVE DISTRIBUTORS RECRUIT
A GIVEN NUMBER OF NEW ACTIVE DISTRIBUTORS EACH TIME PERIOD)

TIME PERIOD	YOU RECRUIT	CUMULATIVE TOTAL LEVEL 1	LEVEL 1 PERSONS RECRUIT	CUMULATIVE TOTAL LEVEL 2	LEVEL 2 PERSONS RECRUIT	CUMULATIVE TOTAL LEVEL 3	LEVEL 3 PERSONS RECRUIT	CUMULATIVE TOTAL LEVEL 4	LEVEL 4 PERSONS RECRUIT	CUMULATIVE TOTAL LEVEL 5	TOTAL PERSONS WHOLE GROUP

Key: Time Period—Indicate whether weekly, biweekly, monthly, etc.

You Recruit—Indicate the average number of new active distributors you recruit in that period.

Cumulative Total Level 1—Make a running cumulative total of your new recruits as of that period.

Level 1 Persons Recruit—Assume that your Level 1 recruits do not become active until the next time period. Then write down the total number in Cumulative Level 1 for each time period in the column: Level 2 Persons Recruit for the following time period.

Cumulative Total Level 2—Make a running cumulative total of your Level 1s' recruits.

Level 2 Persons Recruit—Assume that your Level 2 recruits do not become active until the next time period. Then write down the total number in Cumulative Level 2 for each time period in the next column: Level 3 Persons Recruit for the following time period.

Continue this procedure for all levels in your organization down to Level 5. See Chart 9 for an example.

CHART 4.14: THINGS TO DO LIST

DAY OF WEEK _____

DATE _____

THINGS TO DO . . . (RATE IMPORTANCE FROM 1–5)	ESTIMATE OF TIME NEEDED
_____	_____
_____	_____
_____	_____
_____	_____
_____	_____
_____	_____
_____	_____
_____	_____
_____	_____
_____	_____
_____	_____
_____	_____
_____	_____
_____	_____
_____	_____
_____	_____
_____	_____
_____	_____
_____	_____
_____	_____

Calculating Your Financial Returns

After you have figured out the amount of time and effort expended, look at your financial returns for your personal sales and, if you have one, for your sales group as a whole.

Financial Returns from My Direct Retail Sales

Assessing your own financial returns is relatively simple, based on asking yourself these key questions:

- On the average, how much product volume am I moving personally?
  - each month?
  - each week?
- What is my total commission on these sales?
- On the average, how much am I earning relative to the time I am spending (that is, approximately what is my average return per hour)?

You can use Chart 4.15 to fill in the answers.

CHART 4.15: EARNINGS FROM MY DIRECT RETAIL SALES

Month _____

My Total Product Volume _____

My Total Commission on Sales _____

Number of Hours Spent on Direct Personal Sales _____

Average Earnings per Hour:

$$\frac{\text{Commission}}{\text{Number of Hours}} = \text{_____}$$

Financial Returns from My Sales Group

To figure out your returns from your sales group is a bit more complicated, since you don't have all the data yourself. If you can, get some information directly from your first-line distributors on their product volume, and where possible, ask them to report on how their own immediate distributors are doing (though don't be pushy about this; only ask as you feel your distributors will be willing to share this information). You should also be able to get specific product volume data from your company's monthly statement, but getting it from your distributors gives you some advance information. Also, getting information independently from your distributors can be a way of checking on the accuracy of your printout. (Yes, computers sometimes make errors!)

Using this data, ask yourself the following key questions:

- What is the total product volume of the distributors in my group?
- How much product volume is each distributor moving on the average?
- How are my first- and second-level distributors doing compared to their distributors in my organization?
- What is my average commission per distributor?

To help you figure out the answers, use Chart 4.16, Earnings from My Distributor Group.

Then, knowing your average commission per active distributor, you can estimate how your earnings are likely to grow as you increase the number of active distributors in your organization. Also, since you know how much time it takes to find an active distributor, you can estimate how long it will take to increase your earnings to a certain level.

For example, say it takes you an average of 40 hours to find one active distributor, and each active distributor brings you an average commission of $100 a month.

CHART 4.16: EARNINGS FROM MY DISTRIBUTOR GROUP
(Get information from company's monthly statement)

Month _____

Total Product Volume _____   Total Distributors _____
   Product Volume per Level: Distributors per Level:
     1. _____   1. _____
     2. _____   2. _____
     3. _____   3. _____
     4. _____   4. _____
     5. _____   5. _____

Average Product Volume:

$$\frac{\text{Total Product Volume}}{\text{Number of Distributors}} = \underline{\hspace{3cm}}$$

Average Product Volume per Level:

$$\frac{\text{Product Volume on Level \#}\underline{\hspace{1cm}}}{\text{Number of Distributors Level \#}} = \underline{\hspace{3cm}}$$

Total Commission: _____   per Level (if available):
     1 ____   2 ____   3 ____
     4 ____   5 ____

Average Rate of Commission:

$$\frac{\text{Total Commission}}{\text{Total Product Volume}} = \underline{\hspace{3cm}}$$

Average Rate of Commission per Level:

$$\frac{\text{Commission from Level \#}\underline{\hspace{1cm}}}{\text{Product Volume Level \#}} = \underline{\hspace{3cm}}$$

Average Commission per Distributor:

$$\frac{\text{Total Commission}}{\text{Total Distributors}} = \underline{\hspace{3cm}}$$

$$\frac{\text{Commission from Level \#}\underline{\hspace{1cm}}}{\text{Distributors on Level \#}} = \underline{\hspace{3cm}}$$

Therefore, to increase your earnings by $500, you need to find five additional distributors—or to spend about 200 hours in recruiting, making presentations, and training (5×40 hours average for each active distributor). Of course, as these distributors bring in other active distributors, that will increase your income even more.

To estimate how much time you will need to sponsor the distributors for your group to achieve a desired level of earnings, just plug the appropriate figures into the formulas on Chart 4.17, An Estimate of Earnings and Distributors Needed.

**CHART 4.17: AN ESTIMATE OF EARNINGS
AND DISTRIBUTORS NEEDED**
(Get Information from Earnings from My
Distributor Group Chart)

Month _____

| Total Commission | = Average Commission per Active Distributor | × Total Number of Active Distributors |

_____ = _____ × _____

Number of Active Distributors Needed to Achieve Desired Earnings $= \dfrac{\text{Desired Commission Earnings}}{\text{Average Commission per Active Distributor}}$

_____ = _____

| Time Needed to Obtain Needed Distributors | = Number of Active Distributors Needed | × Time Spent to Recruit and Train One Active Distributor |

_____ = _____ × _____

| Time Needed to Obtain Additional Distributors | = Number of Additional Distributors Needed | × Time Spent to Recruit and Train One Active Distributor |

CHART 4.18: ASSESSING MY GOALS FOR SUCCESS

Date:

1. What are my current goals? How important are they to me? (List all your goals; then rate them on their importance to you from 1 to 10.)

2. What is my most important goal? (This can be a single goal or an overall goal combining several of those listed above.)

3. When do I want to achieve this goal? The date desired is: _____

4. What must I do to achieve this goal? (Work backward and list the steps.)

Finally, review your overall goals in light of your assessment of your progress to date. Consider these questions in your review:

- What are my current goals?
- My most important goals?
- Do I want to change any goals?
- What is my time line for achieving these goals?
- What must I do at these different times to get where I want to be?

If you have previously reviewed your goals, you can compare your current goals with your past goals. Ask yourself, what kind of changes have occurred, if any? You can use Chart 4.18 to look at your current goals. To compare, simply look at how you have previously answered these questions. (And, of course, keep your current review, so you can compare it with your new goals assessment in the future.)

Part II

ACQUIRING CUSTOMERS AND SPONSORING DISTRIBUTORS

Chapter 5

BASIC PRINCIPLES OF MULTI-LEVEL SELLING

Whenever you are marketing your product through direct sales or multi-level marketing, you are selling as well as sharing information with others. Whether you are talking to people in person, calling them, placing ads, passing out brochures, or sending letters, you are selling something.

FIVE BASIC STEPS OF SELLING

There are five basic steps to selling:

1. Attracting the prospect's attention
2. Getting and keeping his or her *interest*
3. Conveying the *conviction* that this is a beneficial product
4. Stimulating the prospect's *desire* to obtain that product or service
5. Making a successful *close,* so he or she takes the desired action: buying a product or service, signing up as a distributor, or otherwise agreeing to participate further.

Salespeople are also aware of and use the major motivators to promote attention, interest, conviction, and desire and to close the sale. These motivators have been variously described as

- self-preservation, protection, or security
- comfort and ease
- romance, love, and affection
- recognition or pride
- financial gain or profit

Abraham Maslow has suggested that these basic motives or needs can be organized in a hierarchy, in that a person seeks to satisfy a lower-order need first. Then as he or she fulfills that need, he or she becomes interested in achieving a higher-order motivation. According to Maslow, beginning with the most basic, these needs are

1. The need for survival or self-preservation (which would include attaining a basic financial livelihood)
2. The need for safety and security (which would include a desire for comfort and ease)
3. The need for belonging (which may also involve a desire for romance, love, and affection)
4. The need for self-esteem (which may stimulate a desire for recognition, pride, and financial achievement to show self-worth)
5. The need for self-actualization (such as through creative expression or setting and accomplishing goals, which could include attaining financial wealth)

Although financial gain or profit is not a primary goal in Maslow's list, it is actually intermixed at every level, since one's income is instrumental to achieving each one of these other goals. You need money to survive: it gives you security, it helps you find acceptance and love, it is a source of self-esteem, and it gives you the funds you need to pursue creative expression.

DIRECTING YOUR MESSAGE TO YOUR PROSPECT'S WANTS AND NEEDS

The key to being persuasive and successfully selling anything is appealing to the wants and needs that motivate someone. It's also critical to recognize that wants and needs can be quite different. This way you can best sharpen your appeal, depending on whether you are trying to fulfill a need, a want, or both. The difference is that a *want* is something a person desires, sometimes very intensely, sometimes not, while a *need* is something a person must have fulfilled to function well. While an intense desire can turn into a need, a person also can intensely want what he or she needs. But the two are not the same. For example, a person may want a beautiful car and house, but he or she *doesn't need* them to survive. Conversely, a person may *need* to lose weight for health reasons, but he or she may not want to make the effort to do so.

While some wants and needs are very common (such as the desire for a good income, nice house, and freedom and independence), people have particular motivations that are essentially appealing to them, as well as different priorities in attaining these desires. Therefore, successful salespeople learn to listen and probe to find out what wants and needs motivate a certain person—they search for his or her "hot button"—to be able to push it in pressing their appeal.

Broadly speaking, there are five different types of people with different hot buttons, based on their greatest priority in responding to one of the five basic needs. These are the following.

People Who Want Security: These people don't care very much about being rich. Mainly, they want to take care of their monthly bills and give them a secure retirement.

Frequently, they have low or below-average incomes, and their main concern is getting by successfully from day to day.

People Who Want Comfort and Ease: These people are satisfied to be comfortable and a primary goal is being able to take it easy and relax. They want to do more than just get by and pay the bills. They want an easy, comfortable life, with perhaps a nice home in the suburbs, a car, and the usual conveniences. Occasional vacations are nice, too. Frequently, these people are blue-collar workers and office workers with middle-level jobs who are satisfied or resigned to being where they are.

People Who Seek Romance, Love, and Affection: These people are especially interested in being with other people and in living an exciting, interesting life. They crave travel, adventure, and a circle of fun, interesting friends. They are not primarily interested in money for itself, but seek it because it enables them to achieve their goal of having fun and meeting interesting people.

People Who Seek Recognition: These people want power, prestige, and respect from others. They want to prove their self-worth through their success. Typically, you'll find such people among the strivers who are trying very hard to make it in some field or among those who have already attained a position of power in business, politics, or the arts. Sure, they may want a high income, because money is a measure of success in our society. But primarily, they enjoy achievement for its own sake and for the power and prestige that comes with success.

People Who Seek Financial Gain: These people are especially interested in the trappings of success and the status associated with it. They have or want fancy cars, big homes, furs, diamonds. When they travel, they go first class. While some may pursue the same life-style as many of the people who seek recognition, their primary motivation is money and status, rather than power, prestige, and accomplishment. In fact, they typically want more money than they have—no matter how much they have—because acquiring money becomes a kind of game in which they want more and more.

THE BASIC PROCEDURES FOR MAKING A SALE

Before you make your sales pitch, determine if your product will meet your prospect's needs by asking questions and listening to what your prospect wants. Then, judge for yourself if your product is appropriate, and if so, go on. Otherwise, why waste the time and effort? Your prospect will respect you more if you say you don't think the product is right for him or her, and when you approach the person again with something he or she does need, he or she will be much more receptive.

Assuming your product does seem suitable, go ahead with your presentation, keeping in mind that you want to emphasize how your product's features provide benefits that will satisfy the person's needs. Your stress should be on benefits, not features. Also, involve your prospect as much as possible, by letting him or her experience the product through as many senses as possible. For example, besides talking about showing the product, so the person *sees* and *hears* about it, let him *touch* the product, and if appropriate, *smell* and *taste* it. And let him use the product if possible, too.

Have a rough outline in your mind of the major points you want to cover. But let the presentation flow spontaneously to suit each prospect. This way, your pitch won't sound canned.

Also, don't be concerned if you forget something. Your prospect will probably never know, since you're the expert on the product. Besides, most people only recall about 10 to 20 percent of what you say—experts claim we forget about 80 percent of everything we hear in a day and about 90 percent in a week. So if you try to fit in everything, your prospect probably won't remember it anyway. Rather, what your prospect will tend to remember is the overall theme of the presentation and his or her overall impression—positive or negative—toward you and the product. Thus, rather than trying to say too much and overload your prospect with too much detail, it's usually more effective to repeat your main points a few times, because people learn through reinforcement (which is why the same commercial runs again and again), and emotions help to further reinforce the message (which is why most commercials try to tap the person's feelings by stimulating excitement, humor, or good feelings so they *like,* or feel they need, the product).

If time allows, spice up your presentation with some anecdotes, testimonials, demonstrations, photographs, color brochures—anything to make it more vivid and convincing.

Allow some time for questions—either during your presentation or afterward. But don't let too many questions disrupt the flow of your presentation or get you bogged down in details. If there seems to be too many, ask your prospect (or prospects) to hold questions until later and cover any minor points quickly.

Then, press for the conclusion of the sale. If your prospect wants to think about it, try to overcome any questions on the spot to push for a decision. But if your prospect still wants time to consider, set up another meeting if you can. Or at least leave the door open by suggesting that you will call to follow up in the next few days or week.

Sometimes, emphasizing that you are offering a money-back guarantee may help to convince the person to try it now. After all, if he or she is at least slightly interested, the guarantee will help to persuade that there is nothing to lose. Also, it's better to offer a guarantee than a free sample, because this way a person will make an investment in using the product. It's easy to say yes to a free sample without really caring about the product being offered. But when a person puts down money, even with a money-back guarantee, that investment is an added incentive to try what he or she has bought.

Finally, ask for referrals to get the names of other prospects. When you do, it's best to mention categories of people who might be interested in your product. This helps people think of names and phone numbers more easily than if you ask vaguely, "Is there anyone you know that . . . ?" Instead, ask for specifics, such as if they have any "neighbors," "people at work," "members of groups" they belong to, and so on that might be interested. Then, after you mention each group, pause to give the prospect a chance to think. Then, when people offer suggestions, ask them to get you the addresses and phone numbers at that time. Otherwise, it's too easy to forget. Or they may be busy later.

If someone does give you a referral, and you are building a sales network, this can be a good time to mention the advantage of being a part of this network, for then the referral could become the person's own customer instead of yours. If the prospect wants to know more, you can talk about the business opportunity—or suggest a follow-up meeting to go into that. But if the person seems hesitant, don't push. Just accept the person's position so you don't risk alienating customers or contacts by being too pushy about getting them more involved than they are ready for now.

Once you conclude a sale to a customer, explain how to place additional orders, if these are likely. If reorders are direct from the company, indicate this. Or, if you will be supplying your customers directly, invite the person to call you, or explain that you will call at a certain time to check if he or she needs anything more.

HOW TO MAKE THE FIVE KEYS TO SUCCESSFUL SALES WORK FOR YOU

Once you determine that a person is a likely prospect, your sales presentation should include the five key sales elements described earlier—getting a prospect to (1) pay attention, (2) be interested, (3) develop a conviction, (4) have a desire, and (5) take action. Here are some techniques to achieve these results in any type of MLM or network-marketing program.

Gaining Attention

When you know how to use the five motivators effectively, gaining someone's attention becomes easy. Avoid trite, overly general openers such as, "Can I help you?" Usually the person will say no.

Instead, say something interesting and attention getting, such as, "How would you like to earn twice what you do now, work with a fun group of people, take that trip you've always wanted, and use your creative abilities to achieve this end?"

Notice that in a few words you have introduced most of the motivators, which should make the prospect perk up and listen to what you have to say next. Other possibilities are short to-the-point statements and questions such as, "Are you the weight you would like to be now?" Or "This is the number one diet in the United States today."

Having a few opening lines prepared, use them appropriately. To determine which one is working best, pay attention to the responses you get, since different approaches will work best depending on your own style, the social environment in the community, and individual personality traits. Then continue to use those that work best for that situation. Note that your initial approach is extremely important. You have about four to ten seconds to make your first impression and get the person's attention. Then, in this short time, your prospect will decide if he or she wants to listen to what you have to say next and will develop a mind-set about how to receive what you say. When you make the right approach, the person will be receptive; if not, he or she will tune you out or may listen with a kind of prove-it-to-me attitude, even while seeming to listen to you respectfully. So, if you come on with a bad impression that serves as a turnoff, you have to struggle to reverse that first impression.

Thus, it's critical to gain attention from the beginning in the right way.

Building Interest

To build interest, stress the product benefits that appeal to the five major motivations. Don't just explain how a product works and why, but describe the benefits these features offer. *Stress benefits, not product functions.*

For example, in promoting a health product, say something like this, which tells what the product will *do* for the prospect:

> You'll be able to lose five to ten pounds a week. You get all the nutrients you need, because this formula contains all the essential amino acids, vitamins, and minerals doctors recommend.

Don't start with something like this that says *what* the product has so it can do what it does.

> This product has been tested and contains 8 amino acids, 15 vitamins, and 20 minerals.

This explanation may be fine later—and someone interested in what the product does for him may want to know this—*why* it works. But first the person wants to know that *it works.* The whys, wherefores, and hows can all come later, if at all.

Also, to be effective in sales, find out about the person's particular motives and interests, so you can relate the benefits of the product to these specific concerns. Thus, ask questions and listen to find out what the person wants. Drawing the person out is also valuable because it gets the prospect involved in the conversation, and this involvement builds interest.

Yet, while you should invite the prospect to speak, keep control of the conversation, so you encourage him to say only so much. Then, if the person starts asking too many questions or shifts the presentation off track, bring it back to the main points you want to make. Likewise, when you make a call to arrange a meeting, keep the conversation short, and cut off any attempts to draw it out.

Developing Conviction

Once you have the person's interest, you want to convince that you have a good, valuable product and that you are someone worth listening to. *For, besides selling the product, you are selling yourself.*

The first impression you make starts the process. Now in the rest of the presentation, continue to back that up. For example, a professional appearance from your initial contact helps to build conviction, because you look successful, so the prospect imagines that whatever you are doing must be good if you have been successful at it. In turn, for that success look, dressing stylishly, keep your clothes freshly cleaned and pressed, have your shoes shined, and carry any sales material in an appropriately professional way (such as in a leather binder or carrying case).

Likewise, reinforce your image of professional success with an environment that implies success, too. For example, pick a meeting place that is nicely furnished to convey a success image (no seedy coffee shops, please). And if you drive to a meeting, make sure your car will make a good impression, or if not (say you're just starting out), park a few blocks away. Since people judge you initially by the symbols of success, outfit and present yourself accordingly to acquire the credibility you need.

Then, to this first impression, add your own conviction, belief, and enthusiasm that the product is good and you are sure that it is. To be convincing, you must show confidence in yourself and your product. And to *appear* confident, you must *believe* in your worth and in the worth of your product. Initially, you may need to act as if to develop this belief and confidence, as discussed in Chapter 3, Thinking Success. But whether you really feel it or just start off acting that you do, you need to acquire this confidence and belief to sell yourself and your product, for your faith and conviction will inspire others to develop this conviction and confidence in you and the product, too. Confidence and conviction are contagious.

Encouraging Desire

Recognize that desire springs from interest and conviction and represents an emotional response or reaction to an appeal to the emotions. You can arouse interest or convince someone of a product's merit by appealing to the intellect. But to make someone *truly desire* something, you must engage the emotions, too.

Successful salespeople do this in many ways. One is by painting a very attractive picture, so the person can literally see, taste, smell, or otherwise experience possessing the product. Or they make the person feel a sense of losing out or of not being "with it" without the item. For instance, "Everyone is getting it" or "It's the latest fad" reflects this appeal to the desire to be trendy, up to date, and to belong.

Also, many salespeople will sometimes say, to appeal to the person's feeling of self-importance or self-image, "you'll be the first one to get this, and everyone else will want one, too." Or they may try to appeal to the person's desire for financial wealth: "Just think. If you get in now, you're getting in on the ground floor. So you'll have the potential to make much more than if you wait."

Making a Close

When you make the close, in which you ask your prospect to do something, you must be sensitive that the person is *ready* to act, that he or she is ready to respond to your push to close. It's a bit like deciding whether the timing is right to ask for a date, for a favor, for a vow of marriage; for in life, timing is everything. Likewise, in selling, you must watch for the appropriate "buy signals" indicating that the person has been sold on you and the product. Then, when he or she seems ready to respond (for example, by making receptive comments showing interest and enthusiasm, such as "Boy, this really sounds good" or "You're right, I think this would be a good program for me"), it's time to close by asking for some action.

If you feel very confident and you like a more direct style, you can ask for this action directly. For example, say something like: "Why don't we take care of signing you up now?" or "Would you like to order a case of this product?"

If you prefer a more subtle finale, which many sales-people do, use an assumptive close in which you act as if the customer has already agreed to buy or sign up, and you are just asking them to affirm that. For example, you might say: "Okay (pulling out an order form), where would you like your first order and distributor kit to be sent?" or "Would you prefer to start with one case of product or two?"

Using Your Prospect's Way of Taking in Information in Your Sales Presentation

Knowing how your prospect takes in information can help increase your sales, because, as successful sales-persons know, people respond to presentations in differ-ent ways, regardless of the particular things that motivate them. The reason for this is that people perceive and receive information differently. Some people are more visual and like to see pictures and details. Others are more auditory and prefer to take in information by hearing it. Still others tend to react on a feeling or gut level and respond based on their actual or imagined experience of something. Finally, some people tend to listen to their inner voice in reacting and making decisions.

I once belonged to a group that divided people with these different perceptions into four personality types—the visionary (visually oriented), the intuitive (aurally oriented), the feeler (feeling oriented), and the prophet (attuned to an inner voice). At many meetings, the group leader would seat people according to their personality type, and when people responded to questions and related experiences, the differences were highlighted dramatically in the way people experienced and described things. The visual people painted pictures, the feelers talked about how things felt to them, and so on.

Thus, when you talk to people about your product or business opportunity, get a sense of where they are coming from so you can tune in on their wavelength. Here are some illustrations of how to do this.

With the *visual* person, for instance, paint a vivid picture. Use visual metaphors, and say things like: "When you drink our health drink, you'll *see* those pounds melt away." Or "With all the money you'll save on this program, just *imagine* all the things you can buy that you want. You can redecorate the house with some beautiful drapes. And *imagine* giving your next party there. Your guests will love it."

If you are with an *auditory* person, use auditory references to appeal to this person's hearing sense, such as "You'll love this travel program. Just think about being on our tour to Peru now. You're lying in your tent *listening* to the gurgle of the brook near you. You *can hear* the singing musicians, accompanied by flutes."

With the *feeling* person, tap into this person's emotions by emphasizing how he or she will *feel* as a result of the experience. Some examples: "You'll really *feel great* when you try our new vitamins. You'll *feel extra energy,* and you'll just charge through the chores you have to do each day." Or "The trip will be an *experience* you'll never forget. You'll *experience* the excitement of traveling through the wilderness and discovering new plants and animals. Then, at night, you'll *experience* a marvelous tranquility, when the moon rises and the whole world around you seems absolutely still."

With people who respond to the inner voice, suggest that they can experience *knowing* the product or program is right for them. This taps into their intuitive or gut-level sense. For instance, "When I heard about this health program, *I knew* instantly that it was right for me. And that's the way it is for many people. There are many diets. But when they hear about this one, they experience the magic. *They know instantly:* 'This is the program for me.'"

OTHER WAYS OF INCREASING YOUR SALES

Be Aware of Every Opportunity to Tell Your Story. Wherever you are, whomever you are with, look for an opportunity to talk about your product or business and how it has helped you. For example, suppose someone mentions a problem (such as being tired). You might offer a solution (try your product). However, when you do share what you are doing in a social or nonbusiness situation, don't sound like you are giving a sales pitch. Simply share about the value of the product or the company, and how either has improved your life.

Drop Teasers about Your Product or Business. You can even do this in the course of everyday conversation. Then let others *ask you* for more information. The advantage of this approach is that people get intrigued and reach out to you for information, instead of your persuading them to do something. As a result, they don't think you are trying to sell them something and get defensive.

This strategy is particularly good with friends, who might be sensitive to your using their friendship to make them act. But you can employ this approach with anyone. Just dangle out some information—such as how your new business helped you save on taxes or get a new car—and see if people bite. Then, like a person who's good at fishing, let out plenty of line, and if people pull on it, reel it in.

Avoid a Canned Sales Pitch. When people think you are giving them a preprogrammed or rehearsed story, it sounds very phony and is a real turnoff. Instead, speak with sincerity and from the heart about how your product has helped you and how it might benefit others. Have the key points you want to mention in mind, but adapt your presentation to your listener's interests, wants, and needs. Also, only share what you believe yourself. If you don't have the conviction and are just trying to sell something without real knowledge, it will show.

Sell Your Prospect on You First. To make people respond more positively to your product or business opportunity, sell them on *you* first. You may have an easier time with people you know, because they are already sold on you, though some may still have to be convinced. However, the people you don't know need even more reassurance.

So take time to get to know your prospect (if you don't already) and let that person get to know you. Show that you care. For example, ask a few questions about his or her family, job, or recreational interest to create a feeling of rapport between you. Then, only after you have sold yourself should you try to sell your product or opportunity, for doing so helps to smooth the way.

Use Yourself as an Example. It's a good way of persuading others if they can see how you have benefited or succeeded. One approach is to tell people how using a product has changed you or how well you have done in finding others to join your sales team to market the product. Or let the way you have changed speak for itself with people you know. For example, suppose you have lost 20 pounds or have gotten a new car. People will notice. And when people see your success, they will start asking how they can have what you have, too.

So, as a sales opener, use *you!* Your own actions and success are more powerful than anything you might say. They not only grab attention, but they have the power to convince, too.

Get as Much Information as You Can about Your Prospect in Advance. This way you can find out who your prospect is and what motivates him or her before you make your sales presentation. Essentially, in this preapproach phase, you want to gather information to find out the person's primary motives. What does he or she want out of life?

What does he need? Then, you can show how your product will fill the bill.

Also, gaining advance information has several other advantages. You avoid mistakes, such as telling someone about a great vacation plan when he or she has just lost a job. You avoid wasting time contacting or making a presentation to people who are not likely to be interested. Also, you can make your presentation with more confidence, because you know more about what your prospect wants. And having extra information gives you an advantage over your competition.

The two main ways to get this information are to (1) ask people who know the prospect about his or her interests and needs, or observe yourself when with this person or at his home (for example, you can get insights from the way a person's home is furnished or the books he reads), and to (2) ask your prospect what he or she wants or needs, or how he or she thinks his or her problems might be solved.

Qualify Your Prospect at the Outset.   Determine if your prospect really might be interested in and able to purchase and afford your product or business opportunity at the beginning of your discussion or presentation. You don't want to spend a lot of time explaining something to someone who doesn't qualify or already has what you are selling.

To qualify your prospect, ask a few leading questions. These can be excellent attention-getters, too.

Follow Up.   Frequently, one contact—whether by phone, letter, or in person—is not enough. After you set up an appointment, things can happen or the person can forget. So it's a good idea to call back to reconfirm, and then, if necessary, be prepared to change the arrangements or reset the appointment. If you send a letter, it is often helpful to call a few days afterward to find out the response—or even to remind the person to read the letter. Likewise, after a presentation, if a person wants to think it over, be prepared to contact that person in a few days if you don't hear from him, since your call may be what's needed to spur him into making a positive decision.

And when you follow up, do it quickly—while your initial contact or presentation is still fresh in people's minds. This is when they are most interested. Don't give them a chance to cool off, though also be careful not to be too pushy. If you find your follow-up is making the other person become defensive, respect this and back off, though if you can leave an opening for further follow-up, such as suggesting "Sure, I understand you need to think it over. So when would you like me to call you back?" or "Well I can get back in touch with you in a few weeks, if you like."

Employ the Principles of Good Communication. An essential component of being persuasive is being clear about what you want the other person to know and presenting this so he or she understands how it will benefit him or her to take some action. So know what you want to say. Be clear about the purpose of your message and the ideas you want to present. Also, keep these principles of good communication in mind.

- Know who your audience is and orient your message to that audience.
- Consider the interests, needs, and wants of your listeners, and appeal to these.
- Talk about things people can readily identify with to develop rapport with your audience (for example, make your point by telling a story or sharing a joke).
- Use simple, concrete words to promote understanding.
- Communicate only a small amount at a time so people can readily follow your message. Then you don't overwhelm and confuse listeners with too many points or too much detail.
- Use repetition and associations with familiar ideas to promote retention of your message. In other words,

say the same thing several times in several ways so people remember it!

- Use the appropriate tone, manner, and gestures in presenting your message, because these are part of your message, along with your content. In fact, the *way* you say something can be more influential than *what* you say, because people react on an emotional, feeling level.

- Emphasize the areas where you and your listeners are in agreement. This promotes rapport. Then, if you want to promote change or the acceptance of new ideas, start where your prospect is; then once you have that kind of rapport that comes from being on the same wavelength or in tune with someone else, you can gradually work toward shifting that person's point of view. But you need to start from that point of commonality and agreement first to help make that person more receptive to change.

- Get feedback by asking questions and listening.

- Anticipate the objections that might come up and learn how to overcome them.

Chapter 6

ANSWERING
OBJECTIONS

Inevitably, in selling, you will encounter objections and need to be ready to respond. Often an objection is a request for more information, and then you need to have the appropriate information on hand. Other times people raise objections because they are seeking reassurance, and then you must be able to reassure them so they feel more confident about your product, company, or you.

As long as any objection exists, it stands as a barrier between you and your making a sale. So you need to know how to answer and eliminate objections to proceed to a successful close.

One key to answering objections effectively is knowing what objections are likely to come up and being prepared in advance to answer them. Or if you are just starting to contact people, take notes as objections arise, so you can think about them later and develop good responses to them. Then you will be more prepared to respond next time.

A good way to answer objections is to acknowledge the objection respectfully but then do one of the following:

- Turn the objection around to show how it is really an advantage.

- Pass over that objection to stress a benefit that out-weighs it.
- Ask why the person feels that way (if you feel that this is not a strongly held objection or that it is based on incorrect facts which you can correct).

You also need to respond calmly and confidently without getting nervous and flustered, and being prepared will help you do this.

Be aware, too, that some people raise objections or say that they are not interested when you first approach them, simply to test you. They want to see how much you believe in the product, how persuasive and convincing you are. Then, if you persist and show them you are sincere and knowledgeable, they will come around.

While some objections will be specific to your product, company, or industry, many may come up when you describe any multi-level or network-marketing program. Commonly, they fall into these key categories:

Concerns about selling

Concerns about having enough time

Concerns about the legitimacy of the company or about MLM or network marketing as a sales method

Concerns about the amount of investment involved

Concerns about using or marketing the product

Concerns about being successful

Concerns about conflicts because of other marketing commitments

General feelings of uncertainty

RESPONDING TO PROSPECTS' CONCERNS

Here are some of the most common objections in each category, along with some possible responses to them when they arise.

Concerns About Selling

I'm not sure I can really sell; I don't like selling.

"You're not really selling. You're really sharing information about the program with a few other people."

"There's nothing wrong with selling. Many people have a misconception about it. They think it involves hard sell or convincing someone to buy something they don't want or need. But selling really involves conveying information to people and showing them how something you have can benefit them. It's learning about and understanding other people's needs and figuring out how to satisfy them."

"The most successful individuals in multi-level (or network) marketing programs are not salespeople. Rather, they are people who want to help and teach each other. Salespeople often want to sell someone something right away and move on to the next person, so this kind of selling doesn't work for them. By contrast, teachers are usually very successful in this kind of selling, since they know how to teach others, and they have learned how to be patient in working with people."

I don't know many people; I'm new in the area and don't have many contacts.

"You don't have to contact only the people you know. We can show you how to contact many people you don't know. Our organization has all sorts of aids to help you, including sample letters, phone scripts, and ads. And we'll teach you how to use these effectively."

"You really know more people than you think. You know the people you deal with everyday, such as the clerks where you shop and the letter carrier who delivers your mail. And you know the tellers at your bank, the gas station attendant down the street. And if you go to any group meetings, you'll get to know people there, too."

"You don't have to know many people to be successful in a multi-level (network) marketing business. You just need to share with a few people; then they will tell others about the program. And these people will tell others. Then, all these people become part of your sales network. So you only need to know a few people because the network builds from them."

Concerns About Having Enough Time

I'm very busy; I don't have much time.

"You have more time than you think. Even if you're a very busy professional person, you'll find you have some extra hours each week. For example, you can figure this out now by looking at how you spend your time. I'll help you do this. So first let's calculate how much time you spend working, eating, engaging in leisure activities, and visiting with your family. Also, let's see how much time you spend relaxing and not doing much at all. Now think about your priorities. If this project is important to you, you could take an hour or two a day and find that you have about five to ten extra hours a week you could devote to this project."

"You don't have to spend much time in a multi-level (network) marketing program to make money. You only need to work with a few people."

I like to spend my free time with my family and friends.

"You can in this program. That's the beauty of it. Many families participate together in a multi-level or network marketing program, because it's possible to work the program right out of your home. And when people in a family share the work together, that lightens the load for everyone. Plus, it will bring you closer together.

"You can involve your friends in this program, too, and you'll all work together as a group. In fact, you can plan social activities together as part of promoting the program."

Concerns About the Amount of
Investment Involved

The distributor fee is too expensive; the sales kit costs too much.

"It's not really that much when you think about it. If we break the fee down, you'll see that it only costs a few dollars a month or a *few* pennies a day."

"Think of this fee as an investment in yourself."

"The fee is really very little when you consider the opportunity you are getting. There are very few businesses you can start for less than a hundred dollars. Most businesses cost several thousand dollars, maybe more, to start. And when you consider the fantastic earnings potential in this business, you'll realize the distributor fee is not that much."

I can't afford to get involved right now; I need a job and don't have enough money.

"You don't have to give up your present income. That's the beauty of a multi-level (network marketing) business. You can do it part time and choose your own hours. So you can keep working on your regular job until you have enough money from your business, and you don't need to work for anyone else."

"If you only think about getting a job and working for someone else, you'll never become really successful. The only way to succeed and attain financial independence is to be in business for yourself. And this business requires only a minimal investment in return for the potential of earning a large income. What other business can you enter for so little? Also, think of the high income that is possible for you in the future when you start now."

"But can you afford not to get involved? Just think how much you will save and all the benefits you will get by buying this product. And think of the chance that you have to make a good monthly income, too, if you act now.*

Concerns About Using or Marketing the Product

I don't think I would use the product; it's not a product for me.

It helps if you use the product. But you don't have to use it to market it, as long as you agree it's a good product. If you see this as a good business opportunity, you can simply promote the program.

Some very successful distributors (sales reps) don't use the product themselves. But they actively promote it to people who do use it.

I'm not interested in marketing the program.

That's fine. You can simply be a consumer.

You don't have to market an MLM (network marketing) program when you become a distributor. You can be as active or inactive as you want. But if you are going to be using the product regularly, being a distributor gives you a chance to purchase the product at wholesale. So you can save a lot of money that way.

Concerns About Being Successful

I'd like to see how you do first in an MLM (network marketing) program.

Fine. I'll be glad to get back to you later. But right now you have a chance to get in on the ground floor and help build the program in this area. If you wait until you see that I'm successful, you won't have as much opportunity, because the area will already be developed and many others will be involved.

"The people who are extremely successful in multi-level (network sales) are those who get in on the ground floor of a good, well-managed, fast-growing program. If you wait, you may find the opportunity has passed you by,.because most of the people you know will be involved by then, and you'll have to work harder to find other people to sponsor into your sales group."

"I'm inviting you to be one of the individuals who can help make it happen. There are three kinds of people—those who make it happen, those who wait for it to happen, and those who don't know what's happening. That's why I decided to get involved—to make it happen—and that's why I'm inviting you to join me now."

"Okay. I'll contact you later."

I'm not sure if I will be successful; I don't know if this program will work for me.

"It will work for you if you believe it will. It already has worked for thousands of people in other areas. But if you don't believe this is the program for you, it won't work. It's up to you. If you decide this is a program you like and put your energies behind making it work, then it will."

"I'll do everything I can to support you in making it work, if you join my sales group. But you have to be committed to making it work for yourself, too."

"Is there anything I can do to help you become more certain? Would you like more information on the company, the product, the management, what our group will do to support you?"

"Okay, maybe it won't work for you. This program isn't for everybody. Think about it and let me know. I'll check back with you in a few days. If you decide you want to get involved, we'll do everything we can to help you become successful."

General Feelings of Uncertainty

I'll think it over; I can't make a decision right now.

"What do you need to think over? Is there some objection you have? For example, do you have any reservations about the company? About its management? About the product? Do you feel the membership fee is too high? Do you want to discuss this with your spouse?"

(The point of asking questions is to find out exactly what is leading the person to be indecisive. You want to know because frequently people express general uncertainty when they still have some objection, but do not want to come right out and say this for several reasons. Say they don't have enough money. They may feel embarrassed to tell you this. Or they may not want to admit they must talk to someone else before making a decision. Or they may not be sure what the objection is; they just feel somehow uncomfortable but can't put their finger on why. Thus, to cut through all this uncertainty and clarify what's really going on, you can encourage and guide the person to raise specific objections. Then, once you know what they are, you may be able to overcome them.)

"Okay, if you really must think it over, I'll get back to you in a day or two to find out what you decide."

Concerns About the Legitimacy of the Company or MLM

How do I know this is a legitimate program? I'd like to check it out first.

"The company is listed with the Better Business Bureau and Chamber of Commerce. The company also has a full description of its management in its literature, and I'm truly impressed with their background."

"The company already has several thousand distributors marketing its product, and the company is well funded. The company describes its financial backing in its literature."

The MLM Company sounds like an illegal pyramid.

"Multi-level is very different from an illegal pyramid because . . ." (Then describe the differences explained in chapter 1.)

"Many people have been incorrectly using the name 'multi-level' to refer to illegal pyramids and chain letter schemes. But, in fact, multi-level marketing is a completely legal form of marketing, since it moves a valuable product or service, whereas an illegal pyramid involves only the movement of money, and people get hurt. There are many important differences which include . . ." (then describe them).

I've already been burned in a multi-level (network marketing) program; I was with another organization and didn't make any money.

"Every multi-level program is different. Some programs are not as good as others. And sometimes there are other reasons why a program doesn't work for you, such as a sponsor who doesn't help you enough or a product people don't like that much. I think this program is very good and *will* work for you because . . ." (then go into the specifics).

"That doesn't mean you should give up on multi-level. If you get a bad apple once, that doesn't mean you should give up on eating apples. Or if you have a car accident, that doesn't mean you should stop driving. It's the same in multi-level. You can learn from the first experience, and when you have the right program and work it right, it can really work for you."

I don't believe people in MLM (network marketing) can really make that much; I can't believe I'll really make that much money.

"But it's true. People do make incredibly large amounts in a successful multi-level (network marketing) program when they get in on the ground floor and build a large organization. For example, there are people in Amway who are getting checks for $500,000 and $750,000. Most distributors don't make that kind of money, but it's possible."

"You have to realize that you can make a high income and you will. You won't overnight. It takes about six months to a year or two of hard work to build up your business in an MLM (network-marketing) program. But if you build a strong organization, you can be earning several thousand dollars a month in the near future and then increase your business even more."

"Your income grows by the principle of multiplication of effort in MLM. So, as your organization multiplies in size, your income does too. It takes time to build an organization in depth—perhaps four to six months before you start seeing a substantial income develop. But if you work at it, in two or three years, sometimes sooner, you can be earning a very good income. In some programs, some distributors have started earning $50,000 a month after eight or nine months."

"You have to believe you will keep working toward this goal. Many persons get stuck in believing they will keep earning what they are earning now. But if you start imagining yourself making these big amounts you'll find your thinking will help you change. So you'll become the prosperous person you want to be."

Concerns About Conflicts Because of Other Marketing Commitments

I've already heard about the program from someone else; I'm already in another MLM (network marketing) downline.

"Just because you heard about the program from someone else doesn't mean you have to join that person's sales group. You should consider how much support you will get from your sponsor or sales leader. You may find that our organization gives you much more help and support if you are really serious about marketing this program. So we may be better able to help you become successful."

"Our organization can offer you a great deal of support that you won't get from most other groups marketing this product. For example, we offer special training, sales litera-ture we prepare ourselves, and regular presentations. We will put on some individual presentations for you when you get started. Also, we have meetings all over the area, which you and your guests can attend. Plus, we send out a regular newsletter to keep you informed."

"If you already have a commitment to another person and can't change downlines or switch sales groups, perhaps we can still arrange to support you if you aren't getting enough support from the group you are in. For example, you can have another member of your family sponsor into or join our group, or perhaps a friend can sponsor in or join for you."

"We'd like to work with you, but like many distributors, our policy is to work only with the people in our downline or sales group. The reason is that we do all we can to make you successful. But if you are in another downline or sales group, we are just building up our competition. After all . . . does Macy's tell Gimbel's? However, if things change so you can join us, please let me know, and we'll be glad to work with you then."

I'm already in another MLM (network-marketing) company; I don't want to confuse the people in my organization with another product.

"There is no reason you can't be involved in two or more marketing programs at the same time, as long as they are compatible. Many distributors today handle sev-eral products."

"Being in another marketing program will help you sell this. You already have a downline or sales group you can start with, and this program will supplement the product line you already have. Besides, if you don't contact the people in your organization, someone else probably will, and many of your people may join under this person, since many distributors are involved with several programs."

"Some people in MLM (network marketing) handle two programs, but keep their downlines (or sales teams) separate. Now that you've got a solid organization in one program, you could build another organization with this new program and market it to completely different people as long as you have the time to do both adequately."

AND IF YOU GET A NO . . .
HOW TO HANDLE REJECTION

Whenever you are selling anything, you'll get some nos. No matter how terrific your presentation, no matter if you've done everything right—you'll still get them.

So accept this. The nos come with the territory, and you need to learn how to handle rejection when it occurs.

First, regard every rejection as an opportunity to learn something. Review your presentation or approach. Was there anything you might have done to make it better? How can you improve for next time? Or perhaps the person you contacted would not have been interested regardless of what you said. If so, what can you do to better assess and qualify a prospect in advance to better target whom to spend your time with?

Second, remind yourself that multi-level or network marketing, like any form of sales, are numbers games, and a certain percentage of the people contacted are going to say no. You can't hope to bat 100 percent every time. You can increase your batting score by improving your presentation and your assessment of people. But still, some people will say no. So think in terms of percentages, and remember that if a certain percentage says no, a certain percentage will say yes. Thus, every time you get a no, you are that much closer to getting a yes next time.

Finally, do not take the nos as a personal rejection and get upset. Instead, look at the nos as part of the sales game. Sometimes you win; sometimes you lose. And the nos are merely strikes—but not outs. So keep going up to bat—and eventually, your strikes will turn into home runs.

Chapter 7

HOW TO START PROSPECTING

DIFFERENT APPROACHES FOR
DIFFERENT PROGRAMS

Your approach to prospecting for customers and distributors will vary depending on whether you are just seeking to sell directly to customers or are also seeking distributors to join your sales team. In the first case, your only concern is with potential buyers, but in the second case, you will also want to recruit or sponsor new people into your organization who may or may not be consumers.

This chapter focuses on what to look for in building a sales team, since you should be aware of what to look for in prospects as you market the product yourself. If you're only seeking customers, you can skip ahead to the next chapter.

PUTTING YOUR EMPHASIS IN THE
RIGHT PLACE—ON PRODUCT SALES

Whether you are selling to the ultimate customers or building a sales team, too, always *emphasize product sales.*

This statement may seem self-evident when you are selling direct yourself. But some people lose sight of this principle when they seek to build an organization of MLM or network-marketing distributors, since the big success in these programs comes from building a large group. So they focus almost exclusively on creating such a group.

But, initially, whatever kind of program you are marketing, you must work on promoting and selling the product itself, because that's the only way anyone makes any money—through product sales because commissions are only paid for that. Then, once the focus on selling the product is properly emphasized, create a sales team and look for key distributors who will likewise focus on marketing and promoting the product while building a sales team too.

The reason for this emphasis on product is that whether you personally sell the product or have a sales team working with you, you and/or your group must move the product. It also helps if you or your people actually like and consume the product. Some distributors who are interested only in the business opportunity are very effective because they are able to tap a large market for the product among others. But one risk of going after distributors who are mainly interested in business is that you may build up a big organization but not move much product, because no one is using it.

So *emphasize product sales,* whether you are appealing to prospects as consumers, as business opportunity seekers, or both. The product should be in the forefront of what you are selling—not just building an organization to sell it. It's like style and content in a presentation, gas and a steering wheel in a car. You need to have both working together to get where you want to go.

LOOKING FOR LEAD DISTRIBUTORS

Once you are ready to go with a program, your first task is prospecting for consumers and/or prospective distributors. In seeking your distributors, do this as soon as possible to increase the chances of your contacts joining your down-line. For if you wait, someone else may contact them first, so you may find your hot prospects already signed up under someone else when you call.

The first stage of prospecting is developing and con-tacting leads. One common approach is to list all the persons you know and contact them first. While some suc-cessful distributors recruit only those they know, many others go outside their circle of friends and sponsor mostly strangers, as Debbie Ballard suggests in *Secrets of Multi-Level Fortune Building.*

Either strategy will work. It depends on your circle of friends and acquaintances. If you know a large number of people who have been in sales, business, or promotional work, you may be able to recruit easily from your own network. But if your contacts have limited business experi-ence or come from fields that are traditionally far afield from business, such as the arts or academia, you will prob-ably have to reach out much farther.

The key is to decide what works for you. Some people don't have to go beyond their own network for active distrib-utors. But most do.

Thus, most of your customers and distributors will probably be strangers. But that can have certain advantages too, since often these strangers will be more receptive to your message, whereas people you know may be most skep-tical since they already have an image of you as one kind of person. So when you start marketing a new program and changing your life, people may be dubious or wait to see what happens, but after you start to succeed, they will generally become more receptive, for you have proved yourself.

So, of course, contact the people you know first—some may be your most ardent supporters and most loyal distribu-tors. But if some are critical or ridicule what you are doing, don't let that discourage you. Just go on to others who are more receptive, and let the skeptics come around when they are ready.

GETTING YOUR FIRST
FRONTLINE DISTRIBUTORS

Choosing the best frontline distributors is important, because these are the people you will devote the most time to working with; you will work with them the closest. Until you know which people will become truly committed, you may want to recruit a large number of first-level or frontline people, so you can see who really works out. But, eventually, you want to narrow down your focus to work with a handful of frontline distributors—usually a maximum of five to ten at first—and teach them what to do. But, as must be emphasized, *you typically have to go through many prospects to find those effective, committed distributors and train them.* It's a kind of unknowing process till you find those few key people to focus on working with.

LOCATING LEADS AND MAKING
YOUR FIRST CONTACTS

Targeting Your Market

To locate potential consumers and/or distributors most efficiently, you must focus on those prospects who are most likely to be receptive—and that means *targeting your market* to choose people with certain characteristics, such as where they live, their age, sex, education, life-style, interests, group memberships, and so on that contribute to their being more receptive. Even though a product has broad appeal, you still need to target the particular market you want to focus on to conserve effort and energy, and then, having selected this market, you need to determine the best approach to reach it.

To help determine your market, make a list of all potential types of users. Then prioritize which categories of people you think would be most receptive and therefore best to contact first by rating them from one (least important) to five (most important). You can use Chart 7.1 to do this.

The chart is divided into two sections: types of individuals (e.g., teenagers, children, mothers) and types of groups (such as health clubs, travel clubs, singles groups). Think of as many types of individuals and groups as you can who might be interested; then rate them to indicate the most likely prospects.

For example, if you have a weight control product, your list might start off looking something like this:

Types of individuals—overweight people, mothers, single people

Types of groups—health clubs, health stores (if you can contact stores), Weight Watcher groups, singles organizations, PTAs, MLM people in another diet program

Sources for Leads

Once you have targeted your market, you must seek leads for prospects within that market. And such leads are everywhere. Among people you know and see everyday, among the groups to which you belong, among the names of people in your local business directory or telephone Yellow Pages—everywhere. And even if you start off contacting just persons you know, you'll find you know many more people than you think. A *Reader's Digest* research survey once showed that the average American knows over 400 people.

To come up with the names of who you want to contact within your market, start by systematically making a list of leads. Use the target market list (Chart 7.1) to help you think of groups that might have a special interest. Also, go through your personal telephone books, business card files, membership lists of groups to which you belong, and combine all of these names together onto one master list.

To help think about whom to contact, list each category or type of person you want to contact. Then think of all the people you can in this category. Using this system of breaking things into categories will help you come up

CHART 7.1: THE TARGET MARKET FOR
MY PRODUCT OR SERVICE
(first list all the markets you can; then rate each market from
one—least likely—to five—most likely)

TARGET MARKET	RATING	COMMENTS
Types of Individuals Who Would Be Most Likely to Use the Product or Service		

TARGET MARKET	RATING	COMMENTS
Types of Groups That Would Be Most Likely to Use the Product or Service		

with ideas through the process of association which is more effective than just trying using a broad question to yourself, such as "Now, who can I think of who would be interested?"

Later, when you contact these people, ask for referrals, if they don't want to purchase the product or learn more about the business opportunity themselves. These referrals will not only give you new leads, but will help to open future doors when you call. Or if your contacts get involved in your program as distributors themselves, help them make their own contacts.

Some of the categories to contact are:

Relatives

Neighbors

Current friends

Old friends

School friends

Work associates

Members of groups you belong to—church groups, social groups, interest groups, service clubs, and community groups

Fellow commuters

Merchants or store clerks where you shop

People who have services you use, such as doctors, dentists, hairdressers, postal carriers, repair people, gas station attendants

People you meet at parties

People you meet at classes, seminars, workshops

Referrals

Initially, list everyone you can think of in each category. You never know who might be a prospect until you ask. At the same time, maximize your efficiency by rating the

CHART 7.2: PERSONS I KNOW, TO CONTACT

Relatives
1. _____
2. _____
3. _____
4. _____
5. _____

Neighbors
1. _____
2. _____
3. _____
4. _____
5. _____

Current Friends
1. _____
2. _____
3. _____
4. _____
5. _____

Old Friends
1. _____
2. _____
3. _____
4. _____
5. _____

School Friends
1. _____
2. _____
3. _____
4. _____
5. _____

People at Work
1. _____
2. _____
3. _____
4. _____
5. _____

Friends at Church
1. _____
2. _____
3. _____
4. _____
5. _____

People in Groups I Belong To
1. _____
2. _____
3. _____
4. _____
5. _____

Fellow Commuters
1. _____
2. _____
3. _____
4. _____
5. _____

Merchants or Store Clerks
1. _____
2. _____
3. _____
4. _____
5. _____

People Who Serve Me
1. _____
2. _____
3. _____
4. _____
5. _____

People at Parties
1. _____
2. _____
3. _____
4. _____
5. _____

People from Classes, Seminars
1. _____
2. _____
3. _____
4. _____
5. _____

People I Play Sports with
1. _____
2. _____
3. _____
4. _____
5. _____

people you plan to contact with a priority system from one (maybes) to five (probably not prospects). You can use Chart 7.2 to make your list and rate your prospects.

While you should be contacting people as you meet them anyway, making this list will remind you to make these contacts.

Also, make a list of special groups and types of individuals who would be especially interested in the program and are part of a large network of people. The heads of groups are especially good to contact, because they can turn their whole group onto the program, if they are interested.

Some of the groups and individuals with wide contact networks include:

Churches and temples (contact the minister, priest, or rabbi)

Religious or church groups

Community service clubs, such as the Lions, Rotarians, fraternal lodges, and women's service groups

Youth groups, such as the Boy Scouts, Girl Scouts, and local youth center

Self-improvement groups, such as toastmasters

Entrepreneur groups

Local business networking groups

Homeowner associations

Tenant groups

Political groups, such as Young Republicans, Young Democrats, and special-interest groups

Activity clubs, such as sports clubs and travel clubs

Singles groups

Senior citizen groups

Insurance and real estate agents

Schools

CHART 7.3: SPECIAL GROUPS AND TYPES
OF PEOPLE TO CONTACT

Churches and Religious
Groups

1. _____
2. _____
3. _____
4. _____
5. _____

Community Service Clubs

1. _____
2. _____
3. _____
4. _____
5. _____

Youth Groups

1. _____
2. _____
3. _____
4. _____
5. _____

Self-improvment Groups

1. _____
2. _____
3. _____
4. _____
5. _____

Local Trade Associations

1. _____
2. _____
3. _____
4. _____
5. _____

Entrepreneur/Business
Groups

1. _____
2. _____
3. _____
4. _____
5. _____

Homeowner/Tenant Groups

1. _____
2. _____
3. _____
4. _____
5. _____

Political Groups

1. _____
2. _____
3. _____
4. _____
5. _____

Singles Groups

1. _____
2. _____
3. _____
4. _____
5. _____

Activity Clubs

1. _____
2. _____
3. _____
4. _____
5. _____

Senior Citizen Groups

1. _____
2. _____
3. _____
4. _____
5. _____

Schools and School Groups

1. _____
2. _____
3. _____
4. _____
5. _____

CHART 7.3: *(Continued)*

Real Estate/Insurance Agents	People in Other MLM Businesses
1. _____	1. _____
2. _____	2. _____
3. _____	3. _____
4. _____	4. _____
5. _____	5. _____

People in other MLM businesses (particularly if they are promoting a related product to the same market)

People looking for jobs

You can use Chart 7.3 to make your list. Or if you decide to focus on a particular category (say churches or real estate agents), use (Chart 7.4).

Then, when you contact people, keep a record, either on a single form like the Leads Contact Sheet or on an index card for each person or group. Or even better, use a computer if you can to keep track of your records. A form you can use for your index cards is on Chart 7.5.

When you are targeting particular categories of individuals or groups, see if you can get a directory of members of that group (e.g., a list of all real estate agents who belong to a local trade association). Or use your telephone Yellow Pages and look under the appropriate heading to make your list (e.g., "Churches" and "Real Estate Agents").

Keep track of your referrals too. Thus, when someone refers you to someone else, indicate the name of the person making this referral in your Local Leads Contact Sheet or index card. This way you can say who referred you when you call which may give you more confidence and can help you make a sale.

Besides giving you ideas about *who to contact,* keeping these records is very important to help you keep track of *who you have contacted,* when, and the response. Then, you

CHART 7.4: LEADS CONTACT SHEET

DATE	NAME, ADDRESS, ZIP	PHONE	REFERRED BY	INTEREST Y/N	MEETING Y/N	ATTEND Y/N	MEMBERSHIP Y/N	COMMENTS

CHART 7.5: LEADS CONTACT CARD

Name: _____

Address: _____

City, State, Zip: _____

Phone: _____

How Referred: _____

Program(s) Described: _____

DATES CONTACTED	ABOUT WHAT	INTEREST Y/N	MEETING Y/N	RESULT Y/N	COMMENTS
_____	_____	_____	_____	_____	_____
_____	_____	_____	_____	_____	_____
_____	_____	_____	_____	_____	_____
_____	_____	_____	_____	_____	_____

have a clear picture of who is or is not interested, and whom to contact again, when, and about what.

Instructions for Using Leads Contact Sheet and Card

Obtain and record the following information from your contact:

Date: Note dates of *any* contacts, and if you need to call again, the date when you are supposed to do so. When you do follow up, note that date, too.

Name, Address, Zip: Whenever you contact someone, always try to get that person's name and address.

Phone Number: Unless you are contacting a company representative, try to get the person's work and evening phone numbers, and indicate which is which. Note the best time to call (day, evenings, weekends).

Referred By: Note the original source of the referral—a person, newspaper ad, etc.

Interest: Indicate whether interested (*Y*) or not (*N*). If the person is uncertain, sense what direction they are leaning in and add a question mark (*Y?, N?*). If you're not sure, just put down a question mark (*?*).

Meeting: If the person is interested in meeting with you personally or coming to a general meeting note this (*Y*) and indicate the day the individual plans to come. Then, you can easily call to reconfirm the day before or the day of the meeting.

Attendance: Indicate if he or she attended (*Y*). If not (*N*), you may want to follow up to find out what happened. Or at least you have a record of the results.

Membership: Indicate if the person decided to join (*Y*) or not (*N*). If the person is still considering, note this for follow-up later.

Comments: Record your observations or reactions, such as "sounds like a hot prospect," "especially interested in fishing." Then, when you call again or meet together, you can orient your presentation accordingly.

Getting Referrals

Referrals are a way to keep your leads list growing rapidly and effectively. You not only get more names to contact, but the names of people making the referrals help to open doors to people being more receptive to listen and ready to buy. Thus, whenever you talk to someone who is not interested (or even someone who doesn't become a distributor himself or herself), ask for a referral to others who might be interested either in the product, the business opportunity, or both, as appropriate. Try to get at least three referrals, and note any special comments (such as "mention the boat trip"). Then, when you contact these persons, if they are not interested, ask for a referral too. And so on. This way, you have an ever-expanding network of people to contact. Later, if you build a sales group, you can refer these names to people in your organization, so you don't do it all yourself and find that your growing file of names becomes unmanageable. But more about that later.

Getting referrals is extremely important, because when you mention a personal reference, the person you are contacting is much more willing to listen. So keep track of who referred you to whom, and use these names to open doors when you make your first contact.

The referrals chart (Chart 7.6) will help you keep track of these referrals. Then, when you contact someone who is interested, transfer his or her name to your list of active prospects.

Some Easy Ways to Get Started

After targeting your potential market and thinking about leads, the next step is starting to contact potential consumers and distributors. An easy way to get started is to do things close to home and talk to others about the program as you go about your everyday business. Then, after you have some experience, you can gradually try other ways, such as advertising and contacting the leaders of groups.

Here are some things you can do with little or no effort or expense.

- *Invite a few friends and neighbors to a presentation at your house.* If you feel comfortable, do the presentation yourself. Otherwise, ask the leader of your sales group or sponsor to do a few presentations you can observe or assist with to get you started. Generally your sales group leader or sponsor will be more than willing (or should be) to help you get started in the right way, since he or she will benefit from your sales ability as well.

CHART 7.6: REFERRALS

DATE	NAME OF LEAD	ADDRESS AND ZIP	PHONE	PERSON MAKING REFERRAL	COMMENTS

- *Invite a few friends, neighbors, or business associates to a nearby meeting about your product or business opportunity.* And if they agree to come, arrange to take them there yourself. Otherwise, people often say they will meet you there and don't show up.

- *Tell the group leader or program chair of an organization you belong to* about your new program and offer to put on a free event for them (possibly your sales group leader or sponsor will do it).

- *Carry little packets of literature with you.* Include an introductory flier on the product and company; a list of meeting locations, if available; your name and phone number; and a small sample of the product, if feasible. Now when you meet people you consider prospects, hand out these packets to them, suggesting they might like to try the product. Or, as appropriate, indicate that this information will also tell them about a business opportunity, if they want to earn some extra money. You can hand out these materials to almost anyone. Some possibilities are the toll taker where you pay your toll; the gas station attendant who sells you gas; the waitress in a restaurant who serves you; the bartender who sells you a drink; the store clerk who sells you merchandise; the teller at your bank; the person you sit next to on a bus, train, or plane; a person you meet at a party or meeting; customers or exhibitors at trade shows and fairs; people waiting on line with you; people leaving an event that suggests they might be especially interested in your product (such as people at a health fair if you have a health product); and anybody else you meet as you go about your daily life.

- *Put up posters or fliers at places you go to,* such as campus buildings and bulletin boards, churches and community centers, supermarkets, coin-operated laundries, stores or restaurants that display posters and fliers, and so on.

- *Leave fliers for displays* at parties, meetings and conferences, and at your office or school. If you are at an event or in a place where you can do so, make an announcement about your program and afterward pass out or post your fliers. Your announcement will focus attention on your message and give you more credibility. It suggests you have the support of the leader of the group or organization.

Start Talking About Your Program Wherever You Are

Promote your product or business wherever you are, whatever you do. Just look for the opportune moment to say something about it, and then you can bring it up casually in the conversation when you talk to your friends, business associates, whomever you meet. Then once you have established a lead-in into your product and people seem receptive to listen, emphasize the *benefits* of the product or the business opportunity, as appropriate.

For example, if someone mentions having trouble losing weight and you are promoting a health program, that's a perfect opener to describe how your products can help the person on his diet.

If you are starting to become successful, you can promote your business by bringing up some of the ways your life has changed (for example, a new car, a vacation to Hawaii) as you talk. If a friend observes that she wishes she could take some time off to travel, you can explain that you just took a great trip there—all made possible by your new business. Then, you can explain how she can get involved in this business, too.

Similarly, if you are at the post office buying stamps, you might comment, "You know, you've been seeing a lot of me these days, because of my new business. I have people writing to me from all over the country."

Or, when a friend mentions that he's saving for a new camera you might tell him, "Say, I'm in this terrific new program where you could earn that money by working a few extra hours a week.' The point is that every situation may provide some natural openers. So look for these openers, and if you find them, push ahead.

Learn How to Market to
Your Target Audience

Slanting your approach to best appeal to the target market you have selected is critical, since everyone you contact has different wants and needs, and certain groups or types of individuals have special identifiable interests. So consider how you can slant your presentation to appeal to your own markets. This way you emphasize the features of your program that are likely to be of most interest to the particular individual or group you are contacting.

Most salespeople tend to vary their approach on an ad hoc spur of the moment basis as they contact people. But it is more efficient to develop a systematic approach to the different markets you have selected, particularly if you are going to be advertising, creating fliers, sending letters, or otherwise seriously promoting your program. This way you are more apt to hit your target. It's like using a rifle with a cross-hair viewfinder so you see what you are aiming at, versus shooting off a shotgun that spews out bullets everywhere, most of which don't hit the mark.

Chart 7.7, The Target Market—Products Benefit Form, is designed to help you do this audience targeting by determining what features might best be promoted to each selected group.

To use the matrix, do the following:

1. List the key features or benefits of the program in Column 1.
2. List the groups you think might be most interested in the program across the top.

CHART 7.7: TARGET MARKET—PRODUCT BENEFITS FORM
What Product Benefits Appeal to Different Target Markets

PRODUCT FEATURES AND BENEFITS (List the key features or benefits of the program)	TARGET MARKET (List the types of individuals or groups the program is most likely to appeal to; then go down the column and check off the features or benefits you think would have the most appeal to that group)						

3. Go down each column, and for each group, place an *X* in the box if you think that group might be especially interested in that product feature.

4. Indicate how important you think each feature checked might be to members of that group by rating it from one (least important) to five (most important).

5. Tailor your advertising, fliers, letters, or other promotional efforts to emphasize the features that appeal most to that group. You want to focus on the most important features—highlight one or two, at most three, for the most effective ad. This focus helps provide added impact.

Chapter 8

TAKING YOUR PROSPECT TO AN OPPORTUNITY MEETING

Many MLM marketing programs feature business opportunity meetings to recruit new distributors. These meetings range in size from small home gatherings to large splashy presentations with all the excitement of a massive company rally or political convention.

Some distributors take their prospects to opportunity meetings regularly. Others rely mainly on small one-on-one presentations and take prospects only occasionally. These meetings can be very valuable sales tools, so if your company or an upline sponsor sets these up in your area, consider taking a prospect to one of these meetings. These can help to do your selling for you and even close the sale.

The reason that a good opportunity meeting can be such a powerful sales method is that it creates a high level of excitement—particularly when it's a big one because of the dynamics of the group. Also, such meetings usually have a good professional polish commonly more than you can provide yourself, especially when you are just getting started, so these can be a good, persuasive way to introduce your prospect to the product or business.

Most good sales leaders or sponsors will put on these meetings for you and other distributors in their sales group, or they will be part of a network of people active in the program and can tell you when and where these meetings occur.

THE KEYS TO GETTING SUCCESSFUL
RESULTS AT A MEETING

You can up your chances for success when you take a prospect to a meeting by following these key guidelines:

- *If you have set up the appointment several days in advance, call to confirm that you are going to the meeting that day.* This way you increase chances that the person will go as previously agreed. When you call, simply restate the arrangements you agreed to and advise the person that, as planned, you will pick him or her up (the better way) or that you will meet at a certain location (and indicate that you plan to wait, so the person feels committed to show up).

  Also, when you call, *don't ask* if the person is still planning to attend. That provides the person with a chance to rethink the original decision and perhaps to have a change of mind, since the excitement of your original pitch may have faded. Just assume he or she is coming, and you are calling as a courtesy reminder.

- *Pick up the person if you can.* This way you make it as convenient as possible for your prospect to attend; you know that he or she is coming. Otherwise, people may frequently agree to meet you at the meeting, but don't show up, because they feel less enthusiastic than when you first spoke to them. But if you pick them up, you can resell them along with providing the added convenience.

- *Go to the meeting early, preferably about 10 to 15 minutes before the scheduled time.* This gives you a chance to sign in (most meetings have some form of registration) and get a good seat so you can easily see and hear everything. Also, you can introduce your prospect to other people, advise about what to expect, and generate enthusiasm about the benefits to be presented in the upcoming presentation. As a result, your prospect will be more attentive and feel more positive when the meeting begins and thus will show greater interest in the program.

- *Have your distributor agreement and a packet of materials readily available to give your prospect at the end of the meeting.* This way you can build on the enthusiasm created by the meeting, and you may be able to sign up your prospect immediately as a new distributor. In fact, the meeting leader will typically end by inviting prospects to get together with their sponsors to discuss the program in more detail and sign up.

    Once the meeting ends, invite your prospect to sign up, and if you notice any signs of hesitation, ask for any questions and answer them. If you can, finish your discussion and sign up at the meeting site. But if you have any trouble doing so (for example, the room is noisy or everyone has to leave the room because of a deadline), invite your prospect to a nearby coffee shop or cafe to discuss the program there.

- *Try to get your prospect to sign up after the meeting, if you can't follow up in a day or two.* When you discuss the program after the meeting, be prepared to handle any objections, and if your prospect wants to think it over, try to encourage a decision now by asking the prospect to indicate what he or she wants to think over. Perhaps you can answer this concern now. In short, do all you can to get the person to sign up now, when the enthusiasm of the meeting is at a peak.

    But if your prospect is determined to wait, accept this graciously and say you will call in a day or two (unless, of course, your prospect adamantly asks you not to call because he would rather call you if interested, though this is rare). Then, assuming your prospect is receptive to your calling, do that. Don't let more than a few days go by, because your prospect is more likely to remember the meeting and be more receptive to an early follow-up. He or she is much more likely to cool off after a long delay.

Chapter 9

PUTTING ON A PRODUCTIVE ONE-ON-ONE PRESENTATION

A small one-on-one presentation of your product or business is an excellent way to get started. Just invite a friend or contact to meet with you at your house, at the prospect's house, or perhaps over coffee, and then you share your story.

If your prospect is married, invite husband and wife together so they see the program at the same time. Then, you won't hear the excuse, "But I have to talk it over with (my spouse) first." They both may still want to discuss and think about it, but they are better able to decide now.

Another possibility that can save time and energy, once you feel confident enough to do this, is the expanded one-on-one format, which some distributors use. At such a meeting, arrange for about three to eight people to attend at one time. Some distributors do this because they believe it is too expensive in time to give a presentation to only one person or couple. Also, they may set up an appointment and the person doesn't show up. But if they have a small meeting for a few people, their time is spent more productively, since the meeting is more likely to occur, and someone is more likely to sign up. At the same time, the meeting remains small, so it preserves the intimacy of the one-on-one presentation.

HOW TO PUT ON YOUR PRESENTATION

When you make your presentation, be prepared. Plan in advance what you are going to say. This way, you can keep your presentation short, compact, and to the point, which makes for a more powerful presentation than a long rambly one.

Preferably keep your presentation to about a half hour to an hour. Otherwise prospects may start to lose interest.

CHART 9.1: PRESENTATION CHECKLIST

ITEMS I PLAN TO USE IN MY PRESENTATION	ITEMS I NOW HAVE (CHECK)	ITEMS I NEED TO GET FOR MY PRESENTATION

CHART 9.2: ORDER OF PRESENTATION CHECKLIST

The order in which I plan to use materials in my presentation:

1. _____	16. _____
2. _____	17. _____
3. _____	18. _____
4. _____	19. _____
5. _____	20. _____
6. _____	21. _____
7. _____	22. _____
8. _____	23. _____
9. _____	24. _____
10. _____	25. _____
11. _____	26. _____
12. _____	27. _____
13. _____	28. _____
14. _____	29. _____
15. _____	30. _____

But if they have lots of questions, you know they are interested, and you can go longer.

Also, have any supporting materials organized and close at hand, so you can readily refer to specific items to make the point you want.

It's important to have more than a general idea of what you want to say, because if you prepare only casually, you are likely to forget major points. Or if you cover them, you may do so in a haphazard way.

Thus, *have an outline or script firmly in mind (or even written), and assemble your supporting materials in the order you want to refer to them.* You can use the Presentation Checklist (Chart 9.1) and the Order of Presentation Checklist (Chart 9.2) to help you prepare.

Do some practicing initially until you are familiar with the major points you want to make and the sequence in which you plan to present them. If you prefer, have your outline or script with you when you make your first presentations; so you are sure to cover everything and will feel more relaxed. Later, when you know the material, you won't need to have the written copy with you.

SUPPORTING MATERIALS

Supporting materials are useful for creating interest and providing proof that you represent a good company with good products or services. Following are some suggestions on supporting materials to include. Choose among them to help build a more powerful presentation.

Testimonials. Use either tapes or letters (video-tapes if you have them). It's best to get these from several types of people to show that interest in your product is broad based. Also, it is even more persuasive to have a testimonial from someone in the same field as your prospect, so he or she can more closely identify with that person. If you can, order your presentation to present those testimonials first.

If you use testimonial letters, try to show each one on a nice letterhead from the person giving the testimonial. Such formal testimonials are much more impressive, if you can get them, than are handwritten notes. And if necessary, be willing to draft or even write this testimonial for some-one who pleads a lack of time to do this himself or herself.

Include, too, some identifying material about the person giving the testimonial, if this is not already provided in the letter or tape—such as the person's name, town, occu-pation, sales record (if good), and how long he or she has been a consumer of the company's products or a distributor for that company.

Slides. Some companies have professionally pro-duced slide-sound or slide-script presentations. Or if you feel creative, produce your own show or add some of your own slides to the company presentation to make it more personal. For example, show yourself and some friends using the product or service.

Graphs, Charts, Posters.   Visual aids make your presentation seem more solid and interesting, and they graphically support the points you make.

Combining Your Support
Materials into a Presentation Manual

Ideally, combine the suitable supporting materials you have created or assembled into a presentation manual. Some companies and sponsors have already produced these, and if so, use them. Or, if you prefer, adapt this material, or develop your own, to suit your personal style. (However, check company guidelines as to how free a hand you have, and get any necessary approvals.)

One advantage of a manual is that you can go over the major points of your presentation in a step-by-step fashion, because your manual keeps you right on target and helps you to avoid forgetting major points—so you cover everything. Use a loose-leaf or other binder that permits you to change the sequence of materials around; then you can shift sections of the manual around for different presentations, or you can vary the sequence in which you present different sections in response to your prospect's interests.

Another advantage of a manual is that it looks impressive and backs up what you say graphically. Some techniques for making a good manual are described in the last section of this chapter.

Using Your Supporting Materials for
Handouts after Your Presentation

Another way to use supporting materials is to create a packet of materials you can hand out after your presentation.

While some people may be convinced from your presentation to buy or become a distributor on the spot, many will want to think it over, and if so, it is important that they can review something tangible, which reminds them of the major benefits you discussed in your presentation. In addition, these *review materials can include additional supporting documents not mentioned in your presentation,* such as testimonials from satisfied product users or successful distributors, and information on why the product works (particularly needed if you have a health or nutrition product or a high-tech product). These materials show that the program is really solid and that you are truly professional. Just giving out your business card after a presentation is not enough.

WHAT TO COVER IN YOUR PRESENTATION (AND IN YOUR MANUAL)

Organize your presentation and your manual to suit your personal style—though in general, your presentation should cover the major areas described in this section. If you are using a manual with supporting materials, arrange them to follow the same sequence as your presentation, so your presentation flows easily.

Depending on your program and the interests of your prospect, vary the sequence in which you make your presentation to emphasize the consumer benefits or the business opportunity or just the consumer appeal alone. In some cases, if the prospect is only interested in being a consumer it's better to present only the consumer benefits to avoid alienating a good customer for the product with a business opportunity pitch. Conversely, some people may be primarily interested in the business opportunity, and with them, you will want to emphasize that, although in this case, it's usually best to emphasize the product benefits, too, since a person must be sold on the product first before he or she can sell it.

Start with something to get your prospect's *attention*—the first step in selling anything. Next *build interest* by showing how the benefits of the product or business opportunity will fill his or her needs. Then work on *arousing the person's desire* to become involved in the business.

As questions or objections surface, be ready to answer them with good answers; these will increase your prospect's *confidence* in the product, the company, and in you.

Finally, help your prospect *make a decision and take action* on the grounds that this action will be beneficial and result in his or her satisfaction. If possible, encourage the person to act now, but if someone hesitates and is unwilling to decide now, give him or her the space to review the product or opportunity, and ideally, provide an information packet to help him or her decide.

More specifically, include the following topics, as relevant, in your presentation and/or in your manual in any sequence that works best for you.

Introduction

Offer some attention-grabbing information that shows the value of your product and establishes credibility. This might include testimonials by users, claims by researchers, your experience using the product, a description of the company's fast growth, and a demonstration of the product or service. In your manual, you might include pictures or illustrations to show it being demonstrated whether you actually do this demonstration in your presentation or not.

A Description of the Product or Service

Include a discussion of how or why the product works, but don't get too detailed, unless the prospect asks questions. For example, some people find it sufficient to learn that a diet program worked for you and don't care what exactly is in the products. Others do. So sense the depth of your prospect's interest and knowledge, and respond accordingly. Also, you might include in this section a hands-on demonstration (if not part of the introduction) and photographs of the product or service in use. Likewise, your manual section dealing with this topic might include some summary descriptions or photos or illustrations of your product in action.

A (Very Brief) Discussion of the Company for Consumers Only; A More Detailed Discussion for Business Opportunity Seekers

Talk about how solid and stable the company is and discuss its ability to produce the product or service. Some topics to cover include the company history in the business, names and backgrounds of key company officials, and reasons the company was formed and how it was organized. With people primarily interested in being consumers, keep this discussion fairly brief; say just enough to establish credibility. With business opportunity seekers, go into more details, since they will have more interest in the company they will represent. Here your accompanying manual section might include things like news clips on the company, a list of company leaders, a brief description of past credits, photos of the company headquarters and operations, and the like.

Backup Support You Will Provide

To Consumers.   In some programs, your backup support doesn't matter much to consumers, since they order direct from the company. But in other cases, consumers may look to you for advice and assistance to help them in using the product or service. This is particularly true in the case of diet programs or health products, which require ongoing follow-up for proper use.

To Potential Distributors.   Prospective distributors need the assurance that you will be there to assist. Since some now shop around for the best sponsor or sales leader to help them in marketing a particular product line, you should be convincing in explaining what you will do to help. So play up your background and your plans to support them. For example, some topics to cover are:

- Your knowledge or expertise in the product area (for example, if you're promoting a health or diet product, it's great if you're a nutritionist)
- Your background in sales or marketing
- The team of distributors you are working with
- The kinds of activities organized by you or your sales organization (such as local meetings, rallies, newsletters, and so on)

A Brief Introduction to Network or Multi-Level Marketing

Many people still have not heard of multi-level or network marketing or have misconceptions about it as a pyramid scheme. So if you are looking to build up such a sales group, include a section on how this form of marketing works for people who are not knowledgeable.

In your explanation, illustrate how a marketing network grows, and show the difference when each person on the average contacts two, three, four, and five persons. However, point out that the program works differently for each individual, depending on how much effort he or she puts into it. (You can use Charts 1.1 and 1.2 in the beginning of the book.)

Since the issue of illegal pyramids may arise in discussing MLM, it helps to show the difference. (You can use Chart 1.3 in Chapter 1.)

After a general discussion of this marketing approach, talk about why your company is an especially good opportunity in this field, and give your reasons (now fill in the strengths of the company: top-quality products, management, marketing plan, and so forth).

A Description of the Marketing Plan

If you are seeking distributors in your presentation, explain how the marketing plan works, too. Include some diagrams showing the plan's basic structure as well as how the plan might work in practice. But be conservative. Use actual data from the company or other distributors if you have it. Alternatively, make conservative projections about how the organization is likely to grow or how much someone is likely to make.

Because of various regulations about what MLM companies can say and cannot say in literature, you may not be able to get detailed information on potential earnings from the company or your sponsor. (Legally, companies cannot make projections about hypothetical earnings, or they can get in trouble with the post office and other authorities. They are, however, generally permitted to provide some examples of how much a distributor needs to sell to qualify for different levels of bonuses or what a typical distributor makes.)

Despite these restrictions on showing hypothetical earnings, people are likely to ask anyway, so work out a few projections yourself if you can't get them from your sales group leader or sponsor. But when you use them, emphasize that they are completely hypothetical, and make sure people understand you have developed them yourself.

It is also useful to include testimonials from distributors who have been successful. Other materials and diagrams you might use are a chart showing the structure of the plan, a chart showing how the plan might operate in practice, and copies of checks showing the earnings of other distributors, including yourself. You can use a big check someone has earned to illustrate, but don't imply that everyone is likely to do this well, because people don't earn that kind of money when they start a new sales program, and most don't make huge incomes each month. Simply say that this check shows what one person has earned and what is possible. Also, to be more realistic, perhaps show your first few checks with the company or the checks of a few other distributors for their first few months. People have an easier time identifying with this.

A Close That Encourages
People to Get Involved

If it seems appropriate, *ask for the order.* Simply show your prospect an order blank or distributor agreement, and urge placing an order or signing up now.

However, if your prospect seems sincerely hesitant, don't be too pushy. Instead, send the person home with some literature and possibly some samples. (For example, if you're promoting a health company, recommend that your prospect take some vitamin pills and call you in the morning to say how he or she feels.) Then follow up later yourself.

Other Keys to a Successful Presentation

Besides being prepared with an organized presentation and supporting materials, take into consideration other elements that contribute to an effective presentation. These are the following:

Adapt Your Presentation to Your Prospect. Use what you already know about your prospect and probe further during your presentation, if need be, to determine how to slant your talk to what the prospect wants or needs.

One decision is whether to emphasize the product advantages for the consumer, the business opportunity, or both. You want to find out what people are most interested in. Some may be interested only in the product, some mainly in how much they can make marketing it; some are receptive to both alternatives. Adjust your talk accordingly.

In the case of the person who is now interested in being a consumer only, respect that and don't try to push the business opportunity now, which can be a customer turnoff. Instead, wait until after the person becomes a customer; you can always bring up the income earnings possibilities later. In fact, people in multi-level marketing find that some of their best distributors have started off as consumers only.

Be ready to modify your approach, too, based on whether you are speaking to someone who is only interested in part-time work or someone seeking a full-time business opportunity.

Also, adapt your style to what feels comfortable with that person and to the circumstances of the presentation. For instance, you can be more informal with a friend, while it's best to be more professional and formal with a person you don't know. Similarly, give a more structured and slick presentation to a businessperson who is used to this professionalism. But when you talk to someone in another field, a musician, for example, present your case accordingly.

Then, too, pay attention to personal style preferences; some people are more relaxed, casual, and friendly, while others feel more comfortable when you keep your distance.

In short, play every presentation by ear, and in adapting you presentation to your prospect, take into account such factors as

- your relationship to this person (friend, business associate, stranger)
- your prospect's occupational background, educational level, and main interest in the program (consumer only, part-time distributor, full-time distributor)
- your prospect's experience in MLM, network, or direct sales (e.g., no knowledge, some experience, very experienced)
- your prospect's personal style (relaxed, casual, informal, warm and friendly versus distant, reserved, aloof, and formal)

Frequently, you will find you make many of these adjustments automatically, since everyone makes many adjustments intuitively as he or she interacts with people. But being aware of these factors can help you fine-tune these adjustments you make.

Know Your Facts.   This way, you can come up with the answers if your prospect asks for details. Many prospects never ask. But some may, and you should know what to tell them. Otherwise, if you hem and haw, answer evasively, deflect the question, or admit several times that you don't know, you will lose credibility.

Don't Make Unrealistic Claims.   Some limited hype can give a product or a company pizzazz. But if there is too much puffery, you will lose credibility. For example, don't make extravagant claims for what a product can do. People may not believe you, and if people start using the product themselves, they will soon find out what you claimed isn't true, and your credibility will decline.

Likewise, avoid making untrue claims about a program's earning potential. Don't assure prospects they are guaranteed to make "big bucks" or any kind of income, because earnings depend on how much work a person does and consumer response, among other factors. Furthermore, only a small percentage of distributors make the fantastic sums widely talked about in multi-level sales.

Also, if you make wild claims about possible earnings, using the incomes of the most successful distributors, most people will feel it impossible for them to achieve this much, even if they believe you, and they may not want to undertake a project that seems so overwhelming. By contrast, if you quote figures they can realistically aspire to based on how active they plan to be in the program, they are more likely to act.

Don't Argue.   If your prospect doesn't like the product or business opportunity, accept this. Not everyone says yes, and if you can't convince your prospect after presenting your program and answering questions and objections, don't feel you have to keep struggling to gain acceptance, and don't feel you have done anything wrong if you can't convince someone. Just accept the fact that different people have different likes and interests, and go on and present your program to someone else.

HOW TO MAKE AN ATTRACTIVE
PRESENTATION MANUAL

Once you decide on the general order of your presentation, organize your supporting materials and put them in an attractive binder to make your presentation more professional. As noted earlier, a binder allows you to shift pages around, so you can change the order of your materials if you want to adapt your presentation to your prospect.

While you may be able to use the training manuals or marketing kits provided by some companies for presentation purposes, often these are extremely detailed and are more for your use than for making a presentation to others. Still, it is important to have this detailed product information on hand, or include it in the appendix of your manual, so it's readily accessible if someone asks about it.

You can dress up your manual by placing individual sheets of paper in plastic sheet protectors. These protectors come in various styles and usually have a three-hole-punched side panel, so you can slip each sheet of paper into its own plastic pocket and don't have to punch holes into the paper itself.

In organizing your manual, separate each section (such as "Introduction," "Product or Service," "The Company," "Sponsor Support," and "Marketing Plan") with a divider or introduce it with a title page. You can use rub-on letters to make headlines for this page. Either rub them directly onto the divider or title page or make a master copy of your title page layout on white paper. Then run off a copy on colored paper or good bond paper.

Other excellent additions to your manual include charts, graphs, photographs, and other visual materials. If these are not provided by your company or sponsor, you can develop your own fairly easily. For example, cut some pictures out of magazines to illustrate a point. Or transform raw sales figures into a bar graph showing how sales have grown each year.

Some local touches help, too, to show how you have been using the program yourself, who is in your local organization, and what your group has been doing. For example, a section on the backup support your organization provides might include

- a directory of local people and where they live
- a calendar of local activities
- a copy of the local newsletter
- a chart showing your immediate sponsor and the people in your immediate downline, so prospects can see how they will fit into your organization
- copies of checks received by local distributors or sales reps or by leaders of your sales group

You can also include an appendix for more technical product and marketing information. You won't plan to discuss this in your initial presentation, but you have it readily accessible for backup support if anyone asks.

Finally, after you decide what to include in what order, prepare a table of contents so you can easily refer to everything, and if you change the order, change the table of contents accordingly. Also, if your prospect wants to flip through your manual, a table of contents will facilitate this.

Chapter 10

DEVELOPING CUSTOMERS AND TURNING THEM INTO DISTRIBUTORS

One effective approach for building a sales group in MLM is developing customers first and then turning them into distributors. Many people don't use this approach; they prefer to zero in on people who want a business opportunity and almost exclusively try to recruit distributors. But in doing so, they not only eliminate potential customers, they exclude many customers who may subsequently decide to distribute the product, too, because they like it so much or because their life circumstances have changed and they now are looking for ways to make money.

This turning customers into distributors makes great sense when you consider the vast number of people who are potential customers versus those who are likely to be serious distributors in an MLM business (a ratio of about 10 or 20 to 1). There are many more prospects for likely customers than for likely distributors. But then these customers can be a source of other customers, because once people get hooked on the product, they almost automatically tell others about it. Then, when you show them how they can save money by becoming distributors and purchasing wholesale or point out they can easily make money by doing what they are already doing—telling others about the product—you can readily gain a new distributor.

If you had tried to pitch the business opportunity first, the individuals might have been turned off. But now they like the product and have an ongoing relationship with you, so they are more receptive. Besides, they may realize that if it's so easy to become a distributor and recruit others, as you did in sponsoring them, then why shouldn't they do it too?

SOME SUCCESS STORIES

I have met dozens of MLM distributors who tried the business opportunity/recruiting approach with little success. People didn't show up at meetings. Or if they did, they didn't join. Then, if they did join, the distributor found it hard to keep them motivated. Or these people had a similar "recruit other distributors" mentality, resulting in a marketing structure overloaded with distributors and few customers. So there were few sales to ultimate customers, and nobody made much money, including the company. The sales structure might be growing, but the product volume wasn't keeping pace.

But then, when these distributors shifted their approach to emphasize the product and being a customer first, that worked for them. For example, Bob, a distributor of health foods and vitamins, clipped a few vitamins to the back of his business card, and when he met someone who seemed tired, he would whip out his card and say, "Try them. They'll make you feel really good, and then call me in the morning." Janet, representing a travel program, would invite single people to a social evening at her house, and then she showed some slides describing how they could go on exciting low-cost trips. "I don't even try to market the business to people," she confessed. "But people sign up, and they bring others to sign up, too."

One key to this consumer-into-distributor approach is using the products yourself and telling the people you meet every day about them. For example, Joan, a former high school math teacher, built a business grossing over $10,000 a month in three months by talking to the people she met in supermarkets, at the post office, at the gas station—everywhere. She began by using the products—vitamins and a water dome that purified water. Then, she started talking about them enthusiastically to everyone she met. "I ask them if they're concerned about the water—and what vitamins they take." Then, she recommends what she is using and offers to get the products for them.

But Joan doesn't tell people about the business opportunity in the beginning, because she feels that might turn them off. As she explains, "Many people think multi-level marketing is like knocking on doors. But a satisfied customer is really your best distributor. When they see how good the product is, they think of other people they know who might use it. Then, they realize they could sell the product, too."

Another distributor, Barry, who also doesn't go out of his way to contact people, uses an effective three-phase approach to turn customers for his health products into distributors. First, he always has a few sample packs with him, gives out free samples, and asks people to call him the next day to let him know the results. When they call, he finds out about their level of interest. Do they want to only be a consumer and get the product wholesale? Would they like to tell a few friends about the product and make money, too? Would they like to start or expand a home business using this product?

Then, depending on their level of interest, Barry invites them to one of the following: (1) a small product seminar to learn more about the product and other health products, (2) a business opportunity meeting put on by some distributors in the company, or (3) a lunch together to discuss the business opportunity in depth.

Other distributors combine advertising, phoning, and other sales techniques with this consumer-first approach. For example, several distributors I know have promoted diet and nutrition products successfully by advertising their products in a few local papers, and when people call, they talk only about the product. Then, they invite the callers to come to their office to try the product or arrange to meet in the prospective customer's office or home.

When they have this first meeting, they focus on the product, too. They may mention in passing that there is a business opportunity for people who like the product. But they defer any discussion about this until the person has become an active consumer. That way the person develops a real commitment to the product and doesn't feel under any pressure to make it a business, which is what makes some people resist becoming consumers in the first place.

However, once persons become active consumers, they can be turned around. And some become extremely dynamic distributors. For example, Nancy was seeing a holistic physician who recommended a particular herbal remedy. She used it for several months. Then, after seeing dramatic changes in herself due to the product, she became a strong advocate and began telling others. Gradually, she built a business, and a few months later, her husband joined her in what had become a full-time effort.

MAJOR STRATEGIES

In summary, the distributors who have turned consumers into distributors use most of these strategies:

- They use the product themselves and are highly enthusiastic about it.
- They use every opportunity to talk up their product, and they slip it into the conversation in a casual, informal way by describing it as something that turns them on or can help someone else.
- If the product lends itself to free samples, they give these out and ask the person to call them to report the results, or they call a few days later to follow up.

- If they advertise or use other promotional techniques, they push the product only, although they may indicate there is a business opportunity, too. But they mention the business only as an aside and focus on getting the person to try and use the product.

- They have some product on hand to supply the needs of their retail customers, and they order it for their customers, as needed.

- They not only supply their customers with product, but they help them use it successfully. Such assistance is especially important with health or high-technology products, for consumers can easily use the products incorrectly and hence feel dissatisfied or frustrated.

- They invite people to product meetings or demonstrations to get more information on how to use the product and why it works the way it does.

- Once the consumer seems sold on the product, they explain that he or she can purchase the product at wholesale by signing a distributor agreement.

- They also tell the consumer that he or she can make money just by telling other people about the product. Then, if the consumer is interested they invite the person to a business opportunity meeting or make an individual presentation.

- If the consumer decides to become a distributor, they continue to support and train that individual, just as they would any other distributor.

Chapter 11

HOSTING MEETINGS OR SALES PARTIES AT HOME

After you feel comfortable giving individual presentations, you can put on product demonstrations or business opportunity presentations in your home for small groups. These might include prospects you have invited. Or, if you are working with a few active distributors, invite them to bring guests, too.

Follow the same steps as in a one-on-one presentation. Perhaps add a few gracious touches to make your presentation seem more like a social occasion. But keep things comfortable and informal. Some guidelines for a successful small home meeting are the following:

- *Keep your livingroom or other room where you are meeting arranged as it usually is.* You want to make the place feel warm and homey. You don't want people to feel as if they are in a classroom or theater. If you need extra chairs, scatter them around the room or bring them out later.
- *Have coffee or light refreshments on hand and invite people to help themselves before the meeting starts.* This way people can be more relaxed and can mix

and mingle with each other. Some hosts enjoy making special hors d'oeuvres and creating a small buffet, though some distributors feel it is better if you don't do anything special particularly if you are meeting with people you don't know well, because then your guests don't feel you will be trying extra hard to pitch them something they may not want.

- *Dress comfortably, but well.* Dress well to present a good, serious, professional impression. But don't overdo it, because you will seem insincere, and if you dress much more formally than everyone else, others may feel uncomfortable. Essentially, you want to dress just a notch above everyone else, but not much more.

- *If guests are late or don't show, start the meeting anyway, no later than 15 minutes after it was scheduled to begin.* Frequently, people don't come, so don't worry about this or express concern to others. And don't hold the meeting up for latecomers, because that shows a lack of respect for the people who are there. They have shown enough interest to come—and on time—so pay attention to them. They are the people who are important to you—not the latecomers and no-shows.

    Thus, put on the meeting for them, and if latecomers appear, invite them to quietly join the meeting. Indicate that you will be glad to meet with them later to answer their questions about what they may have missed. And *don't* try to start the meeting over for them—a sure way to antagonize the people who were on time.

- *To begin the meeting, get everyone together in the meeting room, invite them to sit down, and start by making everyone feel comfortable.* If everyone knows everyone, a few introductory quips or comments are fine. But if some people are new, start off with introductions. Introduce yourself, and say a little about what you do and how you happened to get into this program. Next ask the others to introduce themselves in turn and say what they do and why they are here, too.

Then, go into the presentation. As in the one-on-one meeting, you can organize your presentation in a variety of ways, as appropriate for your group, to cover such topics as

- information on the product or service (including reports on the experience of users, such as yourself).
- a demonstration or hands-on experience with the product.
- a discussion of the company.
- a discussion of the backup support you and your organization provide.
- an introduction to multi-level or network marketing (if any guests are unfamiliar with it).
- a close, in which you urge people to order or sign up.

PUTTING ON A SALES PARTY

The sales party or party plan approach is an excellent way to sell certain products. Pioneered by Stanley Home Products about 50 years ago, the party plan has been the mainstay of companies whose names are now household words, such as Mary Kay, Tupperware, and Avon.

Basically, to put on a sales party, you go to someone's home to sell to a group of individuals who may be interested in the product. Also, you look for consumers at these parties who would like to organize and host parties in their own home or perhaps put on a party like yours.

This approach lends itself particularly well to a product that needs to be demonstrated or needs a personal touch. For example, some products commonly sold via the party plan include cosmetics, jewelry, lingerie, household supplies, gifts, fine glassware, and recently, food. Typically, these products appeal to women, and usually women are the main participants at these parties. The salespeople for companies with these plans commonly have titles indicating they are specialists in the product, such as "beauty consultant" or "fashion representative."

Organizing the Party

Usually, to put on a sales party, you invite a woman to act as a hostess and invite several friends to her home to see your products. (Or if you have a product that appeals to men, too, ask a couple to host the event.) In return, you offer the hostess or host a free gift or percentage of the sales revenue. Or alternatively, some distributors offer the host or hostess $1 for each person present, apart from any gifts or percentages, on the grounds that the host's job is to get the guests there, while the distributor's job is to sell them.

As a variation on this approach, contact leaders of social and church groups and offer to put on a party for their group. In this case, the incentive for putting on the party might go to the organization as a whole.

To make sure the hostess or host understands what to do, go over some basics. The hostess should make the setting as comfortable and conducive to selling as possible. Most offer their guests something simple like coffee and cookies; others include fancy hors d'oeuvres or even turn the event into a potluck before the presentation. Suggest the possible alternatives, and leave it up to the hostess or host to decide, based on the crowd that will be coming and personal preferences.

Whatever the arrangements, the hostess should advise the guests they are coming to hear a sales presentation and should bring their checkbooks if they want to purchase anything. This way they come prepared to buy—and no one is miffed because they find the evening is more than a social occasion.

With this proper buildup, the sales party is a good setting for making sales. People who attend usually come for a mixture of reasons, including getting out of the house, doing something different, and finding a good bargain or unique product. A good presentation helps whet their appetite for the product, because it makes the product more exciting and desirable by showing how it is used. So the person can experience using the product, and your role as an authority on the product helps sell it, too. For example, you demonstrate how the cosmetics look and should be used by giving a facial, or you show how a decorative item would look on the wall.

Another reason a sales party can work well is that some guests may view making a purchase as part of the price they pay for an entertaining afternoon or evening. Then, too, some feel an obligation to buy because you and the hostess have spent time putting on the event and entertaining them. Further, the sales party creates a captive audience setting, where the excitement of one person is transmitted to everyone else, much as at an auction. When a few people start buying, suddenly others want to buy, too.

You can also use your creativity to turn a sales party into a theatrical event. For instance, Donna, a distributor for a high-quality lingerie and loungewear line, found eagerly attended sales parties and great success in sales by turning the party into a kind of performance event. She read poetry while the models walked about to show off different items, led the audience in a creative visualization technique dealing with love, and had soft music playing in the background. Then, everyone had a chance to try the clothes on, and Donna concluded with a drawing for a door prize. She described the event to me as being akin to a theater piece, though its purpose was to get the participants to visualize themselves in these clothes and therefore in the mood to buy.

Although your parties may start off small, with perhaps 8 to 15 persons, they can become quite large as you do much more than put on a simple sales presentation. Donna, for instance, gradually built her programs to the point where she got invitations to put on parties for groups that sometimes drew hundreds of participants.

Attracting People to These Parties

While it is the hostess' job to attract people, help her do this by giving her some guidelines which you know work, such as

- *Advise the hostess that when she invites people, she should ask them to confirm if they are coming and call to cancel if they can't make it.* Explain that it is important to do this, because otherwise people can get very lackadaisical about coming or not, and it becomes very difficult to know who will really be there and therefore plan for the event.

- *Urge the hostess to check out the date in advance before she sets it to be sure there are no major conflicts that might prevent the people she plans to invite from attending or lead them to arrive late or leave early.* For example, one hostess failed to check in advance and scheduled a house party for the date of a big office party most of her friends were attending, so the sales party bombed.

- *Make up an attractive flier, give the hostess a white master copy, and invite her to make up fliers and send to her friends.* The flier should announce the sales party and make it sound exciting. For example, use descriptions like "fun," "new," "a chance to see unique products." Also, the flier should include a phone number to RSVP and directions to the event, unless the hostess is inviting only neighbors or people who have been to her house before. By sending or giving out a flier, the event seems even more important. Then, after a few days, the hostess should call anyone who hasn't responded to check if they are planning to come. Should anyone be still wavering, she can use the call to further encourage them to attend.

- *Give the hostess an incentive for attracting people.* While some distributors offer the hostess a 10 to 20 percent discount on her own purchases or a free gift, it's more motivating to give her a percentage or bonus as an incentive for recruiting people to come. One common approach is to give her a percentage—say 10 percent—of the purchases made by people she invites. Another is to give her a flat payment—say one dollar per person—for each person who attends.

How to Put on a Good Party

When you put on the party, use your imagination to provide some dramatic flair. For example, one friend was the hit of the party when she presented a line of sensual items with a running commentary of deadpan humor. Another created a ministage show when she put on cosmetics demonstrations. A third put on fashion shows using the guests as volunteers to show off a clothing line. Use your own creativity to put "oomph" in your own program.

Also, be sure to let everyone know in advance that the products are for sale. Some distributors pass out a list of sales items and prices at the beginning of the program, so people can follow along as they show particular items. Others pass out their order forms after the presentation.

In either case, people should know they have an opportunity to buy something. Then, at the end of the presentation, invite people to order. It helps to include some incentive to persuade them to buy now, rather than letting them send in their order after they get home, because many people won't follow through. For example, if they order now, perhaps offer a 10 percent discount or a free gift.

Just before the program breaks up so that people can buy, invite the guests to give parties of their own. Let them know they will receive a special gift if they do (although don't talk about getting a percentage of sales, because that makes them think about how the hostess will get a percentage of what they buy now). Also, if you are looking for additional distributors, say that you'll be glad to talk to anyone who might like to put on a party as a representative of the company like you. Indicate that you want to take care of any sales first, but you can meet after that with anyone who wants to set up an appointment to talk further.

After your presentation, ask people to bring up their orders. Meanwhile, as you fill these, the others can socialize and enjoy the snacks the hostess has prepared. Afterward, meet with anyone who wants to host a party or put one on by becoming a distributor for the company like you.

Finally, thank the hostess and give her any share of the sales or gifts that are due.

The Importance of Follow-Up

At many parties, you will find that most of the guests want to become customers, and a few may be interested in hosting a party. Finding a potential distributor takes longer.

But whatever the attendees' level of interest, follow-up after the party is important because it gives you a chance to make extra sales from customers, firming up arrangements with potential hosts for future parties, and recruit new distributors. You can also change initial ideas about involvement with the product or company because even if no one wants to host a party or get involved in representing the company at the time, you may be able to convert customers into hosts or part of your sales team later. The way to do this is through follow-up to either sell more product, or encourage participation as a host or distributor, or both.

Some programs already have a system for this. For example, the Mary Kay representative normally follows up with each customer to find out how she (and sometimes he) is using the products and whether she (or he) needs anything else. The rep also uses this time to explore whether the customer might like to organize or put on a party, too.

You can do the same in any program. Just call your customers within a few days and offer to help if the person would like some consulting or needs more product. If the person seems to have become an avid consumer, ask if she (or he) would like to host a party, learn how to get the products wholesale, or put on a party like yours.

Then, tailor your follow-up according to what the person wants. As appropriate, set up another meeting to provide more product or show how to use it, demonstrate how to organize and host a party, or explain how to become a distributor for the company like you.

Chapter 12

OTHER CREATIVE WAYS TO PRESENT YOUR PROGRAM

The possibilities for marketing your program creatively are endless. And the more exciting, the more interesting you make your activities, the more enthusiasm you'll create for your product or service.

ATTRACTING PEOPLE TO HEAR YOUR MESSAGE BY CREATING AN EVENT

One way to attract people who may be potential customers or distributors is to present your program as part of an interesting event that serves as a draw. Such events are also a way to keep the present distributors in your organization excited and involved.

The important thing is to make your event enjoyable and fun. You want to appeal to people as consumers first—so they really like your product or how you present it. Then, if they are sold on the event, they may not only want to be customers but may be interested in promoting the product or service, too.

You are only limited by your imagination. Use the following ideas as a jumping-off point. Then plan events that fit your own product, personal style, and the tastes of the people you expect to attend.

For example, we have used social interaction and communication games as a means of attracting sizable groups of people to a fun event (usually about 10 to 20 persons each time), and before that event we presented one or two product demonstrations, for instance, a Get Healthy with Games Night; a Food, Fun, and Games Night; a Travel and Games Night; and more.

At another successful series of events we had a mini-trade show in conjunction with what we called a Gala Game Fair, attended by about 35 to 50 persons. We invited people to bring their literature and demonstrate their products, and we provided an area with table space for this purpose. Usually 6 or 7 persons came armed with products, and everyone had a chance to mix informally for about 45 minutes to learn about the products. Then we played games. You might want to use some activity other than games yourself, but the trade show idea could be a good way to work cooperatively with other people where you share expenses and are able to draw many more people to the event than you could individually.

Still another possibility might be a theme party that ties in with your product, such as a food tasting party if you are marketing a food line; or a travel party if you are marketing travel. For example, a woman from Beverly Hills used a travel party approach to market a travel program to singles. She sent out invitations, using her list of hundreds of single partygoers, and prepared for a swinging Beverly Hills–style party with all the trimmings. She charged ten dollars at the door, served up exotic salads and party dips, let people mingle for about a half hour, and showed a brief travel slide show which described both the program and some highlights of the marketing plan. Afterward, people had a chance to sign up with their sponsor or take literature home. Finally, those who wanted— usually about half the guests—were able to party in earnest.

Other Possibilities

Here are some other suggestions for events to stimulate interest in your program.

Potluck Dinner and Product Presentation. Invite everyone to bring a dish, and coordinate what people bring, so you have a good mixture of courses. Before or after the dinner show your product, and if you're marketing a food product, make it the main event.

Get-Together for the Neighbors. To invite them, leave fliers for them at their doors or in their mailboxes, preferably after the regular mail delivery comes since postal workers sometimes confiscate unofficial mail. On your flier, explain that you are involved in an exciting new program, and you would like to invite your neighbors to a festive occasion to tell them about it. Also, if you don't already know your neighbors, well, note that this is a chance for the neighbors to get together to know each other better.

Show-and-Tell Evening. Invite everyone to bring whatever they want, and encourage the performers to perform. You, of course, demonstrate your product or service.

Movable Feast. This is a party that moves from one house or location to another within a relatively small area. You set up a few stops along the way—typically one for hors d'oeuvres, another for the main course, a third for dessert, and possibly a final blowout party. Then, at each place, you feature something different. For example, you might have an amateur performer at one, a dance lesson at another, a game at a third, and, of course, at one site your product or service presentation.

Barbeque or Picnic. In this case, it's best to have a product that fits in with the ongoing activities, such as low-calorie candy, a bakery product line, or toys and games. Then, in a fun way, people get to sample the product or perhaps buy it on the spot. Or you get leads for follow up if people aren't ready to buy now.

Workshop or Class Dealing with a Topic Related to Your Product. This is a powerful way to get some free exposure, because you present yourself as an expert or authority, which raises your credibility and makes people even more receptive to listening and being persuaded by you. Plus, you may even get paid for your advice. For example, suppose you're marketing a health product. You can work up a lecture or program on a subject such as "Techniques for Getting Healthy." Or if you're working with a food program, try offering a class on "Good Nutrition." You can advertise your classes or workshops locally or offer to put on the program for some group.

Health Fair, with Demonstrations of Health Techniques. It helps if you're promoting a health product, but since health is defined broadly these days, almost any product that helps people feel better in any way (emotionally as well as physically) can be worked in. The event might include people giving massages, demonstrating exercises, or leading a meditation. Plus, you give a brief demonstration of how your product works to promote health. (And if it's not specifically a health product, be creative.)

Entrepreneur Exchange. A great promotional event. Find a group you belong to to sponsor this or join a business group that puts these on. People come to these exchanges prepared to learn about other products and services and talk about their own. Usually, there is a table for product literature where people display their materials and business cards. Also, people have a chance to mix and mingle around.

Sometimes there is a speaker on a business topic; sometimes not. In either case, the usual format is that some or all of the attendees can briefly talk about the product or service they offer, anywhere from a few seconds to a few minutes, depending on the size of the group. Commonly, the gathering attracts 25 to 50 people, though some events may draw 100, 200, even more.

Frequently, the members of these groups are not yet marketing any product or service themselves and are looking for projects to get involved with, so this is an excellent opportunity to recruit potential distributors as well as new customers.

Coming up with Other Ideas Yourself

And you can probably think of many other ideas. However, when you do, keep this in mind. In putting on these programs, you should have two major goals:

1. To show off your product or service so that people will like it but won't feel under any pressure to buy or sign up on the spot. You get their cards; you give out yours; later, you follow up.

2. To show that you are a fun, creative person to work with—so people will want to join your organization. As they can see by your participation in or organization of these events, they are not just buying or marketing a product. They also have a chance to become part of an enjoyable, supportive group of people. And that combination is hard to beat!

Part III

BUILDING A SALES ORGANIZATION

Chapter 13

HOW TO START BUILDING AN ORGANIZATION

As soon as you can, you want to start building a sales organization, since this is where the big money comes from, in the form of overrides or commissions on what your people produce. But remember, when you start building, you also want to be ready to commit yourself to training, motivating, and otherwise supporting your people, so you have people who are really selling and building their own organizations to sell, because this is where the commissions are—in sales. Thus, as soon as you feel ready to start recruiting or sponsoring new distributors, and supporting them, do so. Then, once you have your first distributor, start training and helping that person learn the business, so he or she can start presenting the program and finding customers and recruits.

Initially, plan to spend most of your time looking for new distributors yourself, as well as continuing to make retail sales. But gradually, as you develop a distributor group, expect to spend less and less time yourself on sponsoring. In fact, after you get five or six active, first-line distributors, stop almost all sponsoring activity to concentrate on motivating and training your distributors and helping them build up their own organizations. Perhaps spend about 80 to 90 percent of your time working with them, and most of the rest in continuing to sell yourself. Spend only a very small percentage of your time seeking new distributors, and mainly consider these as fill-ins for your frontline distributors who drop out. Otherwise, if you have a good working group, consider putting fill-ins under one of your own downline people whom you feel is active but does not yet have a full compliment of frontline people to work with. He or she might be able to provide more support than you.

This principle of focusing your energies on strengthening your own frontline group and teaching them to do the same is crucial. Until your distributors have developed their own effective groups, you don't have a solid organization yourself, because your distributors can easily get discouraged and drop out. You'll find they will start to become really enthusiastic only when they see their own organizations develop and grow.

THE IMPORTANCE OF HELPING
YOUR DISTRIBUTORS

You need to do everything you can to help your distributors who are serious. One of the most common reasons for failure in multi-level marketing is not doing this. Frequently, such neglect leading to failure is a problem for people with sales, and particularly direct sales, backgrounds. They get very excited about the program at first and feel like going out to sponsor the world. But if they do, they have no time to work with the individuals they have already signed up. So while they are sponsoring new people, the first recruits are feeling ignored and confused about what to do, and so they drift away.

Thus, getting a lot of people on your front line is not the way to success in building an effective sales group. The secret is building a solid foundation in depth by helping your distributors gain their own success. You'll make less in the beginning, because you'll be giving up some of your immediate retail volume and first-level sales commissions when you take the time to work with your people. And in most MLM or network-marketing companies, the override commissions are less as you go down each level.

But by building in depth, your organization will expand exponentially, and you'll more than make up for the smaller commissions by the size of your organization on which you will collect commissions.

In fact, to promote this growth, many distributors enlist many new recruits under their active distributors—to help the latter build their organizations—rather than putting these new persons on their own front lines.

THE PRINCIPLES OF SPONSORING, TEACHING, AND DUPLICATION

You'll hear it again and again in multi-level marketing. The key to success is sponsoring, teaching, and duplication. That means when you sponsor someone, your responsibilities have just started because you must teach that person how to market the product and recruit others in order to duplicate yourself. Then, you have to teach that person how to teach those he or she sponsors to teach others how to market and recruit, too. Chart 13.1 illustrates this relationship.

CHART 13.1: THE PRINCIPLE OF SPONSORING AND TEACHING

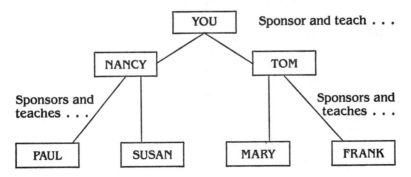

In other words, the key principle is: *Teach those you sponsor how to teach those they sponsor to teach those they sponsor,* and so on down the line. For in this way, by sponsoring and teaching, *you duplicate yourself.* And that's how you build a strong chain of individuals—by sponsoring and teaching each of your first-level recruits how to sponsor and teach others to do the same.

In turn, like any chain, your organization will be only as strong as its weakest link. So if anyone you sponsor drops out of the chain, you want to reconnect links by reaching down to the next link to connect it to your organization.

Thus, if you sponsor John and teach him how to market the product, and he sponsors Nancy but subsequently drops out, then you teach Nancy yourself. For then your organization can continue to grow under Nancy. But if you don't reach down to Nancy, she is probably going to feel abandoned and drop out.

The Principle of Sponsoring Only
People You Can Work With

In order to carry out your teaching responsibilities effectively, you can't have too many people on your front lines, because you won't have the time or energy to give all of them the proper support. As a result, you should only sponsor as many people directly as you can work with effectively.

Many distributors believe you can only work with up to five, perhaps at most six or seven, active distributors at a time. Once one active distributor is successfully launched with his or her own organization and no longer needs your help, you can add another first-level distributor to take that person's place. But if you try to work with more than this recommended limit at one time, these distributors believe you will be spreading yourself too thin.

This type of approach is very much what works well in the military. In each division—in the army, navy, air force, marines, and coast guard—with rare exceptions, nobody directly supervises more than five or six persons, because the military has found that this approach works best. And this isn't only true for the U.S. military. But in other nations and over the course of history, military commanders have passed their orders down the line through a few key officers under them, and wars have been won.

Certainly, some distributors claim it is possible to work with more first-line people by using a more efficient training approach. For example, I have heard some MLM people say that you can work with up to ten or so active first-level people if you supply them with good training materials, so you need to spend less time training them. Their view is that you can ask your distributors to read the materials to learn most of the basics, so you don't have to spend that time explaining fundamentals. Instead, you can use your time more profitably to sponsor others, travel, or learn more about promoting the program yourself.

So, presumably, under this theory, you can give this book, *Success in Multi-Level Marketing* to your new distributors or recommend they get a copy, so they can read it to know what to do. Then, if you urge your own distributors to do the same with the persons they sponsor, they can work together with ten others, and their distributors can work with ten others, too, you can maximize your earnings exponentially, or so the theory goes. For then, supposedly, instead of your organization growing at a multiplication factor of 5 ($5 \times 5 \times 5 = 125$) or a multiplication factor of 6 ($6 \times 6 \times 6 = 216$), it zooms ahead with a factor of 10 ($10 \times 10 \times 10 = 1,000$). And at levels 4 and 5 in your downline, the number of distributors expands at an even more dramatic pace.

Now, I certainly endorse the value of giving out good training materials to reduce the time you spend on nonessentials with distributors. After all, this book is designed for that. Also, I agree this approach may substantially cut down on the total amount of time you spend with each person, so you can work more with first-level persons and perhaps work with some additional individuals by mail. Further, it may free you to spend more quality time with each of your distributors.

However, I also strongly believe that it is important to recognize that much of the time you spend with your distributors is not just for training; it's for providing your personal support and concern, too. And this is necessary because most MLM people also need personal and social contact to stay involved and motivated. For your distributors not only want your knowledge; they look on you as a friend and supporter, too. They don't just want to read about basic principles in a book. Rather, they want to hear about some of this material from you, too, and perhaps see how you put it into practice. So if you just hand your distributors a manual and expect them to get most or all of their training from it and stay active and motivated, that's not enough. *You have to truly give of yourself and show you care about them, too.*

Building Down Three Levels

To make the chain of individuals in your organization really solid, you must build down three deep, and you must advise your distributors that they must build three deep and explain this to their recruits, too. This three-deep principle is illustrated in Chart 13.2.

Until you have taught John to teach Nancy to teach Jack, you haven't fully duplicated yourself, because if Nancy isn't able to sponsor anyone, she is likely to drop out, and that will discourage John. Or if she fails to teach Jack, he may have trouble continuing in the business. Thus, if you don't duplicate yourself, your whole organization can easily fizzle out.

That is why many MLM professionals suggest reaching down to your second and third levels to work with the people there who have the most initiative. To locate them, ask each of your directly sponsored persons who is the strongest, highest-initiative person on his or her first level and indicate

CHART 13.2: THE KEY TO BUILDING AN ORGANIZATION BY SPONSORING AND TEACHING DOWN THREE LEVELS

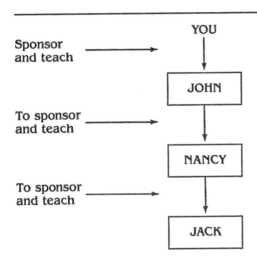

Step 1. You sponsor John.

Step 2. You teach John how to market the product and sponsor Nancy.

Step 3. You teach John how to teach Nancy to market the product, sponsor Jack, and teach Jack.

Then John knows how to do it and has started building his own organization successfully.

you would be willing to work with that person to help increase his or her sales. Then, to get your distributor's input, ask for his or her suggestions on what you might do to help. You'll almost certainly get an enthusiastic yes for your offer, since after all, any increases in sales of that person accrue to the distributor who you are speaking to who is directly above him. Then, when you work with this second-level person, you might take this one more level and ask that person who is his or her strongest, highest-initiative person, and offer to work with that person, too. Most will be agreeable. Why not, with your generous offer? (However, if you do encounter any resistance along the way, don't be pushy. Just say you are making a standing offer and want to help whenever your distributor would like your assistance.)

Once you have located these serious second- and third-level persons, you can offer to help in various ways. For example, call them from time to time or send them mailings to keep them posted on what's happening. Offer to speak at a meeting for them, or include them in your regular meetings and special programs if they live in your area. And be sure to let their immediate sponsor know how they are doing to keep him or her informed and motivated by what these people under him or her is doing.

The value of this approach—working with the hot performers under the distributors under you—is that it helps motivate these distributors in between. They see those under them really moving, and that inspires them to do more, too. (Conversely, if one of your first- or second-level distributors doesn't catch fire, you can always work with the hot performers he or she has referred to you and continue building your organization under them. Then if the distributor under you subsequently drops out, that person under him or her in most marketing plans will come up one level closer to you.)

Likewise, teach your first-level people to use this technique. For then you will truly build your organization in depth—and your distributors will build this way, too.

Reaching down three levels helps to spark everyone upline to the person you have helped. For example, you reach down to help Nancy, so she is able to sponsor and teach others, and that helps to keep John actively involved in the program, because he can see that it is working. Or if you reach down to help Jack, you will encourage Nancy, and her excitement will feed back up to John. It's a little like lighting a fire. The flame of excitement you light down two or three levels in your organization travels right up the line.

In time, when your first-level distributors have built their own solid organizations which are three levels deep,

CHART 13.3: THE IMPORTANCE OF REACHING
DOWN THREE LEVELS

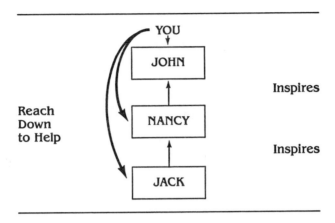

they can carry on without you. And then you have truly duplicated yourself.

Thus, *once you have sponsored someone, it's more important for you to help that person sponsor someone else than it is to find and sponsor another person yourself.* That's the way you build in depth.

THE PRINCIPLE OF BUILDING AN ORGANIZATION ON SOLID FOUNDATIONS

As you sponsor others and they do the same, your organization will gradually take shape.

Initially, this is likely to be a slow process, and in most programs, you shouldn't expect to see any major earnings for several months. Even if your organization approximately doubles every few weeks, it will be quite small in the beginning. For example,

WEEK 1	WEEK 2	WEEK 3	WEEK 4	WEEK 5	WEEK 6	WEEK 7
1	2	4	8	16	32	64

CHART 13.4: NAMES OF SECOND- AND THIRD-LEVEL HOT PERFORMERS

First-Level Person
Sponsored by Me:

Name: _____

Address: _____

City, State, Zip: _____

Phone: _____

Second-Level Referrals:

Name: _____

Address: _____

City, State, Zip: _____

Phone: _____

Second-Level Referrals:

Name: _____

Address: _____

City, State, Zip: _____

Phone: _____

Third-Level Referrals:

Name: _____

Address: _____

City, State, Zip: _____

Phone: _____

Third-Level Referrals:

Name: _____

Address: _____

City, State, Zip: _____

Phone: _____

So, assuming this doubling effect, it is only after the seventh week that you will really see any major expansion. But once your organization takes off, its growth can be tremendous (although, as previously mentioned, don't get carried away with visions of repeated doubling week after week. Rather, think in terms of solid, gradual, and increasingly substantial growth.).

This process is frequently compared by MLM people to building a house. You have to take the time to lay down the solid foundation first. Then you can build. As some say, your initial sponsoring of five or six persons is like digging the foundations with a shovel or spade. Then, as you teach them to sponsor, so that they bring in a growing network of second-level people, that's like clearing the area with a bulldozer. Next, when you teach these individuals to teach others, so the total group size and structure expands even more, that's like bringing in the steamshovels and excavating down to bedrock, where you can build. For now you can start construction in earnest, for once you are four deep, your organization will spurt up quickly, and as long as you have created a strong foundation, it will stay up.

Before you get to this point, it can seem as if it is taking months and months—almost forever—for anything to happen. But if you have built deep, you will see the structure start to rise out of the ground and then grow rapidly.

The key to this rapid growth is building a solid foundation first. And that means working closely with your key first-level people and sometimes a few hot performers on your second and third level, so you train them to know what to do, which includes sponsoring and teaching those under them to do the same.

Chapter 14

HELPING YOUR NEW DISTRIBUTORS GET STARTED

Once you have sponsored someone in an MLM or network marketing program, arrange a meeting with him or her to help get started. Plan to go over the basics with everyone, whether they are experienced in this type of marketing or not, and expect to cover some additional specific topics with newcomers.

WHAT TO COVER IN YOUR FIRST MEETING

Get to Know Your New Distributor

If you don't know the person you are sponsoring well or at all, use this first meeting to get to know him or her better. You can do this informally, if this is your personal style and you are working with only a few distributors. Or if you prefer a more formal approach and have a number of frontline distributors, perhaps use an interview and questionnaire approach—a technique Debbie Ballard advocates in *Secrets of Multi-Level Fortune Building*. She has an interview session with each new distributor in which she gets to know the person by asking about his or her work background, education, hobbies, interests, family life, and goals and objectives. She also asks the person to fill out a questionnaire, explaining that she is not trying to pry but wants the information to serve him or her better. Then, Ballard keeps the results in the distributor's personal file and refers to the card when she calls.

Go Over Company Products, Policies, and Procedures

At this first meeting, also go over the product line, marketing plan, and company background and literature, so the new distributor fully understands the program and knows where to go to find needed information. Usually, a new distributor will only recall the highlights of your original presentation or opportunity meeting, especially if it has been some time since this occurred. So expect to go over key points in more depth, or at least indicate what the distributor should read to review these points.

Also make sure your distributor understands how to fill out the distributor application and product order forms so orders are placed properly and the company can readily process his or her form. Go over them carefully, and ideally, provide a sample of how to fill these out (sometimes, already prepared in company literature or make copies of your own filled-out forms).

This review may sound elementary, but it is extremely vital, since you may lose commissions if orders are written incorrectly or if sponsorship information is unclear. So make sure your new distributor knows how to fill out company forms correctly and will advise his or her recruits about the correct procedures, too.

A good way to make sure everything is correct is to suggest that your new distributor process the first few applications and orders through you. Then, you can double-check to be certain he or she has filled out the forms correctly and has printed clearly and hard enough. If not, you can readily correct any errors and advise the distributor accordingly.

Find Out About Your Distributor's Marketing Interests and Background

Another topic to cover is how active your new distributor wants to be, so you can assist accordingly, and not push your distributor to be more involved than he or she wants to be.

It also helps to know his or her background in marketing and direct sales, because this is an indicator of how much help he or she is likely to need. If someone already has a strong background in other multi-level companies, he or she will already know the basic principles of this type of marketing and many sales techniques. But if the distributor is new to the field, you will have much more training to do.

SUGGEST HOW YOUR NEW DISTRIBUTOR CAN START AT ONCE

The specifics vary from program to program, but some of the things marketing people tell new distributors to do are

1. Make a list of all the people you know.
2. Decide how many hours you want to devote to contacting people.
3. Set up your goals for the week, indicating how many individuals you plan to contact and how many people you expect to sell and sponsor.
4. Allot a certain number of hours for reading about the program and for reading motivational and instructional literature.
5. Start at once!

Connect Your Distributor with Your Local Network

Let your new distributor know where any opportunity meetings are being held. Also provide the names and numbers of key contacts in the area, including your group leader or upline sponsor, because they can provide additional support if the distributor wants this or at least promote a feeling that there is this extra support available. Generally, if you are there providing the support your distributor needs, he or she won't need to go to someone above you, beyond perhaps just saying hello to feel connected to a large unit. Also, your upline distributor can't spend a great deal of quality time with everyone under his or her other distributors, so check on how much actual hands-on assistance he or she can offer. In general, this kind of connecting will be more like making introductions to the boss in a big organization; to help the person feel a part of the larger whole. And then mainly you as the immediate sponsor will work directly with that person.

Offer to put on some meetings for your distributors. Invite them to call you at any time to ask questions and get advice. Let them know you are only too glad to help. And then when they call, be ready to respond to keep them excited and motivated in return.

HOW TO HELP A DISTRIBUTOR WHO IS NEW TO MLM OR NETWORK MARKETING

If people are new to MLM, you need to explain some additional fundamentals to them, and you may need a few extra preliminary meetings to do this. Some things to tell these newcomers to the field are

- *Recommend or give distributors some marketing materials to read.* You can recommend or give them books to read, like this one, that describe basic principles and techniques. Also, encourage them to read some motivational and success books. Explain that if they need help or want to review anything they have read with you, you will be glad to assist.
- *Talk about the importance of setting goals.* Explain that setting goals and writing them down is a crucial

step toward achieving them in MLM, as in other things in life. Also, note how breaking down larger goals into small, manageable day-by-day or week-by-week goals makes them easier to accomplish. Ask them about their own goals and point out that building a sales organization will help them attain other goals, such as financial security or wealth.

- *Advise newcomers to look on their first month as a training period—and start now!* Keep newcomers motivated and reassured about their early progress. Explain that they should get started immediately, but since they are just learning, they shouldn't feel under pressure to produce results while they are getting familiar with the program and the techniques of MLM.

Thus, urge them to sell product and sponsor others as soon as possible, because this will give them a feeling of accomplishment. But make sure they understand that it's okay to take things slow, so they don't feel they are not doing enough or have failed if they don't start selling the product or building an organization right away.

You need to prepare newcomers for multi-level or network marketing in this way because an organization and a sales income can take time to build, so new recruits can get discouraged if things are slow at first. So, emphasize the need to build a strong foundation, and let them know they shouldn't expect to see large returns right away. As needed, go over the principles about how MLM works and how early hard work will eventually pay off handsomely because of the multiplication principle of this type of marketing. But stress that it is especially important for them to concentrate on learning about the product and how to get customers as well as sponsor distributors because the key to success is *building sales volume,* not just a network of salespeople. Finally, tell them you will do all you can to help them do it.

- *Urge newcomers not to compare themselves to experienced people in the program so they don't get discouraged by the difference between them; direct them to focus on what they need to do to get started.* This principle of not comparing a newcomer to his or her higher-ups is important, because newcomers must recognize and accept where they are starting and not think they are hopelessly behind. Frequently, people in MLM look at the success of leaders who have massive downlines and are making tremendous incomes and think, "I'll never be able to catch up." So you need to point out that these leaders were at one time in their position and that new distributors have to understand that it takes time and training to achieve this great success.

- *Prepare your new distributor for rejection.* Help your new distributor understand that not everyone will be interested in the program, so he or she doesn't start out with unrealistically high expectations and get let down. Explain about the typical averages: about three contacts to find one person who is interested, about three contacts with interested people to find one person who wants to sign up, and about three to five sign-ups to find one person who becomes active.

  Thus, your new distributor should discount rejection and continue ahead, because only a certain percentage of people contacted will be interested, sign up, or become active. So the focus should be on finding them, not in regretting past rejections.

- *Tell new recruits a few proven things to do to be successful in your program.* Your new distributors could become successful using other strategies, of course. But if you give them a small list of things to do, they don't get stymied considering several alternatives. Instead, they have an immediate workable plan of action.

  One distributor explains the success of the strategy this way: "I make my recommendations sound like a requirement, and I list these recommendations as specific steps my distributors must follow. That way people feel they have to do it, start doing something right away, and don't have time to think about all the alternatives and get confused about what to do next."

Putting on Meetings for Your New Distributor

In the beginning, your new distributor, even one with some MLM experience, will be uncertain about the particulars of the program and the marketing plan and therefore will lack confidence in presenting the program. Accordingly, to help him or her get started, offer to assist in putting on his or her first meetings—even if these are with only one or two prospects.

Many successful MLM people recommend that their new distributor invite a few people over—then they will come and give the presentation. Others doing ongoing meetings invite the new distributor to bring guests. Or, in some cases, when a new distributor is extremely busy but does have good contacts, an MLMer may offer to speak to the distributor's referrals without the distributor having to be present. Then, if the referral is interested, the MLMer will sign the new recruit up under the new distributor.

Use whatever approach works best for you. Ideally, your new distributors should be present to learn what to do, either by seeing your example or by presenting part of the meeting themselves. Then, after the meeting, a good training technique is to go over what happened at the meeting to make your distributors more aware of what you included in your presentation and why. This is also a time to answer questions about the company or its products and to discuss the elements that contributed to an effective presentation (such as good visual aids, a varied tone, enthusiasm, and so on).

Initially, you may want to handle the whole presentation. But as soon as your distributors feel comfortable, encourage them to give parts of the presentation. Then, in the final training phase, suggest that they do the whole thing, while you offer moral support and backup in case they want your input on some topic or question raised in the meeting that they can't answer.

This three-phase process of training your distributors to put on meetings accomplishes three things:

1. It systematically prepares them to make effective presentations, and thereby gives them the confidence to do so.

2. When you present the meeting with skill, which comes from practice, this gives the program a solid, professional image, which makes the prospects invited by your new distributor more likely to sign up. If the new distributor had presented the program alone to them, they might have been more skeptical, particularly if they were friends and associates. But you are an outside authority figure, so your presence makes the program and presentation seem more impressive, whether you actually lead the meeting or not.

3. Your assistance with presentations helps to inspire and motivate your new distributors, because it shows you truly care about them and want to help them succeed.

Staying in Touch with Your New Distributor

Once you get your new distributors started, continue to stay in touch. Encourage your distributors to call you for help or just to let you know how things are going. But even if they don't call, contact them initially a few times to show you really do want to help.

When you do make contact, do so in supportive way. Don't ask distributors point blank how many people they have sponsored or how many customers they have sold.

That tends to put them on the spot and can make them feel they are working for you. Or it makes them feel that they should be doing more than they are doing or that all you care about is how much money they are making for you. Furthermore, those who have some resistance to the idea of selling will be particularly disturbed if they sense you are trying to judge them based on their sales results.

Instead, when you call, be positive and encouraging, and offer helpful information. This approach works best because you want to make your distributors *want* to do something, and not make them feel guilty if they haven't done enough. Some of the things you might call to tell them about might be

- an upcoming event you are sponsoring
- some company events you just heard about
- a new technique someone is using that is working well
- a training program you are planning for new distributors
- an offer to meet with them personally to go over the program and answer any questions
- a recommendation about an exciting new success or marketing techniques book you have just read
- a request for information you can put in your local newsletter for distributors

Then, as long as your new distributor seems enthusiastic and responsive and begins calling you occasionally, stay in touch.

In time, your new distributor won't be as dependent on you for your assistance. But even so, stay in touch from time to time—maybe not on the daily or weekly basis as is more common in the beginning with new distributors, but perhaps call or get together every week or two, or at least each month. Doing so helps to create a strong family feeling that will spread through your network, for your distributor is likely to emulate you and stay in touch with his or her own people, too. In turn, these bonds help to create and maintain a strong sales network. For with them, you are not just marketing the product, but are developing and continuing to express warm feelings toward one another, which makes marketing the program satisfying and fun. And this helps to keep motivation and involvement high.

Focusing Your Time on Your Best Distributors

At first, be encouraging and helpful to all your distributors, because you don't know who will turn out to be the most serious and committed. But as you find out which distributors want to do the most, devote most of your time to them. They will be your most eager and productive distributors if you help them get started right. So invest your time most productively by giving most of your help to them.

You might think of working with your distributors in the following way. When they first come into the business, they are essentially unknown quantities—like a new born star. Each one has the potential to make it to the top—like a star that becomes a brightly burning sun. Conversely, any new distributor can fizzle out, just as a star might explode or burn itself out. To some extent, you can help an individual become a shining star. But what the person brings to the business—in the form of personal traits, attitudes, values, and skills—will affect the outcome, too. It's just as it is when we're born. We all have a unique potential that can be developed so we can become successful in some way. But then our environment—our parents, friends, experiences, and so on—shapes us, too.

In a similar way, you play a key part in what your new distributor becomes. But if your new distributor doesn't respond, back off. You can only do so much. You can't keep a burnt-out star burning. So *work the most with your distributors who show they really want to succeed and really want your help.* Put your time and energy mostly into them.

The Signs of Success to Look for in Deciding
Which Distributors to Work with the Most

There are certain signs to look for in selecting your most enthusiastic distributors:

- *They are actively interested in the products and the program,* and they indicate this by buying and using the products or taking time to learn more about the business.
- *They are excited and enthusiastic about the business.* They believe the program works, and they are eager to go out and promote it—or are already doing so.
- *They want to learn more,* and they call you frequently to ask for additional information.
- *They ask you to help them in training and sponsoring others.*
- *They are goal oriented,* and have specific things they want to achieve.
- *They have a positive outlook,* so that working and socializing with them is enjoyable.
- *They have made up a list of people to contact* and are continually thinking about whom they might approach.

So these are people to focus on working with and helping, since they are the ones who are most actively and eagerly looking for your assistance. In turn, by helping them, you will help them build your organization.

Conversely, if you devote too much time to distributors who don't have this kind of spark—or don't develop it—this will pull you down. Some distributors are tempted to do this as a way to keep everyone they can active in their organization. But after a certain point, it is best to let the less active, enthusiastic people go, because devoting too much unrewarded time and effort to them will sap your energy. How can you tell? Well, one sign might be that when you call these distributors and offer to help, they will tend not to appreciate your offer. Rather, they may feel you are being pushy or trying to pressure them. Or they might regale you with complaints and gripes. And if you get too much negative input, you can lose your own enthusiasm and sense of direction.

So once you get this pattern of negative feedback from people, stay away and help your responsive distributors. Then, as they succeed, your other less active and motivated distributors may get inspired and come around as well.

Chapter 15

WORKING WITH YOUR DISTRIBUTORS

Besides having regular meetings, other ways to work with your distributors to build a solid organization include

- Organizing cooperative activities
- Passing on leads and sign-ups to members of your sales group or downline
- Developing techniques of communicating with members of your organization, such as telephone trees and newsletters
- Developing fast-start manuals and programs for your distributors

ORGANIZING COOPERATIVE ACTIVITIES

You can help your distributors work together with you as a team by organizing and coordinating cooperative events. These can include some of the following activities:

Jointly Organized Business Opportunity Meetings. You combine forces with other distributors to do a joint meeting. Each person is responsible for a part of the program and contributes a proportionate share to the expenses. You can use various formulas for figuring out who contributes what—for example, five dollars each; two dollars for each guest the distributor brings to the meeting, or a sliding scale of contributions based on one's position in the organization, such as ten dollars for the group leader, five dollars for the area leaders, and two dollars for any other distributors.

An Opportunity-Meeting Network. This is designed to keep members informed of all opportunity meetings put on by anyone in the network. It works like this: A distributor in each area puts on a meeting, and these are announced on a single list or flier that is circulated to all participating distributors and members of their groups. Any distributor in the network can invite guests to a meeting (and perhaps there may be a charge for attendees as noted).

Cooperative Advertising. You jointly advertise with other distributors if you are putting on a joint meeting. Or you pool resources to place a large ad, and all of you share the leads. In one ad approach, individual distributors list their phone numbers in the ad and freely follow up when someone calls. In other cases, the head of the group places the ad, though all participating distributors pay. Then, as the responses come in, the group leader assigns them to the distributors—either by area or randomly.

Joint Participation as an Exhibitor at a Trade Show or Consumer Fair. Again, there are many sorts of arrangements. Several distributors can share the costs of the booth together, then share all the leads generated at the show. Alternatively, one person can pay for the booth, and the distributors who want to work at the event can contribute to the booth cost based on the number of hours they want to be there. In this case, everyone makes his or her own contacts at the show and follows up on his or her own leads. Or create another system that works for you.

Sharing Office or Other Equipment. This is a good idea for expensive equipment such as computers, faxes, and telemarketing devices. For example, one distributor bought a telemarketing system to share in making cold calls (the device dials about 60 people an hour, and if they are interested, it records basic information about who they are). He used it to support his distributors by lending it to each of them for a short-term period. They would use it for a few days to generate a lot of leads; then, they would pass the equipment on to another distributor and spend the next few weeks following up. Another distributor used the same kind of device to develop leads out of a central office, which he shared with several members of his downline. Then, when the leads came in, he referred them to these distributors according to geographical area.

An Open Invitation to a Large Opportunity Meeting You Put On.   Your distributors can bring guests or just send people to your meetings if they can't attend themselves. Then, you sign people up for them. As part of this invitation, you might also offer arrangement for distributors to contribute toward the meeting costs by paying for each guest they bring or send. And if they aren't there, you can always collect later. (Incidentally, don't let guests know about these payment arrangements—guests will feel funny about this and it's in bad taste to talk about these internal workings in front of guests—just keep the arrangements between you and your distributors.)

PASSING ON LEADS TO MEMBERS OF YOUR SALES GROUP

Turning over leads and sign-ups to members of your sales group is an excellent strategy when there is a lot of local interest in your program and your organization is growing rapidly. You act as a central clearinghouse for your organization and pass on leads to first- or second-level members of your sales team or downline for follow-up.

This approach is especially good if you are advertising or are actively promoting your program and are getting many inquiries. Rather than trying to handle all of them yourself and ending up with dozens of frontline people you can't help properly, share your leads with your sales group and distribute them as best you can by geographic area (or according to any other arrangement that makes sense, such as by industry, randomly dividing the leads to people working in the same geographical area, etc.).

Another advantage of passing on your leads is that your active frontline people don't feel you are in competition with them for new recruits—so they can better look to you for support. Think of it as if you are an army commander or corporate head passing on assignments to your troops.

However, be sure your referrals of leads and sign-ups are going to active distributors who are willing to work with the people you assign them. Otherwise, you end up with these further downline in your organization, and you have to work with them anyway yourself, since the sponsor to whom you assigned them won't follow through.

Also pass on people to your downline distributors when you meet them together or if there is any confusion about who should sponsor this person. (For example, you tell Mary about the program, but Mary is a good friend of your distributor Brad.) The reason to give the priority to your distributors is that you don't want your distributors to feel you are in competition with them, for that only breeds resentment and alienation and makes them question your support.

Remember this important rule: Never compete with your distributors.

Besides, when you pass on people to your distributors or let them sponsor the prospect when there is any question about who should sponsor, you benefit anyway, because the new recruit is still in your line. But if you sponsor a person, where your distributor feels he or she should do the sponsoring, only you benefit, and your active distributor may feel offended and less enthusiastic about working on the program in the future.

So practice the golden rule of the MLM approach to marketing. Pass on your leads when you can, and when in doubt, pass on your prospects, too.

COMMUNICATING WITH YOUR ORGANIZATION

As your organization grows, you need a quick way to get your message down to the troops, and you need to be able to inform, motivate, and inspire everyone on an ongoing basis. Good communication is essential.

Two effective approaches are the telephone tree and the organizational newsletter or progress report.

Telephone Trees

Telephone trees are a great way to spread the word quickly. For the best effect, have a short, snappy message that can be conveyed in a few sentences, such as "There will be a great meeting Saturday, since the head of the company will be in town. It will be at the _____ Hotel, and we're expecting about one hundred people to be there. So come early to get a good seat." Keep your messages short, since longer messages can easily get garbled as they are passed on from one person to the next.

To make sure the message gets through accurately, write down everything you want to say and read the message to each person you directly contact. Then, so that person will pass on this message accurately, ask him or her to write down the message as you talk and pass it on exactly in this form.

Structure a telephone tree so each person is assigned a number of calls which he or she *can* and *is willing to* handle—say about four or five people to a maximum of ten—when he or she passes on a message. Be sure each person agrees to participate in the tree before you give out any assignment, and don't settle for "I'll try." You must have a commitment. Then, clearly indicate whom the person will be calling, and ask the person to let you know when the calls have been completed or if he or she has experienced any problems getting through to those on the list. This way you can be sure everyone is called who should be.

It's disastrous to your organization if you think someone is going to communicate a message down the line, but then he or she doesn't. Given the multiplier effect in MLM and network marketing, hundreds of persons could miss out on hearing the message this way.

In the event that there is a problem reaching someone who will in turn pass on messages, then reassign; or if someone who is supposed to pass on the messages doesn't, then reassign these names to someone else accordingly; or if necessary, do some of the extra calling yourself to keep the message moving along the tree.

Newsletters and Progress Reports

Newsletters or progress reports are important communication tools for these key purposes:

> To let people know where you are going in developing and promoting the company's sales program and where you have been.

> To measure and recognize the progress made by you, your directly sponsored people, and notable achievers in your downline.

In reporting the news, emphasize the positive and deemphasize the negative. You want to keep your newsletter inspirational and motivational. Besides informing people, your newsletter is another tool for prompting enthusiasm in your organization and encouraging your distributors to get ahead.

Sometimes local people from different sales organizations may get together to create a newsletter. This kind of group effort is most common in the beginning when the program is just getting going and groups are small. So working together helps generate more enthusiasm to build up the area for everyone, even though distributors may in effect be competing with each other for customers and distributors. Typically, in this situation, distributors have open meetings, too, so anyone from any sales group or downline can come (perhaps contributing a share of the costs, as previously noted). However, whether or not there is already a company or local newsletter produced by other distributors in your area, it is a good idea to create a newsletter for your own sales team once it becomes sizable—say 20 or more people. The newsletter will help everyone in your group stay in touch, and it is another source of motivation, too.

Distributing Your Newsletter

One way some distributors distribute these newsletters is to send copies to their first-level distributors and ask them to make copies to pass on. If this works for you, fine. But sometimes distribution can bog down if someone is inactive down the line.

So often it is better to get the names and addresses of your downline members—either from their immediate sponsors or from the company. Many companies will send you a printout of your downline members at cost—a few cents a name.

Then you decide what's the best approach for covering the costs of the newsletters you send out. Some distributors distribute their newsletters free to the first two or three levels of their downline, considering the newsletter a good motivator and training tool, so subsidizing expenses of distribution is worth the cost. Others ask for a small subscription fee or contribution to cover costs, particularly if they are sending their newsletter to a large downline. Do whatever works for you. Perhaps ask some of the people on your first and second level what they think or what they or their own downline people might be willing to pay for a newsletter, to help you decide.

What to Include in Your Newsletter

Be creative in your newsletter. Let it express your own style, whether formal and businesslike or informal and chatty.

Some good things to include in your newsletter are

- reports about local activities
- a calendar of events
- listings of active leaders who are putting on meetings and their phone numbers
- announcements about recent awards, accomplishments, and large commission payments (which are a great motivator)
- recent news about the company which you but not your distributors have received, because you have a higher status in the company
- descriptions of strategies that have worked well
- a discussion of common problems that come up and how to solve them
- copies of ads and fliers

THE FAST-START TRAINING PROGRAM

A fast-start training program is an excellent approach if you are involved in the early phases of a new company, because it helps you quickly build up an active sales group. Then, once you have recruited, trained, and motivated this team, the team members can introduce the program to other prospects in the more traditional way.

The keys to making this program work include the following:

1. *Have sufficient product and distributor kits on hand, so your distributors can get started right away.* Some companies have their own variety packs and start-up materials. Or if they don't, create your own fast-start kits by purchasing from your company in case lots then repacking these materials in smaller units your distributors can buy from you.

If you are assembling your own fast-start kits, include one or two samples of all products, or if it's an extensive line, one or two samples of the fastest-selling items. Also, include company fliers, brochures, and any material you have prepared for your own group (in keeping with company guidelines, of course).

Use the distributor prices to figure your costs, and keep the cost of each kit to about $50 to $100.

This approach does involve a substantial financial commitment, since you need sufficient product on hand to respond to the demand—perhaps $2,000 to $10,000 in product. If you would prefer not to or can't front this yourself, consider having an investor or a team of investors to put up some money. Say $500 to $1,000 each for a percentage return on their money or perhaps in return for you putting some new active distributors under them.

2. *Require recruits to pay for these kits with cashier's checks, money orders, or cash.* It's best not to use credit or personal checks—because you may be recruiting many people you don't know. Also, unless the company encourages local warehousing and gives distributors a bonus for doing this, add on a small service charge, say, 10 percent, to pay for your time and to encourage distributors to order direct from the company.

3. *Set up fast-start opportunity meetings and invite your first- and second-level persons to come to these meetings with* *at least one or two guests.* Locate a facility, such as a hotel, that is large enough to hold a sizable group and can provide you with expanded space as your group grows. The facility also should have a solid, professional image, to show that you are going first-class.

4. *Organize a good opportunity presentation and close by inviting all newcomers to sign up now with their sponsor.* Indicate that they can take their starter kits with them right away.

5. *Invite everyone to come to the next meeting with one or two more guests.* And this includes the newcomers who have just signed up.

6. *Provide additional training for those who have been to an opportunity meeting before.* This way individuals don't have to sit through the same meeting again and again. Instead, they can learn some new techniques while the regular meeting is going on.

If you do provide additional training at these meetings, consider offering different levels of this training (i.e., more basic, intermediate, and advanced) as your organization grows and you have more and more people in it with varying levels of ability and experience. For example, some distributors in a new health program who used this technique divided their training program into three phases:

1. *The Basics,* covering how to fill out the company forms, how to prospect and invite people to opportunity meetings, the highlights in the company manual.

2. *Advancing in the Program,* covering the techniques of building an organization and how to move up to the next level in the company.

3. *Excelling in Leadership,* covering how to advance to the highest levels in the company by training others to create a strong, growing organization.

The distributors who had been to the meeting before went to the appropriate training meeting, while their guests heard about the product line and the business opportunity.

Encourage your people who live in another area to attend your meetings a few times, even though they may have a long drive. Then, they can see how you organize the program and do the same thing in their own areas. Explain that it's more effective for them if they see what you are doing firsthand rather than just reading about these methods and ideas in the written materials you or the company provides.

Part IV

PROMOTIONAL TECHNIQUES

Chapter 16

ADVERTISING YOUR PROGRAM EFFECTIVELY

The type of advertising which will work best for you depends on numerous factors, especially your target market, product, and how much time, energy, and commitment you want to invest. While some distributors for products never advertise and only contact people they already know, especially those involved on a small-scale business, others use advertising extensively to go beyond their usual network of acquaintances, especially if they are making a serious commitment to the program.

Thus, the best approach for you depends on the type of product you are marketing, your target market, the receptivity of your personal network to purchase or distribute the product, and how actively you want to go beyond your own network. If you have contacts who would love the product or are business and sales oriented, and this is a sufficient pool of contacts for you, you don't need to advertise. But if your personal network is not very receptive to your product, advertising may be an excellent way to increase your sales.

However, it is important here to distinguish the type of advertising I will be discussing from advertising used in a major mail order or direct mail campaign. Certainly advertising can be used in this way, as a way to nationally market by mail a product or to develop a national network of distributors. Many people do work MLM sales programs in this way, either to expand beyond their locally based network or because they would prefer not to have all the people contact traditional MLM and network sales programs.

However, in general, pure direct mail or mail order doesn't work in MLM programs, because most MLM people really do like and need the personal contact to keep them motivated; they don't just want to push paper and stuff envelopes with mailers. Also, while mail order and direct mail can be very successful when done right, it is a completely different advertising approach from what I will be discussing here, and it is one best left to experienced direct sales people who already have built a local sales organization or downline and to people who want to focus on mail order/direct mail selling. It's an approach that could be a book in itself.

Thus, the focus here will be on advertising in your local area to develop leads. Then, after you get these leads from your ads, you or members of your sales group follow up with personal contact through one-on-one meetings, small group gatherings at your home, or invitations to larger meetings in your area.

Have the Right Response When People Call, So They Want to Meet You and Hear about Your Program. At first, you may need to experiment to hit it on the right formula. Also, you will probably need to repeat your message several times to build your audience, since repetition promotes familiarity, and familiarity builds credibility and leads people to become curious about who you are. But then, once you work out the right formula, keep doing it. And if you have an organization of distributors, teach others in your sales group what you have learned works in your ads, so they can start advertising effectively as well, and perhaps instead of you.

CHOOSING THE RIGHT MEDIA

Choosing the right media takes a little research to find out what is available and what has the most appeal to the market you have selected. So the first step is knowing the market you want to reach, as already discussed. Then pick the local newspapers, magazines, or other media directed to that market. For example, if you are marketing a health product, try advertising in a local publication that features articles on health and self-improvement, or if your product would be of special interst to singles, try putting your ad in a paper directed to singles.

If you have a product with broad appeal, you can advertise almost anywhere. You still should have targeted your primary market or markets. Then, with that in mind check out the main markets for the media sources you are considering, and choose those that are best targeted to your primary market in placing your ad. You can ask the ad departments in the various media under consideration to give you information on the number and type of people they reach (often called *demographics*).

A good starting point is the most familiar media in your area. But besides this, there are probably many you don't know about, such as special-interest magazines and newsletters. To explore further, check at your local library for guides listing publications and other media sources in your area. Some excellent sources include *Literary Marketplace,* a media guide for your state (for example, California has the *California Media Guide*), and *Bacon's Publicity Checker.* Ask your librarian for other suggestions.

Besides being directed to your selected target market, the medium you choose should depend on your purpose. Select it accordingly. For example, if you are putting on a special event to promote your product or placing a help-wanted ad to find salespeople, your local newspaper, advertiser, or college paper may be a good place to advertise this. However, if you are advertising the product itself to consumers, a special-interest publication reaching those targeted consumers (like a publication for singles or health) may be ideal.

The key is to choose your media to fit your target market and then use the right advertising approach to reach that market. Chart 16.1 suggests the types of media to use for different types of advertising approaches.

CHART 16.1: WHERE AND HOW TO ADVERTISE

MEDIA SOURCES	TYPE OF APPROACH TO EMPHASIZE			
	HELP WANTED	BUSINESS OPPORTUNITY	PRODUCTS SERVICES	SPECIAL EVENT
Citywide newspaper	x	x		
Community newspaper (usually a weekly)	x			x
Local advertiser	x	x	x	x
College newspaper	x			x
Singles-oriented publication			x	x
Consumer-oriented publication			x	
Business networking newsletter	x	x		
Other special interest publication			x	x
Local radio show			x	x
Local TV show			x	x

DEVELOPING SYSTEMATIC
PROCEDURES FOR PLACING ADS

To get the most mileage for your advertising dollar, you need to be systematic in how you advertise. That means setting up a system to decide how, when, where, and what to advertise, and then you must record the results.

To set up this system, keep track of the schedules, costs, and procedures for placing ads in the particular media sources you are considering. Later, keep track of the response when the ad appears to determine which media sources produce the best results—based on the rate of response and the percentage of responses which turn into consumers or distributors. Also, use this information to determine your approximate costs for each positive response so you can compare the relative costs of advertising in each media. The ads that turn out to have the lowest cost per consumer dollar spent or effective salesperson recruited are the ones that are most effective.

To begin the information gathering process, initially do some research to build up a file of potential advertising sources. Call up potential sources and ask about the costs for classified and display advertising (that is, by the word, line, column inch). Find out about discounts for repeated ads, advertising deadlines, and specific requirements for placing an ad (for example, do you have to have camera-ready copy or can the publisher set your ad in type?). It helps to list the name of a contact person, too.

By knowing this information in advance, you can readily tailor your ads to suit each publisher's specifications. Also, you can plan an organized ad budget and allot so much for advertising in each media source. For ready access, keep all this information in one place (such as on Chart 16.2, the Advertising Placement Form).

In some cases, such as in placing newspaper classifieds, you can call in your ads. But most publications require you send in with your copy a check for payment. Sometimes, you can stop by the office with your copy, but other publishers

CHART 16.2: ADVERTISING PLACEMENT FORM

NAME OF PUBLICATION OR MEDIA SOURCE, NAME OF CONTACT	ADDRESS, ZIP, AND PHONE NO.	AD COST OR RATE	AD SPECS FORMAT	DEADLINE	CIRCULATION, MARKET, AND COMMENTS	DATE AD RUN	RESPONSE			
							CALLS	MEETINGS	SIGN-UPS	PURCHASES

prefer that you mail it in. Find out the appropriate procedures so you can follow them.

Also, ask about special sections, issues, or programs where you might advertise. These might be especially good times to advertise in a particular publication, because these specials attract a larger audience or draw more people from a particular group you want to reach. For example, if a local singles magazine is running a feature on health classes, this is an ideal time to advertise a health product.

When you advertise, list the date (or dates) your ad is scheduled to run, and check that it does. While some publications will send you tear sheets with your ad if you are running an expensive display ad, most publications don't, particularly if yours is a low-cost or classified ad.

After your ad runs, track the response by recording the number of replies received for each ad and the number of callers who arrange to meet with you or indicate an interest. Also, note how many of these subsequently become consumers and distributors. Your records will prove invaluable in helping you assess how well your ads are pulling and whether the cost of the ad is worth the returns. Also, your records will be useful in planning your next ad campaign, because they can help you see what works and is cost effective, so you can do more of that next time, while you drop or modify what isn't working or is costing too much.

USING THE RIGHT APPROACH
TO ATTRACT INTEREST

The response to advertising can be unpredictable—a little like gambling in Las Vegas—but if you follow certain principles in writing your ads, you'll up your odds.

- *Don't say too much in a single ad.* Zero in on the main point and possibly one or two subpoints, and feature these. Also, don't go into too much detail explaining.

You mainly want to pique readers' interest enough so they will respond by calling you. Don't give away your whole story, so a person feels complete and moves on.

- *Emphasize the benefit or advantage to the consumer or business opportunity seeker.* If you feel a certain group may be especially interested, play that up. For example, some distributors I know were very effective in placing ads in their local advertiser that began "*Housewives:* Do you want to save money and obtain a substantial part-time monthly income? Work only a few hours a day at home."

- *Start off with an eye-catching headline and use sharp catchy copy.* Keep your sentences short and simple to understand. Make your ad easy and interesting to read.

- *In a display ad, make your message stand out.* Do this by leaving plenty of white space. Don't crowd your copy together. Use a picture or logo if you can. And vary the size of your headlines, if you have more than one. A sleek, professional-looking ad is appealing and impressive. But if your ad is a jumble of badly organized, badly written ideas, you'll turn potential prospects away.

- *At the end of the ad, as in any form of sales, ask for some action.* "Call for more information." "Act now!" "Take advantage of our special offer, which is good only until (use a specific date)."

- *Use your business name.* Your ad will seem more professional. Don't just say, call "Al" or "Mary" or "Mr. Davis." You'll get more calls—and more serious ones—when you indicate you are a business. For example, "Contact United Business Associates and ask for Mr. Davis."

- *Plan to advertise a few times,* because of the value of repetition. A single ad isn't always a fair test, since the power of advertising builds as your ad is repeated.

- *Experiment in the beginning to see what works best for you.* Try changing one or two things each time. For example, change your headline or copy slightly to see which ad has the biggest draw. By changing a limited number of parts of your ad, you can judge what form of the ad is working better by what gets the best response. Then use that in the future. Also, if you do have an ad that has been drawing well, notice when it starts to taper off. You may need to change your copy or advertise something new. Or perhaps it's time to stop advertising in that media outlet for a while because you have started to exhaust the market.

  There are no hard and fast rules in advertising, since it's something of an art. Basically, you want to explore possibilities and theories about what approach is most productive for you. Then, go with what ads seem to draw the most.

- *When you can, specify where you want your ad to go in a publication.* And if the publication has several sections where your ad might fit, try experimenting with where your ad pulls best, and use different ad copy as appropriate. For example, suppose a publication has these four categories where you might run your ad: business opportunities, miscellaneous merchandise, notices, and help wanted. If you try each one over a month or two you can see which produces the best response.

Also, know the policies of the company you are promoting before you advertise. Some companies allow their distributors to advertise using the company name freely as long as the advertiser states he or she is an independent distributor. But increasingly, companies have restrictive guidelines to keep a certain company image and to protect themselves from wild claims or misstatements from distributors. So you may need to check all advertising with your company first for its approval. On the other hand, some companies forbid you to use the company name, and some distributors prefer not to use it anyway, so they can develop their own company name and image. Thus, check ad policies first and advertise accordingly.

USING DIFFERENT ADVERTISING APPROACHES FOR THE SAME PROGRAM

It makes sense to separate your advertising for consumers and for job and business opportunity seekers. Many people who are involved in building a sales group try to do both in the same ad—for example, they try to reach health-conscious consumers with an ad like: "A fantastic weight control program . . . and make money, too!"

The problem with this kind of ad is that you confuse your appeal, and you may alienate potential consumers or distributors. First, you may turn off some potential consumers, since they view this "make money, too" message as an indication they are going to be confronted with some kind of a business pitch, when they just want to be consumers. It may be that once they try the product and are sold on it, they may become receptive to the business opportunity, but they don't want to be confronted by a business pitch now. On the other hand, you may turn off a person who wants a business opportunity with this double advertising approach, since a person who wants a business opportunity may feel this double program/make-money appeal suggests part-time rather than serious work, so it's not professional enough for him or her.

So keep your ad message simple—consumer, business or job oriented, but not all three.

Then, tailor your ad to your particular market, keeping these key points, previously noted, in mind:

Keep your copy short and to the point.

Focus on a benefit or advantage.

Make your copy catchy.

Make your ad eye-catching.

Ask for action.

Include your business name.

Sample Ads Using These Principles

The following ads illustrate how these principles are used in practice, when targeted to different groups of people. Each ad should end with your company name, contact person (maybe you), and a phone number.

Advertising Your Product to Consumers
Start off by showing how one of the features of your product or service can benefit the customer. For example,

Ad for a Discount Consumer Club

SICK OF HIGH PRICES?

Learn how you can save on almost everything you buy now—discounts from about 20% to 50%, sometimes more, on most items. Call now and start saving.

Ad for a Health Program

DISCOVER YOUR PATH TO TOTAL
FITNESS AND WELL-BEING

with an exciting new health program designed just for you. Let one of our trained counselors show you how. The program includes a weight control diet, healthy gourmet foods you can prepare in minutes, an exercise program, and more. Start now. Call _____

ADVERTISING THE INCOME POTENTIAL
TO BUSINESS OPPORTUNITY SEEKERS

When you are appealing to people who want to make money and have their own business, you want to emphasize the business advantages and the earnings potential, but also include a little about the product. Too many business opportunity ads sound the same. "Make a fortune in your spare time." "Retire in two months with a substantial monthly income." "The greatest business opportunity yet." The problem with these vague ads is that they can sound like scams, and you don't give enough information about what you are offering, so the reader has nothing to distinguish your ad from other similar opportunity ads. So you are not giving the reader much reason to respond to your ad rather than to any other.

So, be specific and briefly describe the type of product or service involved. Or list the kinds of skills needed to run this business. For example,

Ad for a Discount Consumer Club

MAKE MONEY SHOWING PEOPLE HOW TO SAVE

Become a distributor for this fast-growing new program that enables consumers to save 20% to 50% off on almost everything they buy. Find out how you can be in this lucrative business for less than $50. We train.

Ad for a Health Program

SALES MANAGEMENT OPPORTUNITY
IN THE FAST-GROWING HEALTH FIELD

Market a popular new health program which combines weight control, nutrition, exercise, and attitude change into a single program backed by heavy promotion and sales training support. Invest less than $50 and get started now.

Another good business approach is to target a particular group that might be especially interested in this opportunity and direct your ad to them. For example,

Ad for a Discount Consumer Club

TEACHERS! Discover a great opportunity to make money on the side and potentially earn more than you do teaching. Let others know how they can save money buying what they normally buy every day. Use your teaching skills to inspire and train others.

Ad for a Health Program

HOUSEWIVES: MAKE A FORTUNE

in your spare time showing friends and neighbors how to control their weight and enjoy vibrant health with a brand-new health and fitness program. Easy work from your home, and you can involve your whole family, too.

ADVERTISING THE ADVANTAGES OF JOINING YOUR SALES GROUP TO JOB SEEKERS

When you are directing your appeal to people seeking jobs, emphasize the types of skills needed and the earnings potential. Many job seekers who respond may initially be looking for more traditional sales and marketing positions, but they can be shifted to realizing the advantages of going into business for themselves and using their skills in their own business.

So in your ads, emphasize the types of "job" functions they will be performing, such as marketing, distribution, sales, sales management, training, consulting, leading groups, speaking, and making presentations. Also, indicate the product or service they will be involved with when they use these skills. For example,

Ad for a Consumer Discount Club

SALES MANAGEMENT

Exciting new consumer savings program. Use your sales and promotional skills to work with and direct a team of people in marketing this new club that offers everyone savings of 20% to 50% on the products they buy every day. Call now about this terrific career opportunity.

Ad for a Health Program

MARKETING/SALES

Promote a terrific new health program that combines weight control, nutritious foods, exercise, and self-help tapes. Earn a high commission. Unlimited potential if you're motivated to work hard and learn. We train.

USING THE RIGHT APPROACH WHEN PEOPLE RESPOND TO YOUR AD

What to say when people call is covered in more detail in the section on phone techniques, since people may call not only in response to your advertising but because they learned about you from other sources, such as posters, leaflets, letters, and other persons. Yet regardless of how they happened to call, keep in mind several general pointers:

1. *When people respond to an ad, find out which one and note this,* so you can tabulate the results for each ad. Also, try to get names and phone numbers immediately, so you have them readily available for follow-up. A good way to do this is to introduce yourself first: "Hi. This is Dave Smith. And your name is . . . ? Also, let me get your phone number, in case we get interrupted and I need to call you back."

2. *Be prepared for calls and have a general idea of what you want to say.* It's helpful to use an outline or informational script at first, so you cover the major points. Also, by being prepared, you can better control and direct the conversation.

3. *Very briefly and enthusiastically note the main features or benefits of the program.* This way you review, recap, and perhaps expand upon the main points noted in your ad. For example,

    a. *To Calls About a Consumer Discount Program:*

        "Oh, yes, you're calling about our exciting new consumer discount program which saves consumers about twenty to fifty percent on everything they buy anyway. We're looking for some dynamic people who want to move into sales management to help us market this."

b. *To Calls About a Health Program:*

"Yes, I'm glad you called about our exciting new health program, which provides a complete fitness package. It combines a diet program, nutritious foods you can prepare in minutes, an exercise program, and tapes that can help you change your bad habits to become healthier and happier. The program is growing rapidly, and we need people to help us expand even further."

4. *As soon as you can, turn the conversation back to your respondent* by asking a few questions about what he or she hopes to obtain from the product of business opportunity. This way, you find out about the person's wants and needs and can orient your approach accordingly.

5. *Briefly point out how the product or business will suit each person's situation.* But again, don't tell too much. Just tell people enough to get them to want to meet you and find out more. Just as in your advertising, you want to pique their curiosity, but not satiate it by telling too much.

Thus, if people ask for more detailed information, perhaps give some sketchy hints, but point out that this is the kind of material you cover in depth when you meet with them personally to explain the program. Indicate that you will be glad to give them the whole story then. But you can't do justice to the program over the phone, since you have materials to show or give them.

In some cases, people will ask to see something written, like a flier or brochure. Depending on your own personal style, you can respond in one of two ways:

a. *The I'll-be-glad-to-send-you-information approach.* Use this only if you think the person is serious, so you don't waste time and money sending out free literature. Then, if you decide the person is a real prospect, you might say something like "Sure. I'll be glad to send you a brochure. But this will only give you a brief taste of the program. After you see this, we can arrange a meeting and go over the program in more detail. I'll also have much more material to give you then. I'll call you in a few days to set something up."

b. *The no-we-don't-send-out-information approach.* "Gee, I wish I could send you out something. But we've been flooded with calls and don't have time to send out materials before our first interview (or meeting). So I hope you can come in to take advantage of this marvelous opportunity right away." Then, if they are still unsure, you might offer to at least send something if you think the person could be a likely prospect so you don't risk losing the sale entirely. In this case, you might say something like: "But if you do want to see some examples of our program first, I'll be glad to send you a brochure in a few days, as soon as things settle down."

6. *If people do pump you for more information than you want to give,* remember, *you are—and want to stay— in control of the conversation.* So politely, but firmly, explain that you can't go into that much detail on the phone, but you would like to meet with them to explain the program further.

Chapter 17

CREATING PROFESSIONAL BROCHURES, FLIERS, AND POSTERS

DISTRIBUTING YOUR MATERIALS

Brochures, fliers, and posters can be an extremely effective tool for inviting people to call you for individual presentations or to announce upcoming product demonstrations, sales parties, or opportunity meetings. In fact, you should carry some sales literature with you at all times. Then, as appropriate, you can hand someone a flier or packet of materials, put up a poster, or give someone a stack of fliers or brochures to display.

Use the company's handouts, where available, or make your own, as needed. If you do create your own, you may need to get the company's approval if you use its name. (Check the company's policies and procedures.) If you don't mention the company, you are relatively free to say what you want (though, of course, you must be accurate and not misleading).

You can use these materials in a variety of ways to suit your own personal style. For example, one woman who belongs to a number of different groups regularly brings fliers and brochures to meetings and distributes them to participants. In some cases, she gives a brief presentation about the program at meetings and invites everyone to take some of her materials.

Another man regularly takes fliers to parties and events and hands them out. Depending upon circumstances, he leaves them at the door (so people can pick them up as they arrive), scatters them at tables around the room (the refreshments area is particularly good for this purpose), or discreetly hands them out to people after talking to them briefly.

Another woman, who also gives out fliers at parties, finds a way to bring up her program during the conversation. Then, if the person seems interested, she pulls out a flier out of her purse, saying something like, "Well, since you're interested, here's a flier describing the program in more depth and some of our upcoming events. I hope you can come." She does the same thing when she goes shopping or to a meeting.

The advantage of using these materials after a brief conversation about the program is that people have something tangible to look at, and that helps to make the program seem more solid. Also, it's a vivid reminder of your conversation.

How and Where to Distribute Materials

You can always give brochures or fliers to a few people after you talk for a while at any party or meeting. But if you want to do more such as making an announcement, putting fliers at the entrance, or passing out fliers to everyone, check with the host to see how much promotion you can do. In some cases, the host may invite you to say a few words to the whole group or more actively distribute materials. But other times, the host may not want any promotion at a purely social occasion. So be sure to ask first. You certainly don't want to create hard feelings—or worse, be asked to leave.

Other places where you can hand out materials are lines for events or at entrances to places where people who are part of your target market are likely to go (trade shows, fairs, clubs, businesses, restaurants, etc.).

Another possibility is to give them to people you contact as you do whatever you do everyday.

In some cases, you may be able to follow up on your flier by going into more detail when someone is interested (such as someone you meet at the produce counter in the supermarket). But other times, you may be limited to only a few words of explanation, such as one woman who has gotten some good responses by passing out fliers to toll booth collectors as she drives through. She has time to make only a brief remark, such as "Here's a great way to save money," "Here's a way you can make more money than you are making now." But when you do have more time, you may find it cost effective to say a little about the program first; then, if the person is interested, you can hand out a flier that reviews some of the key points you have already mentioned and lists upcoming meetings and activities that guests can attend, or a number to call you to arrange a meeting.

Also, you can put up fliers in key locations (such as at your local supermarket, copy service, or laundromat). If you can, put them in the windows of stores that have other fliers on display, or ask store clerks to put them on the counter so people can take them. You'll find that certain stores are particularly amenable to these displays—typically stores that are already distributing other materials, like free newspapers and magazines. (Commonly, these include record stores, bookstores, magazine and smoke shops, and health centers.)

Places where groups gather are another place to put up fliers, such as

- the bulletin board or display table in a church, youth center, or lodge meeting hall
- school and college bulletin boards
- car windshields when the cars are parked for a particular event related to your product (such as a health conference if you are promoting health products)

An easy way to distribute fliers is to take a few stacks with you when you do your usual errands and drop them off or post them, as appropriate. If you are working with a group of distributors, ask, others in your organization to help you. Another alternative is to hire a postering service, which distributes fliers from different gorups to key distribution points. Or hire high school or college students.

Still another strategy is leafletting at selected locations. For example, hand out fliers on a food product to people leaving a supermarket. Or pass out leaflets on a health product near a health store. However, when you do leaflet, observe some common courtesies and comply with any legal restrictions. For instance, don't stand too close to a store, so that you don't seem to be working for the store and don't upset the owner, who may see you as a competitor. As long as you are not directly in front of a store and are on a public street, not on the store owner's territory, you can usually hand out fliers and samples freely. But wait until people come out of a store—that way you don't appear to be discouraging them from going in.

If you are at a shopping center, the whole complex may have laws restricting the distribution of material. If you see other people already doing this or there's no clear place to go for approvals, it's probably easier to just go ahead and do it. Someone will tell you if you can't. And once you start doing something, people are more likely to let you keep doing it. Conversely, when you ask, people are more apt to say no, regardless of whether you are allowed to do something or not.

Trade shows and consumer events (including flea markets, county fairs, gift shows, arts and crafts shows, and ethnic festivals) are also good distribution sites. However, you may need to do this at the entrance or exit, or in an open public area, and you may not be allowed to do this in a very open way in the exhibit hall, because the event management has rules restricting the distribution of materials to protect the people who have already paid for exhibit booths. Before you hand out things on private property in large scale, check on what is allowable. Alternatively, to keep your costs of materials down as well as avoid restrictions, you may find it best to talk to people first, and then hand out materials to those who express interest. Exhibitors with related products may be especially likely prospects.

You might also try distributing materials at the unemployment office, if you want to appeal to job seekers—though again, talk to people first or hand out fliers outside the office on public property.

Chart 17.1 summarizes some of these key points about where to hand out fliers and brochures.

To keep track of the effectiveness of your distribution efforts, keep a list of where you have distributed materials and the response. You can use Chart 17.1, Flier and Poster Distribution List, for this purpose. When people call in response, ask about what brochure, flier, poster, or other advertising they are responding to and where they saw it, so you can note this, too, in determining what materials are drawing for you and from what locations.

CREATING EFFECTIVE BROCHURES, FLIERS, AND POSTERS

In order for your brochures, fliers, and posters to be effective, they must look good. They must be eye-catching, inviting, and look as if a solid professional organization is behind them. Of course, hiring a professional to design your materials can help. But you can still do a credible, professional-looking job yourself with a limited investment (under $25) and some graphic aids—tools anyone can use.

First, in writing and organizing your copy follow the same principles used in advertising.

- Don't try to say too much on the same brochure, flier, or poster.
- Focus on a few key points.

CHART 17.1: PLACES TO DISTRIBUTE BROCHURES, FLIERS, AND POSTERS

Good Places to Hand Out Fliers
    At Meetings
    At Parties
    At Events
    On Lines
    To People You See Every Day

Good Places to Display Fliers
    Stores and Centers
        Supermarket
        Laundromat
        Copy Service
        Record Stores
        Bookstores
        Magazine Shops
        Smoke Shops
        Health Centers
        Other Store Windows and Counters
    Places Where Groups Gather
        Churches
        Youth Centers
        Lodge Meeting Halls
        Schools and Colleges
    Car Windshields (of cars parked at selected events)

Good Places to Leaflet
    At Stores
    At a Shopping Center
    At Trade Shows
    At Consumer Events
        Flea Markets
        County Fairs
        Gift Shows
        Arts and Crafts Shows
        Ethnic Festivals
    At the Unemployment Office

- Use a different size or type of letter to highlight major ideas.
- Leave plenty of blank space around your copy, so it is easy to read.
- Break up your copy into brief paragraphs to encourage readability.
- Ask for some action, such as

    Come to a particular event (list date, time, place, cost, and indicate if a reservation is necessary).

    Call to ask for more details.

    Call to attend a business opportunity meeting.

Second, use the basic principles of graphic design to create an attractive, inviting look. And if you're not an artist, use the graphic aids to be discussed. To get this professional look, do the following:

- Use bold, eye-catching headlines that convey your key message in a few words.
- Use type or lettering that has the appropriate feel for your message. (For example, use solid, conventional lettering to describe a business opportunity, free-flowing unusual lettering to convey a feeling of fun.)
- Use a picture or two to make the flier look more lively. (You can buy predrawn clip-art books where you just cut out the art and paste it on your copy if you aren't an artist yourself.)
- Use a good-quality typewriter or computer with a letter-quality printer (and if you have proportional spacing, so much the better).

MAKING BROCHURES AND FLIERS

You can use the following graphic aids to help you get this quality look.

Rub-on Letters. Simply press them on paper to create instant headlines. There are many brands, which come in different sizes and type styles: Letraset, Prestype, Instatype, Better Letter, and so on. Just ask to see a book at your local artist's supplies store and choose. The cost is about $6 to $10.

A Burnisher. For rubbing on the letters. You can also use the end of a pencil or pen, although a burnisher—a pencil-shaped instrument with a rounded point—has a nice feel and is made for this purpose. It costs about $5.

A Rubber Stamp Catalog or Book of Clip Art. Great for illustrations. Simply cut out the pictures you like and paste them in position on the layout for your flier. About $3 to $5.

Ruler. Preferably a metal one. Use it to make sure your layout is both centered and straight. About $1 to $5.

Light Blue Pencil. Use this to rule lines for your head-lines. The light blue color won't show in copies. About $1.

Spray Glue. Get the kind that allows you to reposition. Spray it on the back of your copy or artwork and place this wherever you want on your layout. About $6 to $9.

Plain White Paper. Good bond typing paper will do. Use this for creating your layout. About $3 to $8 a ream.

Ko-Rec-Type or White-Out. Use this to clean up your final layout. About $1.

Now, you are ready to go to work.

1. Type up a rough draft of your copy. As much as you can, use the same spacing you plan to use on your final flier.

2. Lay out your copy on an 8½" by 11" sheet. Feel free to cut, paste, and move the typed copy around on the flier until you like the layout. Then, type up the final draft, and make sure there are no typos.

3. Visualize where your headlines and pictures might go.

4. To create your headlines, take your ruler and blue pencil and draw one or more light blue lines. Then, using your burnisher or other implement, rub on the letters to create your headline above the line you have just ruled. Use your judgment to space the letters properly into words and phrases. Choose the size and style of lettering to fit the space and present the image or reinforce the message you want to convey.

5. Cut out the headlines, and position them, along with your final copy, on your layout. Use your blue pencil to mark where everthing should go. Then, place each item in turn facedown on some newsprint or paper, spray-glue it, and place it as indicated on your flier. Use your ruler to make sure the headlines and copy are centered and straight.

6. Now find a picture or two you like from the rubber stamp catalog or book of clip art. Use a picture that fits your message. For example, for a travel party flier, use a picture with an outline of a palm tree on a small South Pacific–style island. For a dance party, use a picture of a couple dancing and perhaps a picture of a messenger announcing the event.

7. Then, cut out the picture (if you may want to use it again, make a copy first) and spray-glue it on your flier, just as you did the headline and copy. But now you don't need to use the ruler. Just eyeball it, and place the picture or pictures wherever it feels right to you.

8. Finally, check over your layout and copy for any errors, smudges, spots, and so on and use the White-Out or Ko-Rec-Type to remove these.

9. Choose an appropriate color for your flier. (I like having several stacks of different colored paper around so it's easier to choose. But if you prefer, get the colored paper you need from the printer. The per copy cost is greater, but you don't have to invest money back in stock.) In choosing the color stock to use, consider using traditional associations to help reinforce your message. For example, green suggests money, yellow or orange suggests kitchens and food. Or choose a color that suggests your own personal style.

10. Now you are ready to make as many copies of your flier as you want. The least expensive way is to take your master layout to your local instant copy center—and *voilà*—your flier can be ready in minutes or overnight.

But one caution. Make a master copy from your original or have the copy center make one for a backup. The reason for this is that the rub-on letters sometimes flake when kept for a while, leaving you with raggedy or missing letters when you go to print more. But if you have a master, you can use this instead. It's better to use the original as long as you can, since it always gives you a sharper image. But if you can't, you have always got the copy.

11. If you wish, make extra copies of your artwork for others in your organization. Then, they can change any necessary details, such as the name and address of the person to contact, to print their own fliers.

Making Posters

For posters, simply use larger headline lettering throughout. And keep your copy very short—25 words or fewer is best.

Choose a poster board of the appropriate color. You can get precut boards at your local art supply store. Usually, these are cut 22″ by 28″. Or cut boards to size on a paper-cutter. (Obtain your own or some art stores may have these.)

To plan your layout in advance, use a ruler and pencil (a T-square is ideal if you have one), and lightly draw the number of lines you need for your copy. Then, measure the space you need for each word (or eyeball it if you are good at this). Finally, rub on the letters. When you are done, use a softer rubber eraser to erase the lines. And presto—almost instant posters.

Chapter 18

HOW TO WRITE IMPRESSIVE LETTERS

When you contact people you don't know or don't see regularly, a good letter can be critical in sparking their interest. Letters can help you contact leaders of organizations, company heads, real estate and insurance agents, and others with a vast range of contacts. By writing a brief and compelling description of what you are doing, you increase your credibility and can overcome initial resistances or uncertainty about who you are, so that the people you contact may want to know more.

Note that this letter is not designed to be a direct mail sales letter that asks the recipient to send in an order or otherwise act now. Rather, it is intended to introduce you and give you credibility, so you can follow up with a personal contact.

THE STEPS TO USING LETTERS EFFECTIVELY

A letter-writing approach involves these key steps:

1. Decide what key groups or types of individuals you want to contact (for example, church leaders, real estate brokers, leaders of social organizations).

231

2. Draft a letter than emphasizes how members of this group can use your product or service or how the group can earn money by marketing to members.

3. Make a list of the groups or individuals you plan to contact. Possibly make a preliminary phone call, either to find out the name of the person in the group to whom to send the letter, or to speak briefly to the contact person about the letter you plan to send. (If you need to do both, it's better to separate the request for the name of the person to contact and your effort to contact that person into two calls. This way you can ask to speak to the person you are calling with more authority—you know who you want already—and you are more likely to get through.) At times, this preliminary phone call may be all you need to interest the person in your program, and you don't need a follow-up letter. (See Chapter 20 on telephone techniques.) But commonly, you will need to send a letter to reaffirm or provide more detail about what you just spoke about.

4. Make copies of the letter and send it out with some literature about your program. Ideally, send the letter to a specific person. To send the same letter to multiple people, one way is to leave space when you type the original to add in the name and address, and then make copies at a copy machine, and afterward, type in a different name and address on each copy. Or use a word processor or word processing service to produce multiple copies with the different names and addresses.

5. Follow up your letter with a phone call after a few days to set up a meeting or invite the recipient to a group meeting.

DRAFTING YOUR LETTER

In writing your letter, emphasize the benefits of your product, service, or business opportunity that are likely to be of special interest to the group you plan to contact. Use the following guidelines to write your letter:

1. *Keep your letter brief and to the point.* Strive for no more than one page.

2. *Make your letter look good.* Use business letter-head, and if you are just starting, you can create one inexpensively by following the guidelines for making fliers and brochures. Also, be sure to produce it on a good typewriter or use a word processor and letter printer. You want to go first class.

3. *Keep your sentences and paragraphs short* (no more than three or four lines per sentence, or eight to ten lines per paragraph). This way your letter is easy to read.

4. *Leave plenty of space for the margins.* Again, this promotes readability—and it looks more professional.

5. *Start off with one or two sentences that attract attention, and quickly let the reader know what the letter is about and why he or she should read more.* This way, you involve the reader and avoid the "junk-mail-toss-it-away" syndrome. If you have a brief conversation with the recipient before writing, mention that the person already expressed interest, and now at his or her request you are sending the information requested.

6. *Select the one, two, or at most three benefits of your product which you think would be most attractive to your prospect and emphasize these.* You are mainly trying to get your prospect to pay attention and stimulate his or her desire to learn more about your program. So don't tell everything now. If you say too much, your letter can get boring or overwhelming. Instead, home in on the key, most interesting points.

7. *Include any details about your product, service or business on a separate sheet,* and note in your letter that you are attaching these materials.

8. *Close with an invitation to action or an indication of what action you will take.* Depending on your personal style, invite the person to call you to set up an appointment, or state that you will call in a few days to set up an appointment.

9. *Address your letter to a specific person, if you know this, or if you are mailing what is obviously a form letter, add a personal note to the recipient to personalize it.* You'll get a better response when you do. However, make sure this is a real personal note based on a past contact or something you know about the person—not just the person's name followed by a general sales comment such as "Marge—this program is really great." Such comments are obviously phoney and some people might get offended at the use of their first name unless they have had prior contact with you.

Later, regardless of how you have written your letter or close, call to make sure your prospect has gotten the letter, has read it, or is interested. This follow-up is important, because even if you have invited the person to call, the person may never have received the letter, may have lost it, may not have read it, may have forgotten it, or may have meant to call you but didn't get around to it.

Regard your letter as a door opener. Then you have to keep that door open and go through it.

SOME SAMPLE LETTERS

To illustrate how these letter-writing principles work in practice, this section includes some sample letters directed to different groups of people. Each group of letters begins with a list of key points on how to slant a letter to that group. Note how each sample letter incorporates these key points.

A Letter to Friends and Neighbors

Key points to remember:

- Make it friendly and chatty.
- Subtly allude to your connection with this person to personalize the letter—but in a low-key way.

- Indicate how you have personally benefited from the product features that are likely to be especially important to this person, and note that now you want to share these benefits, because he or she is a friend or neighbor.

A Sample Letter (Promoting a Consumer Discount Club)

Dear (Name of Friend or Neighbor):

Hi from your friendly neighbor across the street. I just got involved in a new program that has fantastic savings for consumers, and I thought this would be a good opportunity to be neighborly and let my neighbors know about it, so they can benefit from it, too.

It's a consumer savings program that enables you to get most products you are already buying at wholesale prices. It has just about everything, from groceries to more expensive items and familiar brand-name products, too. You can save about 20 to 50 percent on most purchases, sometimes even more.

I've already bought a new camera and saved almost $300, so I know the program works.

Also, you can make money by sharing the program with a few people you know. I know some people who are making a few hundred a week after two months, and one friend recently quit his regular job to do this full time.

I think it's a tremendous opportunity to both save and make money, and that's why I'm so excited about it. I've enclosed some materials describing the program a little more fully, and I'm listing some dates when I will be having a meeting in my house about this program. I hope you can attend, or if that's not convenient, I can let you know about other meetings and take you as my personal guest. Or let's sit down at your house or mine, and I'll tell you about the program personally.

Please let me know when you would like to attend a meeting or get together. Or if you'd like more information, please call. Hope to talk to you about this soon.

Sincerely,

John Smith
(your friendly neighbor
across the street)

A Letter to the Head of a Church
Group or Social Organization

Key points to remember:

- Be professional and businesslike, and use the appropriate business letter form, including your initials and those of the typist (make one up if you wish) in the lower left-hand corner.
- Make your business sound solid impressive. If you're small and want to sound larger, have someone other than yourself sign the letter with an apprpriately impressive title. For example, when a friend did a mailing to ministers, her administrative assistant signed the letter as "Associate Community Service Director."
- Emphasize how the product or service would benefit the group.
- Show how the group or group leader could benefit economically by using the program as a fund-raiser, if this is an option.
- Suggest that you can put on an interesting program for the group, and you would be glad to discuss this further with the group leader.
- Mention any success other churches or group leaders have had using or marketing the product or service.
- If you have had a brief conversation about the program or have been referred by anyone, be sure to note this.

A Sample Letter (Promoting a Consumer Discount Club)

Dear Reverend (Name of Minister):

I was delighted to hear about your interest in (Name of Program) when we spoke the other day. As you may recall, I was referred to you by (Name of Referral), and we talked about how much this program could benefit your group.

In brief, this program is of great benefit, because it offers your members an opportunity to save money on all kinds of goods they are already buying—groceries, general merchandise, and brand name items. At the same time, you can make a substantial monthly income for your organization or yourself, just by letting others know about the program.

I have already spoken at some church-connected social groups about this program as part of a presentation I call "Money-Saving Tips: How You Can Save Without Spending a Cent." And some church leaders have used the program to organize a community project.

I would be glad to put on a special presentation for you and help you organize such a project. I can meet with you personally to discuss this—or if you like, come as my guest to one of our regular meetings.

I am enclosing some additional information on the program and some dates for regular meetings. Please call if you have any questions or to set up an appointment. I can meet with you at our offices or at your church offices—whatever is most convenient to you.

I look forward to hearing from you soon and sharing more about this wonderful program with you and your group.

Sincerely,

Joan Smith
Associate Community Service Director

JS:aj
encl:

A Letter to Outside Sales
People About a Business Opportunity

This letter might go to real estate agents or insurance agents, or other independent sales people.

Some key points to remember:

- Be professional and businesslike in your approach (just as described).

- Make your business sound solid and impressive, even if you're small, by using an appropriately impressive title, such as President, Director, or Marketing Director. For example, in my friend's mailing to real estate agents, her administrative assistant signed the letters "Associate Marketing Director."

- Emphasize the money-making benefits of the program.

- Point out how the benefits of the product will enable the person to make money.

- Suggest why this person might be in an especially good position to promote the product.

- Invite the person to meet with you personally or attend a meeting.

- Mention any successes other salespeople in this person's field have had in marketing the program.

- If you have had a brief conversation about the program or have been referred by anyone, indicate this.

A Sample Letter (Promoting a Consumer Discount Club)

Dear Realtor (Name of Realtor):

I was pleased to hear of your interest in (Name of Program) when we spoke the other day. As you may recall, (Name of Program) is a terrific opportunity for realtors to make a substantial part-time income with only a few hours of work a week. And you can save money on purchases you would make anyway.

I have been contacting real estate agents in my area, because we have found that real estate agents are particularly successful in this business, since they have a wide circle of contacts who are likely to be interested in the program.

Since this program is relatively new in this area and has broad appeal, this is an excellent time to get involved now. Wherever the program has been introduced, it has grown rapidly, and you can be part of this tremendous growth here.

I am enclosing some material on the program and some dates of regular meetings. I would also be glad to meet with you personally at your convenience.

Please let me know when you would like to get together. I look forward to working with you, and will do everything I can to assist you in becoming successful in this rapidly growing new program.

Sincerely,

John Smith
Associate Marketing Director

JS:aj
encl:

A Letter to Merchants
(If Your Program Permits You to Sell to Stores)

Key points to remember:

- Be professional and businesslike in your approach (as described earlier).
- Make your business sound solid and impressive (as described earlier).

- Emphasize that the product line would appeal to current customers, without detracting from products the merchant is currently selling.
- Show how the merchant can benefit from these added sales with relatively little personal effort.
- Point out how the merchant's customers who get involved in the program can help the merchant make money, too.
- Indicate that you will be glad to stop by during the day to present the program.
- Mention any success other merchants have had selling the products.
- Indicate that you are only contacting selected merchants in the area, and if he or she is interested, you will not contact any other merchants on the block (or within a certain radius)—you will let him or her do this.

A Sample Letter (Promoting a Consumer Discount Club)

Dear Merchant (Name of Merchant):

I was pleased to hear you were interested in learning more about (Name of Program) when we spoke briefly on the phone today. As you may recall, you can use this program to expand your present product line, and you can do so relatively easily, since the product virtually sells itself.

It's a program that appeals to almost everyone, since it enables people to save money on all sorts of items. But the products are different from the ones you now carry, so the program won't detract from your own business. It will only help.

I am enclosing some materials on the program, including a full-color flier. The flier describes the full benefits of the program, and many merchants simply pass out fliers to customers in their store. Some hold brief meetings with interested customers at the end of the regular work day. So it's a very easy program to promote, and some merchants are now earning an average of $200 to $500 extra each week, just for a few hours' work.

Also, be assured, if you get involved, we will not contact any other merchants in your area, because we do not want to be in competition with you.

I would be glad to stop by your store at a convenient time to describe the program to you in more detail. Or you are welcome to come to one of our regular meetings. I will call you in a few days to set up an appointment. In the meantime, feel free to call if you have any questions.

Sincerely,

John Smith
President

JS:aj
encl:

Chapter 19

PROVEN TELEPHONE TECHNIQUES

When you meet or call someone for the first time, you have about four seconds to make a first impression. Researchers studying how people meet in bars found that people decide whether to continue their conversation in four seconds. And it's like that when you first call someone on the phone about your product or business opportunity, except you have to make your impression with your voice alone.

Thus, you need to know the basics of making a good phone impression and how to adapt your technique to different situations and types of people.

This section describes the basic principles of good phone techniques and how to apply these in different situations or with different people. At the end of the chapter, there are some sample scripts to illustrate these principles.

SOME BASIC PRINCIPLES

The following principles are basic to all successful phoning, whether you call someone you know, make a cold call to a stranger, follow up after sending a letter, or respond when someone calls your ad. Many of these principles apply in any kind of sales, too. The five key principles are

1. Get prepared before you call.
2. Have the right attitude.
3. Open the conversation with a good lead.
4. Keep the conversation going effectively.
5. End the conversation with a good close.

Here's how to put into practice each of these principles:

Get Prepared before You Call

To get prepared, follow these guidelines:

- *Have a general idea in advance of what you want to say.* Start off with a basic script or outline of the key points you want to cover. This way you make sure you cover your major points and in the order and manner you desire. You can modify what you say as the need arises, and you can train others to do the phoning for you. Use an outline if you prefer to be more spontaneous and ad lib the specifics; some people prefer this greater flexibility. But if you want a more structured, planned approach use a script; some people feel more reassured having it all down in black and white. Either way you can always revise your outline or script for the future, as needed.
- *List the key benefits of your product or service in order of importance.* Then, you can go through those with the most appeal first, and if you encounter any objections, you can try to overcome these or go on to the next benefit.
- *Focus on one or two key products or services when you call.* The company you represent may have dozens of products, but emphasize those that you feel will have the most appeal first.

- *Before you call, review what you want to say and be ready to slant it* according to the interests of the person you are calling.

Have the Right Attitude

When you have the right attitude, basically an upbeat, positive approach, you will stimulate a more receptive, positive response from the person you call. To this end, follow these guidelines:

- *Be enthusiastic and positive.* Then, you convey a spirit of excitement about your products or business, whatever you say. You want to show that you think you are involved in a terrific program which is generating a lot of interest and excitement. Remind yourself of this before you call to help you get in this mood.
- *If you need to, take a few moments to put yourself in a positive, confident, calm frame of mind.* Use affirmations, visualize the caller being excited—whatever you need to get your enthusiasm going.

Open the Conversation with a Good Lead

A good lead helps to get attention and stimulate interest and sets the tone for the rest of the conversation. For a good lead, keep these points in mind:

- *To establish credibility and authority, briefly explain who you are at the beginning of the conversation if the person you are calling doesn't know you.* Give your professional credentials, and convey an image of authority with your tone of voice. Here's an example:

  Hello. I'm Joanne Smith of Health Plus. We're a company that's promoting health and fitness through quality products and helping others earn money by promoting these products.

- *To stimulate interest, start off with a strong lead-in that suggests the listener will gain an immediate benefit in listening to you talk about your product or money-making opportunity.* So say something that's catchy, even startling, to get attention. You can present this as a statement or question, but in either case, keep your opener short and specific to spur your listener into wanting to learn more.

Some good openers include a leading question such as, "Could you use an extra $200 a month?" or a statement suggesting an urgent need to act now, such as, "I just heard about a great new gas saver that has a special offer *on through* this week."

The following examples provide some ideas on different approaches to use with people you know and those you don't. Note that a general lead-in which doesn't get into specifics may be fine for those you know. However, when you are trying to appeal to those you don't know, you need to use a more focused appeal that highlights the advantages of the product or business opportunity. This more focused approach is also fine with people you know. The following examples illustrate these principles.

They also show how the more focused lead-in can be adapted to either someone you know or someone you don't.

Examples of a General Lead-in with Someone You Know "Hi. I just heard about an exciting new idea. Can I come over and let's talk about it?"

"I've been thinking about getting involved in a new project, and I'd like to get your opinion. Can we get together later today or tomorrow to talk about it?"

"I just discovered a great new program, and we both can benefit. When do you have some time so we can talk?"

Examples of an Opener That Focuses on a Product or Service With someone you don't know, emphasize a benefit that you know has broad appeal. With a personal contact, try to personalize your lead-in so it applies particularly to that person.

(To someone you don't know) "How would you like to save $50 a month on your grocery bills?"

(To a friend who has been struggling to lose weight) "How would you like to be able to lose weight and keep it off permanently?"

(To a friend who you know wants something) "You know that new car you've been saving for? How would you like to learn how you can get it in a few months?"

Examples of an Opener That Focuses on a Business Opportunity   With strangers, you can appeal more directly to their need; with people you know, it's best to be more subtle, perhaps even using the third-person approach, so they don't feel on the spot.

(To someone you don't know) "Would you like to make more money than you are making now?"

(To a friend) "Do you know someone who would like to earn an extra $500 to $1,000 a month?"

Keep the Conversation Going Effectively

Some key ways to have a smooth, flowing, effective conversation are:

- *Get to the point of the conversation quickly.* No one likes rambly calls that begin with someone asking a number of questions without explaining why. So establish your purpose quickly, and if someone calls you and isn't clear about why he or she is calling, politely ask the person to explain the reason for the call.
- *Briefly describe the program (or expand slightly upon what the person you are calling already knows).* In making this description, emphasize the main benefits, and show by your confidence and air of authority that you know what you are talking about. And seek to get the person excited to learn more, since this is your

> *main purpose in calling, to get people to want to meet with you to learn more.*

So focus on a few key selling points and describe these briefly. For example, suppose you are promoting a health program and you speak to a college student who is active in athletics. You can briefly say something like this:

> It would be a great program for you. The program will help you in your training. The vitamin pills will give you extra energy. The athletes who have used them report playing better, and even breaking past records.

- *Vividly describe your product, so others can literally see it.* This makes your product more emotionally appealing, and helps to hold your prospect's attention after a good lead-in. Through a vivid description, you make that product really come alive for people. For example:

  It's a fantastic health program. You drink these terrific-tasting drinks that look and taste like malts, exercise about a half hour a day, and listen to tapes that teach you how to change your attitude. In a few days, you'll see the pounds melt away.

- *Mention any special features that make the program stand out,* such as testimonials by name people, celebrity appearances on talk shows, and so forth. For example,

  This famous football player (Name of Athlete) uses these products, and a panel of celebrities who have used them will be appearing on the Johnny Carson show.

- *But don't say too much.* Don't give out details over the phone. If people ask, explain that you need to meet with them personally to go into detail. Or they can hear about all these details at a meeting. If you say too much, you may satisfy their interest, so they feel they don't need to know any more. Also, you take up too much of your valuable time in unproductive conversation.

- *If you talk about the business opportunity, it's better not to mention unfamiliar terms, such as network or multi-level marketing, unless the person knows what these are.* Preferably, call the venture a part-time way to earn extra income or a home-based business. This makes the business sound simpler, and it avoids triggering any misconceptions many people have about multi-level or network marketing. Also, MLM or network marketing can be difficult to explain if people have never heard of these concepts. When you meet personally, you can explain how the business works in your presentation. But for now, keep things simple and brief.

- *Stay in control of the conversation.* Just as in any sales presentation, remember, you are in charge. Be aware of what you want to say and lead the conversation in that direction. If someone asks you a question that gets you off track, gently guide the conversation back or indicate that you will discuss this when you meet each other.

End the Conversation with a Good Close

A good close leads to the desired action you want from the other person. To this end, keep these guidelines in mind:

- *Don't try to complete the sale on the phone.* Unless you know someone really well—and even then—you normally can't close a sale on the phone. People, particularly strangers, need to see something concrete—literature, the product, or other people who are involved in marketing the program. So just focus on getting the person you are calling to want to meet you to attend a meeting.

- *Keep the call under three minutes.* That should be plenty of time to determine if the person is interested, explain who you are, and motivate him or her to want to learn more. A long call will usually just waste valuable time—a shorter call is more efficient and effective.

- *Wind up the call with a request for action, and, ideally, set up a specific appointment.* For example, invite the person to a meeting, or better, make arrangements to pick up the individual so you can go together since this way the person is more likely to attend. Alternatively, arrange to meet at his house or yours. Or agree to send information, and then call to set up an appointment.

- *Ask for referrals.* If people aren't interested themselves, ask if they know someone who might be. And be specific. Mention a particular type of product or business benefit, and ask if they know a particular type of person who might be interested in that benefit. That helps them think of specific people they know, whereas a general question is more likely to draw a blank. For instance, you might ask "Do you know someone who would be interested in losing five to ten pounds in a month?"

  Or "Do you know any other real estate people who might be interested in earning a few hundred dollars extra each week?"

  Avoid more general questions such as "Do you know anyone else who might be interested?"

RESPONDING TO CALLS ABOUT YOUR AD OR LETTER

Before anyone is able to respond to your ad or letter, get ready to respond to calls yourself. To do so, *plan your response in advance*—just as you do when you call someone.

Make an outline or miniscript, so you are prepared and can stay in charge of the conversation. Typically, plan to cover some of these points:

- *A question about why the person is responding to your ad or letter,* and *what is most important to him.* Then you can direct your message to that individual's "hot button." Perhaps start with a question to draw that person out, such as "What most interested you in my ad?" "How do you feel the program I described in my letter can help you?" "What kind of *home-based* business appeals to you?"
- *A brief description* of the product or business emphasizing why it will benefit the person or be a good business opportunity.
- *A brief statement of the type of people you are looking for*—to use the product or participate in the business.
- *A few questions to determine if the person is a likely consumer or business prospect.*
- *A request to set up an appointment* (as usual, suggest you only have a few openings, since you are busy, and determine if these are convenient for the person, or invite him or her to a general meeting).

A Sample Conversation Might Go Something Like This:

For a Call About the Product You Are Advertising
Hello. Let me tell you a little about the product we advertised. We're the XYZ Company, and we have a great line of products for people who are interested in losing weight. We put the ad in to invite people to our weekly health and nutrition parties. We start off with a brief discussion about some new findings about nutrition, and then show you how our program can work for you. Are you someone who really wants to lose weight? Are you in any kind of diet program now?

(Then, if the person says "yes") Well, it sounds as if our program could really benefit you. Would you like to come to our next meeting? We limit the number of people at each meeting, so we can give you plenty of individual attention. I can make a reservation for you for our meeting on _____. (And if the person can't make that one:) Well, our next meeting after that is on _____.

For a Call Responding to a Business Opportunity Ad: Hello. Let me tell you a little bit about our business. We're the XYZ Company, and our company is involved in _____. The company has been growing extremely fast in the last few weeks, so we are looking for some people who would like to assist us and are interested in running their own business to market this product. You would be involved in all aspects of the process—sales, marketing, promotion, business management—and you would participate in training and motivating others, too. We are looking for people who have some skills in this area or who are interested in learning this kind of business; we are scheduling meetings this week. Does this sound of interest to you?

(Assuming the answer is "yes") I need to have a little information about you. What kind of work have you done? Have you had any experience in management? Do you like working with people? Are you working now?

(Then, if the person sounds like a likely prospect) Okay, then, let's set up an appointment. First, let me get down your name and phone number. I have a few time slots available later this week. Which of these would be good for you?

SETTING APPOINTMENTS

Keep in mind these key guidelines:

- *When you set up an appointment, try to pin the person down to making a firm commitment to meet you.*

Make it clear when you set an appointment that it is definite, and confirm that the person understands this. Many people will say, "I'll try to make it" or "I'll let you know." But if you hear signals that the person thinks of this just as a tentative agreement (e.g., he says "I'll *try*"), try to get the person to say that yes, he or she will definitely plan to do this and emphasize why it is to his or her benefit to act now.

For example, if a person sounds uncertain about committing to a one-on-one appointment or you want to stress that the appointment is a definite one, you might say, "Okay, I've got this down in my calendar now. We'll be meeting together at (name the time and place), and I'll be counting on seeing you then."

Or to stress the importance of the meeting, you might say, "Okay, I've got our meeting set for _____, and I'll be over at your house then. If something comes up for you, please give me plenty of notice, so we can set up another appointment. I only have so many appointments I can set up for each week, and my time slots usually get filled very quickly."

- *When people agree to attend a meeting, emphasize how important it is for them to come.* Often people feel free to show up or not since they feel they are just one of many people. So point out that their attendance is important.

For example, tell a prospect, "Okay, I'm putting you on my list for the meeting (date and place). We can only accommodate a limited number of people, and I've made a reservation for you. If something should come up, please give me plenty of notice, so I can invite you to another meeting."

- *Arrange to take your guest to the meeting if possible, rather than meet there.* This way most persons feel more obligated to attend and feel more important personally, because you are going out of your way to bring them to the meeting. Again, make sure your guest knows that it is a confirmed meeting. "Okay, I'll pick you up at (time and date), and we'll go to the meeting together. I'm putting this in my calendar as a confirmed date, and I'll see you then."

- *Instead of asking prospects for a time they can make it, it's better to say you have a few time slots available.* Then, ask which they would prefer. That gives your prospect the impression you are a busy person. If he or she can't make it, you can always work out an alternate time.

- *When you talk to people you know, set up a time to get together before you go into details about the program.* You might, of course, give a very brief description of what will happen at this meeting, although some distributors like to use a "let's get together first" approach in which they "clear the night" first, before going into any sort of sales approach. It's an approach that is usually most suitable to people you already know and might see for social reasons. As an example, you might call a friend and say, "Hello. This is _____. I was wondering if you and your wife had anything planned for next Tuesday." Then, if the person isn't free, you would just try an alternative time when he or she is. One rationale for this approach is that you want to make sure the prospects would be free to attend a meeting before giving your sales pitch to get them there. On the other hand, I think people appreciate knowing what something is about before they commit to go to a meeting and that it's more efficient to screen people out before meeting with them than getting them to come to something and then trying to convince them to be interested if they are reluctant to be there.

- *When you set up a meeting, indicate that you will call back on the scheduled date to reconfirm.* Also ask your prospects to call you at least a day in advance if they can't make the meeting. Again, emphasize that this is important, since you have a very tight schedule. This way, your prospect feels the meeting is especially important, which decreases the likelihood of no-shows.

- *If someone cancels a meeting, put that person off for the next one.* Don't sound as if you are available any time your prospect is. Make such persons feel they have to wait and that the appointment with you is very valuable, so they will be less apt to cancel next time.

Reconfirming Appointments

To increase your chances of people keeping the appointments you set, do the following:

- *Reconfirm any appointments you set for more than a day or two after you call.* This way you reduce the risk of no-shows.

- *When you do call, act as if the person is already coming and you are simply calling to reconfirm this.* This is better than asking the person if he or she is still coming, because that gives a person a chance to rethink if they want to attend and reconsider how interested they are in the program. Also, it gives the person an easy out because he or she just has to say no instead of having to counter your assumption about your previous agreement.

- *Make a few comments to get your prospect reenthused* about attending, such as "I'm calling to confirm that I will be seeing you tonight at seven. We're expecting a record turnout, since the company is introducing its new products tonight. I'm really looking forward to trying them out."

- *Briefly restate your agreed-upon arrangements.* "I'll be by to pick you up at your house, 34 Davis Street, at seven." Or, "I'll meet you at the corner of Davis and

Peach at seven, and I'll be sure to wait in case you're a little late."

- *Don't let the person start asking questions again about the program,* since that will only make him or her reconsider. Instead, cut off any questions firmly but politely by indicating that they will be covered in the meeting itself and that the person will have plenty of opportunity to ask then.

- *If your prospect says he or she can't make it when you call, reschedule the meeting. But probe a little to find out why.* If the reason is a serious matter that takes priority (such as someone sick in the family or a last-minute work assignment), be understanding and try to set the next meeting as soon as possible. Indicate that you are quite busy, but because of the situation, you will try to fit that person in right away.

  On the other hand, if you sense that the person is putting you off because of uncertainty about the program, put the person off a little, too, to make him feel he is truly missing an opportunity. For example, say something like, "Oh, that's too bad. You'll really be missing a good meeting. The regional director is going to be in town, so the meeting should be super good." (Sometimes people reconsider at this point.)

  Then, if you set another appointment, indicate that you have to set it a week or two away because of your other commitments. For example, "Okay, then let's set another meeting. However, it'll have to be next week, because I already have my calendar filled with other meetings, since the program is growing so fast. But I do have two time slots next week—Tuesday at five, and Wednesday at three. Which would be best for you?"

- *Or instead of calling, send out a confirming note to remind the prospect of the time and place of the appointment, if you have set this up more than a week in advance.* Some distributors use this approach because they find that people are better able to cancel an appointment when you call, since the arrangement seems more casual, but they find it harder to say no when something comes in the mail because this makes everything seem more set and formal. Then, too, when they have something in the mail, the burden to call you to break the appointment rests with them. I'm not sure whether you call or send a note makes much difference, and I personally prefer the personal touch of calling. So use what feels most comfortable for you.

Following Up with No-Shows

Even with the best of phone techniques, some prospects will not show up. Distributors have different ways of dealing with this. Some just figure that marketing is a numbers game and drop these people from their list. Others call back the people they know to find out what happened, since they have this personal connection. But they don't feel it's worth the time and effort to call back the people they know, figuring that most just didn't come because they weren't interested.

People may not show up for many reasons and might still have some interest or could be remotivated with a little follow-up that both reminds them of the benefits of the program and also may impress them because it shows your interest in them, leading you to call again. Thus, one effective approach that works for many is to call up the no-shows once in an upbeat way, suggesting that they missed a really great meeting, but they have another chance. The value of this second chance approach is that some people are a little skeptical about whether the program is really solid when you first call, particularly if they live in an area, where many new companies start up, only to disappear in a few months. So the first time they hear about a new product or business opportunity people can easily say to themselves, "Oh, yes, another program." They have seen many companies come and go, and they may think this could be like the others.

However, when you call again after a week or two and report on how well the company is doing, they may be willing to listen more carefully. Furthermore, they may think that if you went to a meeting and are still excited, maybe it's worth looking into the program a little further. That's why I suggest you don't give up on no-shows right away and call again.

If you do call again, don't put the person on the spot about why he or she didn't come. That will only make the person defensive and possibly hostile. For example, one friend hired a student to do some follow-up calling for her, gave her a script, and told the student to use it as a guideline, but put the ideas in her own words. Unfortunately, when the student made her first call, she immediately pounced on the poor man who answered, proclaiming in an accusatory tone, "I'm calling because you weren't at our last meeting for the XYZ Company. So why weren't you there?" Needless to say, he hung up, and my friend fired the student on the spot. But all was not lost. Afterward, when my friend called to apologize, the man's wife said he had been sick, and the man accepted the apology with good grace, and subsequently did go to a meeting and bought some products.

In short, calling no-shows can be productive at times, as long as you keep these points in mind:

- Be enthusiastic.
- Express your regrets that the person couldn't come.
- Let the person give you a reason for not attending if he or she wants to, but don't be too pushy.
- Give new information that makes the program sound exciting and motivates the person to take a second look.

For example,

Hello. This is _____ of the XYZ Company. I'm sorry you weren't able to make our meeting last night.

It was really terrific. And that's why I'm calling—to let you know about some brand-new product features just revealed last night that are truly revolutionary. (Describe them briefly, emphasizing their possible benefits to the person.) I'm sure you'll find them really exciting. We're having another meeting on Thursday, so you'll have another chance to look the program over and see that it's a really solid, fast-growing business opportunity.

When Someone Calls You About Something Else You may be able to get them interested in your own program by bridging from what they have told you about their program, activities, or interests and what your program offers. Thus, as you talk, look for openings and when they come up, be ready to shift the conversation to talk about your product or business opportunity. For instance, when a friend calls to invite you to a party, you might say, "I'd love to, but I'm not sure I can because I have been so busy." When your friend asks why, you explain. "I'm involved in this marvelous program in which I've been making money on the side. It's a . . ." (and then you go on and tell your friend about it).

STRATEGIES FOR CALLING
DIFFERENT TYPES OF PEOPLE

Targeting your phone approach to the type of person you are calling raises your chances for success. This section describes some strategies I have found effective with these key groups you are likely to contact:

Friends, relatives, and acquaintances
Persons who have placed their own ads for
Jobs
Other direct sales programs
Party-plan selling.

People with a wide network of contacts, such as

Leaders of church and social organizations

Real estate and insurance agents

Calling Friends, Relatives, or Acquaintances

As with contacting anyone, decide if your friend, relative, or acquaintance is most likely to be interested in your product, service, or business opportunity, and emphasize that.

Sound enthusiastic and talk about the great product or business opportunity you discovered—how you want to let your friend, relative, acquaintance, or business associate know how to benefit, too. Stress the benefits you think this person might be most interested in.

Also, with personal contacts, personalize the benefits by showing how the program would help, given what you know about this person. For example,

"Hi. This is _____. I'm calling because I've been involved in this fantastic weight loss program for the past month and have finally lost the weight I've been trying to lose for months. I wanted to let you know about it, because I know you've been trying a number of different diet programs, and I thought this might work for you."

Then, having piqued the person's interest, briefly describe some key features of the program.

While being direct about what you are offering a person you know is particularly appropriate when you are trying to market a product or service that person can use, sometimes it may be best to use the third-person "do you know someone who would be interested" approach, particularly when you are promoting the business opportunity. This is the case because then your friend or associate feels under less pressure to show interest because he or she happens to know you. Also, some people don't like to admit they need the money. Here's an example of this more indirect third-person approach:

"Hi. This is _____. I'm calling because I've been involved in this part-time business for the past few months, and now that it's growing so fast, I'm looking for a few other people who might be interested in starting their own part-time business. Do you know someone who might be interested? It's a fast-growing weight control program, and if someone is serious and works the program for a few hours a week, he or she can be earning a few hundred dollars a week on the side in a month or two, and then a few thousand or even more several months after that."

Then, if the person asks, briefly describe some key features of the program and how people make money with it. Your description may, in turn, be just what you need to get your friend, relative, or associate involved. And then, whether or not he is, you can always ask for any other referrals.

Calling People Who Have Placed Their Own Ads

Another good source of leads for people interested in marketing your product or service is people who have ads in your local paper or advertiser, including those looking for jobs (especially in the sales or people contact fields), those already involved in MLM, networking, or other direct sales programs (especially those with a related but not competing line), and those putting on home parties (if your product line would fit in).

When you call, first try to learn more about what the person is looking for or is doing. Then you can slant your presentation accordingly.

Following are some suggested approaches for contacting people who have placed different types of ads.

Calling Someone Looking for a Job

I have found two different approaches for calling job seekers successful.

Offering Three Options: (1) a salaried position for the routine administrative work involved in selling, (2) a commission for getting leads and setting up meetings with contacts, (3) a business opportunity to become distributors. For example, my company advised job seekers that we had three positions available: a salaried position in our office doing routine work (primarily we hired students for this), a commission-based position getting leads and inviting people to our product demonstrations and business opportunity meetings, and a chance to join a business where people can earn a substantial monthly income working on a part-time or full-time basis—from a few hundred a month to much more.

Because we presented these three options, people perceived us as a large organized company, which gave us almost instant credibility. So they were more open to hearing about the commission position and the business opportunity. Some people who originally only wanted a job told us over the phone they were now more interested in the business opportunity. Others came to our meetings with their options open, and after our presentation, most of them decided they were most interested in the business opportunity, too.

Thus, we used this options technique to gently redirect many job seekers into hearing about going into their own business, because the availability of the other options led them to listen to this third business option so they could compare it with the others, and as a result, many were favorably impressed. As for the other options, they were quite real, for if people still wanted a job they were still open to considering this, and we did hire a few of the callers for routine clerical work, such as keeping our ever-growing mailing list.

Advising Job Seekers They Could Make More Money by Going into Business for Themselves Than on a Regular Job. This was especially effective with those having trouble finding a job. Then, if a job seeker expressed interest in hearing more, we briefly described the program, product, and earnings potential and invited them to a regular meeting or to a one-on-one or small group presentation at our office.

What's the best approach for you? It depends on your own style and your assessment of what the person needs and wants. But in either case, since you are calling the job seeker cold, guide the conversation to cover some of these key points quickly to qualify the person, as who you are, and press the benefits you are offering:

- Ask, does the person still want a job? Is he or she interested in part-time work?

- Describe your own credibility as a company with a bona fide income opportunity. The person wants a job, so you need to establish your authority in order to shift his thinking to recognize that starting a business as a distributor offers higher earnings potential.

- Ask about the person's background and major interests. By asking, you show you are personally concerned, and you can better direct your appeal to the individual's wants and needs and make him or her feel a need to sell you on himself or herself too.

- After a brief description of the product, service, and business opportunity, emphasize why the business would be good for this person.

- Provide a brief indication of the earnings potential, without exaggerating too much. To be credible, state figures people can relate to, particularly someone who has always had a job. Yet you can still dangle the carrot that big money is possible, so a person who wants more can imagine it.

- Close the conversation by inviting the person to take some action and meet with you, preferably in a small group or one-on-one meeting where you can talk on an individual basis.

Here's how a conversation with a potential job seeker that covers these points might go.

"Hello. Is this the person who is looking for a job? Are you still looking?" If not, ask, "Are you still interested in some additional part-time work?" If not, thank the person politely and call the next person. If you get a yes, go on.

"We have a position for someone who is looking for the kind of job you want. I represent (your company name), and we have a position that involves (list some of the activities that correspond to what this person wants). But before I go into the details, I'd like to know a little more about your background, and what you are really looking for in a job."

After the person explains, you continue. "Well, good, it sounds like there may be a perfect fit. We're looking for people who want to be independent, choose their own hours, work hard, be self-starters, and work with people. It's a great opportunity to create a real career for yourself and use your initiative and organizational skills in sales management. We help train you, too, and give you assistance you need to be successful. Some people are earning anywhere from a few hundred to two to three thousand dollars a month in a few months. And some earn even more, based on a commission for what they do.

"Now, if this sounds good and you'd like to find out more about this opportunity, I'd like to set up a meeting to go into more detail. I've still got a few time slots available Tuesday morning, if that's convenient."

Calling Someone in a Direct Sales or Party Plan Sales Program

You can locate local direct sales and party-plan people from several sources where they advertise, including your local newspaper in the sales-help-wanted or business opportunity sections (look for small ads that talk about unlimited opportunity, great potential, $1,000 plus monthly income, run a home-based business, sell on a commission only, and so on), your local advertiser or flea market paper (under help wanted, business opportunities, and certain product categories such as health and nutrition products), and a trade show directory from a local home business or income opportunity show.

People involved in these direct sales or party plan programs will respond in a variety of ways when you call. Some may say no, because they are already sold on the product they are advertising and believe in doing only one product at a time. But others will be receptive and be interested in hearing about additional marketing opportunities, especially if they can sell the product to the same market they are already selling and therefore supplement current sales.

You can up your chances of appealing to the person you call and reduce the time spent in talking to someone who is not receptive by doing some brief prescreening to qualify the person.

So when you call, first ask what their product is (people don't always say in their ads), how actively they are marketing it, and for how long. Also, tactfully try to find out how well the product is doing. Then you can better assess how receptive they might be to a new product and how well your product might fit with what they are now doing, and you can approach them accordingly.

For example, if these salespeople are well established and have built up an extensive sales group, they might feel very protective about what they already have and not be very open. On the other hand, if you can point out how your product can supplement what they are doing and appeal to their sales organization, you might get a good response.

Similarly, newcomers may vary greatly in their response. Some who have developed no strong loyalties and commitments might be readily attracted to an appealing new opportunity. Yet others might resist, feeling uncertain, for they are afraid to handle more than one product or fear dropping something they are in for something new and untried.

Thus, get a sense of where the person is when you call. One way is to pose as a potential customer or opportunity seeker for whatever the person is advertising. Then, ask questions. Afterward, you can continue to pose as a potential prospect, but also mention that you are using or promoting this great new product or service, and it sounds like something that might fit in with the advertisers product line. When the person asks you about it (and he or she usually will), describe it, dropping a few teasers to arouse interest. For example, mention how much you have earned, how quickly you have lost weight, how much you have saved, or whatever, to highlight some major benefits. Then, if the person still seems interested, you can suggest that perhaps you can work together on these two programs. So subtly, you have shifted the conversation from the advertiser's program to include your own.

The direct approach can work well, too, if the advertiser has put enough in the ad to indicate the product or at least the product category (such as health and nutrition). In using the approach, call the advertiser, ask what company or particular products are represented, indicate you are familiar with the line and think highly of it, and then say you called because you represent a related but noncompeting product that would help increase his sales.

Whichever approach you use, guide the conversation to cover some of the following key points, as appropriate (unless you already know the answer from the ad):

What product or company does the advertiser represent?

How long and how actively has he or she been marketing this product?

How committed is he or she to this company?

Does he or she currently market any other product lines?

Or does he or she believe it is possible to market more than one product at a time?

How fast is his or her product selling? Or how fast is his or her organization moving? (Ask questions to get this information tactfully, such as "How much product does the *average* distributor move?" or "How many new people is *one* likely to recruit each month?")

Finally, point out how your own product or service can increase sales.

Some Sample Conversations

A conversation with an advertiser using the "I'm a customer" approach and covering these points might go something like this:

"Hi. I saw your ad for the XYZ health and nutrition company, and it sounds interesting. Can you tell me more about your products? . . .

"That sounds interesting. How long has the company been in existence? . . . How long have you been doing this? . . .

"Hmmmmmm. That sounds like something I might like to do. How much money might I be likely to make if I spent about 10 to 20 hours a week marketing this? For example, what's your experience, or the usual experience? . . .

"Well, that sounds really good. I might be able to work with this in with the program I'm already involved in (then you go on to describe it)."

A conversation employing a more direct approach might go something like this:

"Hi. I see you're marketing the XYZ Company's line of health products. I'm familiar with that product and think it's a great line. And that's why I called.

"I'm involved in the ABC Company, which also has some health products. But they're different, and ABC has a nutritious food line, too. So I thought you might find this is a great way to increase your sales with almost no extra effort, since many people use the products of both companies."

Pause to see if this person has some interest. If so, continue.

"I have several people in my sales group who are marketing both products. I don't think you should spread yourself too thin, of course. But if you've got two or three complementary products, that can work. For example, are you currently marketing any other products? . . .

"Well, then, if this is your main product, I think you'll find our product can really add to your line. It's not at all competitive, and it virtually sells itself."

Now, if the person still sounds receptive, you conclude:

"So, why don't we get together and talk some more?"

Then you set the appointment.

CALLING THOSE WITH A WIDE NETWORK OF CONTACTS

Persons who are the heads of organizations, in outside sales, or in public contact positions where they see many people every day are especially good to contact because they know a large number of people. Some examples are heads of church groups or social organizations, real estate and insurance agents, and merchants.

These people will probably want to see a letter or materials they can review before they agree to meet with you (see the section on writing letters). But you can pave the way with a brief introductory call, in which you explain to them or their secretary why the program might interest them and their group. The call should only last about a minute. If they are interested, send them literature, and after a few days, call again to follow up.

What to Say in Your Initial Call

In your initial call, get to the point quickly: how the program benefits these individuals and their group. Start off by saying you are calling about a program with these benefits and you would like to send them some literature if they are interested.

The advantage of this quick-to-the-point approach is that they know you intend to be brief, so they will be more receptive to listening—because they don't have to face a long sales pitch.

Finally, find out where to send the literature, and depending on your style, invite them to call back after they receive it or indicate you will call in a few days to follow up. In either case, plan to call back yourself, whether you invite them to call you or not.

A call might go something like this:

To a Leader of a Church or Social Organization (about a Consumer Discount Club)

"Hello. This is _____ of (your company name). I'm calling about a new program that might benefit your group, since the program offers an opportunity to save money on all kinds of goods that people are buying anyhow. It would also be a great fund-raiser for your group, since you could organize it as a group project.

"I can tell you about it very briefly in about a minute over the phone. Then, I've got some literature I'd like to send you. We have a number of presentations on the program in your area. Or if you prefer, I can meet with you personally, or one of our members can put on a presentation for your group."

To a Real Estate Agent (about a Consumer Discount Club)

"Hello. This is _____ of (your company name). I'm calling about a new program that real estate agents are finding very popular, because they can increase their goodwill by telling their clients about a new way to save money on all kinds of goods. Also, you can earn extra income when your clients get involved in the program.

"I can tell you about it very briefly in about a minute over telephone. Then, I've got some literature I'd like to send you. We have a number of presentations on the program in your area. Or if you prefer, I can meet with you personally to discuss this further."

To a Merchant (If You Can Sell Your Product to Retail Stores)

"Hello. This is _____ of (your company name). I'm calling about a new program that many merchants are getting involved in, because they can substantially increase their income by putting out a few brochures about some exciting new products.

"I can tell you about it very briefly in about a minute over the phone. Then, I've got some literature I'd like to send you. We have a number of presentations on the program in your area. Or if you prefer, I can meet with you personally at your store to discuss this further."

What to Say in Your Follow-up Call

Sometimes people will call you after reading the literature you have sent. But usually, you need to follow up yourself. The key points to cover in your follow-up calls are:

Have they read the material? (If not, recap some major points or offer to send them another brochure and call again.)

Do they have any questions about anything they read?

Are they still interested and do they want to learn more?

When can you set up a meeting? (Usually, they will want you to meet at their place of business. Or invite them to a meeting and offer to take them there yourself.)

As in the initial call, don't go into too much detail on the phone. Your main objective is to gain interest and then, if the person is receptive, set up a meeting to talk about the program in depth.

Chapter 20

PARTICIPATING IN A TRADE SHOW

Trade shows can be a good source of new contracts and leads. You can participate by yourself, although most distributors combine forces with others to share costs or take turns working the booth.

In consumer-oriented shows, you can sometimes generate a high retail sales volume for a high-demand product, whether at the show itself or through follow-up with potential customers who express interest. Also, some products, such as office supply products, move very well in business and trade shows.

But if you're looking for new distributors for your sales group, don't expect to be a major source of on-the-spot sign-ups. Some people may decide quickly. But generally, look on each show as a source of leads for prospects. Then, you or your sales group members can follow up after the show.

Some distributors do very well going to trade shows all over the country. However, unless you have a product that sells very well at the show or you are prepared for long-distance follow-up for selling customers or recruiting new distributors, stick to the shows in your area. You have a greater chance of sponsoring new recruits locally, where you can offer your strongest backup and training, and any follow-up for customers is of course cheaper—and local customers are probably most apt to buy because you are in the area, which is reassuring, particularly if this is an expensive product or one which may need some follow-up service and support.

TYPES OF TRADE SHOWS

The two main types of shows are

- Consumer shows, which
  - feature a particular product line (e.g., health products or computers)
  - are part of a fair or festival (such as county fair)
- Professional and trade shows, which include
  - conventions, workshops, and seminars for a particular profession
  - product shows for the trade (for example, gift shows and stationery shows)
  - business opportunity shows (such as franchise, home-based business, and MLM shows)

Some of these shows, such as county fairs, are sponsored by your city or county. Others are organized by trade or professional groups; some are put on by private promoters.

Choose the shows that best feature your particular product. For example, if you are promoting a health product, you might consider a health fair, a county or city fair, a convention of health professionals, a home products show, or a business opportunity show featuring home-based or direct sales businesses (assuming you are seeking additional distributors).

SHOW POLICIES ABOUT COMPETING PRODUCT LINES

Shows have different policies about allowing competing products lines or sharing booths. Some shows—particularly consumer shows—have an open-booth policy, so that any number of product lines can be featured in the same booth and more than one company can sell the same products. However, in other shows—most notably in those featuring business opportunities offered by MLM and network marketing companies—the usual policy is only one booth per company and only one product line per booth. This way you are not competing against others with the same product. But you will have to act fast to get the space if you have a popular product.

So find out which policy the show is using. If it has open booths, find out about the likely competition before you sign up for a booth, and decide whether it is to your advantage to be in the show or not. If there are already or are likely to be other booths with your product, it might be better to skip the show, since each additional booth dilutes your potential market. On the other hand, an open-booth policy gives you a chance to try out additional lines or perhaps do something a little bit extra so you make the sale rather than a competitor with the same product.

Conversely, if you decide to go into a one-booth—one-product show, make your commitment early so that you are sure to get it.

COSTS OF TRADE SHOW PARTICIPATION

Trade show fees range from a low $25 to $100 for a standard-sized booth at a small local show to about $500 to $800 for such a booth at a professionally produced show. There have been shows where the cost was as much as $1,000 to $2,000 for a booth, but the $500 to $800 fee is more common.

A standard booth is usually 8 by 10 feet. Corner booths and booths at the entrance to the show commonly cost about $100 to $200 more. And larger booths or double booths cost proportionately more, too, though sometimes these are discounted to encourage larger-size booth sales.

To figure your full costs of participation, include the cost of any product samples and literature you plan to give away, the cost of the products you hope to sell, and your expenses getting to the show and while at it (travel, hotel, food, and so forth).

If you are sharing a booth, figure out your share based on some agreed-upon arrangement. If you are sharing the booth with a person or persons with different product lines, the usual way is to determine your share based on the relative amount of space you have; then your percentage of the cost is your percentage of the space. Alternatively, if you are sharing the booth with other distributors of the same product, a common arrangement is for all to share equally, and then participants divvy up the number of hours in the booth or work out some understanding of who approaches prospects, so these are spread equitably among participants. Still another possibility is to base shares on the number of hours distributors will spend in the booth. Then, too, whoever is the sponsoring distributor of the other distributors in the booth may pay a larger share, while other distributors pay according to their level in the MLM structure.

However you work it out, use these figures to decide if your participation is likely to be profitable and whether you want to participate on that basis.

For example, if you mainly expect sales to consumers, figure out how much you are likely to sell based on the size of the crowd expected and what your average profit is likely to be if you attain your sales goal. Then, compare your profit to the cost of being in the show. Also, add your time and effort into the equation. Your expected profits should be greater than expected costs to make participation worthwhile. If your expected profit isn't great enough to cover both your costs and some reasonable payment to yourself and anyone else running the booth (say at least $15 an hour), perhaps you shouldn't have a booth.

On the other hand, if the show is an arena for recruiting potential distributors as well as selling retail customers, take that into account in figuring your profit potential. To do this, make some projections about how many potential distributors you are likely to contact and how much income you might gain from those distributors.

To make a reasonable projection, make a rough estimate of the percentage of the population at the show that might be interested in your product line. (For instance, maybe 10 percent might be interested in a new time management system, but 50 percent might be interested in a health product.) Then, if available, use the attendance estimates provided by the show organizer, or make your own estimate based on the type of show and previous attendance at similar shows, to figure out how many people might be attending and, of these, how many might be interested in your product.

Then, if you are looking for new distributors, estimate your potential earnings from those you are likely to recruit. In general, figure that about one-third of the persons you talk to will be interested in hearing more, about one-third of these will be interested in signing up as distributors, and about one-third to one-fifth of these will become active distributors. In other words, you can estimate that about 2 to 4 percent of those you talk to will be interested in a serious business opportunity working with you. Then, estimate how many distributors that might be and how much each is likely to earn for you.

Finally, if appropriate, combine your expected profits from retailing to consumers and signing up distributors, and ask yourself: Is that enough? How much profit am I likely to make from consumers? How many distributors am I likely to sign up? And will these earnings or potential earnings make my costs and my time for participating worthwhile? Then, make your decision on whether to be in the show or not on that basis.

Of course, you may have other goals besides immediate profits, such as getting your name known or conducting a market test, which may more than offset not making a profit. Just be clear when you consider entering a show about your goal, expected profits, and costs, so you can make a good decision. Chart 20.1 will help you weigh the various factors.

CHART 20.1: ESTIMATE OF COSTS AND PROFITS AT A TRADE SHOW
Cost of Participation

	TOTAL	MY SHARE OF A SHARED BOOTH	
		%OF COSTS	TOTAL COSTS
Basic Show Expenses			
Booth fee	————	————	————
Cost of samples	————	————	————
Cost of literature	————	————	————
Cost of products for sale	————	————	————
Total	═══	═══	═══
Other Expenses			
Travel	————	————	————
Hotel	————	————	————
Food	————	————	————
Entertainment	————	————	————
Other	————	————	————
Total	═══	═══	═══
Total Cost of Participation	————	————	————

Projected Gross Profits on Retail Sales and Earnings from New Distributors

Projected Profits on Retail Sales
1. Number of Consumers Expected at Show ————
2. Percentage of Consumers Likely to Make Purchases ————

CHART 20.1: *(Continued)*

	TOTAL	MY SHARE OF A SHARED BOOTH	
		%OF COSTS	TOTAL COSTS

3. Number of Consumers Likely to Make Purchases (multiply #1 × #2) _____

4. Average Value of Each Expected Purchase _____

5. Total Value of All Expected Purchases (multiply #3 × #4) _____

6. My Share of the Profits (if shared) (multiply your percentage of profits by #5) _____

Projected Earnings from New Distributors

1. Number of Persons Expected at Show _____

2. Percentage of Persons Likely to Be Interested in My Product Line _____

3. Number Likely to Be Interested in My Product Line (multiply #1 × #2) _____

4. Number of Persons Interested in My Product Line Who Are Likely to Become Active Distributors (multiply #3 by 2–4 percent) _____

5. Average Amount of Income Expected from Each New Distributor per Month _____

6. Total Amount of Income Expected from New Distributors per Month (multiply #4 × #5) _____

7. Total Amount of Income Expected from New Distributors in One Year (multiply #6 by 12) _____

Projected Net Profits or Costs of Participating in Show

Projected Gross Profits on Retail Sales (use total from #5 or #6) _____

Projected Earnings from New Distributors (use total from #7) (+) _____

(−) _____

Total Cost of Participation _____

Projected Net Profit or Net Cost of Participating (subtract the cost of participating from the projected gross profits) _____

SHARING A BOOTH

Although it's ideal to take a full booth to feature your product better, many distributors share a booth to cut down costs.

If you share a booth with another company, try to do so with a product line that is compatible but not competitive. For example, if you sell vitamin products, sharing a booth with someone who sells a diet program is fine. But if both you and the other person sell vitamin products and diet plans, it would be better to find two separate booths. It also helps to share a booth with someone whose product line can enhance your product. For example, if you are selling health products, a line of soothing relaxation tapes would be a nice draw.

If you want to share a booth but don't know anyone, many shows with open-booth policies permitting sharing will help you find someone. They keep a list of those seeking to share booths, and will give out their phone numbers to you or put your name on the list to be given out to others. Then, it's up to you to make the arrangements. So let the show people know you are looking, and then if you don't connect with someone right away, call in from time to time to see if they have gotten in new people on their list. This way you keep your own name in the forefront for referrals, as well as get an edge in making contacts, just in case the show people don't give out your name to callers or individuals who get your name on a list haven't gotten around to calling you.

To be sure you have a booth and have control over it, you can contract for the whole booth and then seek people to share with you. Or if you don't want a booth unless you find someone to share with, try to find someone who already has a booth or someone who wants to share first, and then sign for the booth together. Perhaps some local advertising or calls to people you know might help you find someone with whom to share.

Usually, distributors who share booths apportion costs based on the amount of space used. But who gets what space where is negotiable. Typically, the person who rents the booth and subcontracts it is the final arbiter.

DISPLAYING YOUR PRODUCTS

Organize your display to feature your most popular or eye-catching products. If you have room, set up a demonstration to get potential consumers and distributors involved. For instance, if you are marketing a food product, do a cooking demonstration or set out some free samples. If you sell vitamins, hand out a few on the back of business cards.

Using Posters and Literature

Put up a few posters which quickly relay the major benefits of your program. For example, in a travel club booth, you might feature a colorful poster of Hawaii and next to it a sign that boldly telegraphs your message: GO ANYWHERE IN THE WORLD YOU WANT AND PAY LESS.

In using posters, keep anything you say *short.* You don't want to be too wordy on your posters. A short, to-the-point message is much more effective than a lot of words. In a consumer or trade show, people pass by quickly, and you have one to four seconds to catch someone's eye. If a poster is too wordy, no one will read it. You want catchy slogans, perhaps accompanied by pictures, to get someone's attention. Then use smaller flyers or handouts to go into detail on the key benefits of your program.

Similarly, select your literature carefully. Display only a few pieces that will highlight your product's major benefits. If people want to know more, they will ask, and you can always have additional materials on hand for backup, when they do. By the same token, if you start chatting with someone, selectively hand out the literature you think would appeal the most, based on the person's background or interests he has expressed.

Arranging Your Booth

If you have the whole booth, the overall booth layout is up to you, and depending on your product and style, there are various possibilities. The most usual arrangement is with the product or demonstration in front and you standing behind the booth. This format provides a sense of separation between you and the potential consumer or distributor, which helps to make you seem authoritative and professional.

On the other hand, if your product lends itself to an open booth with a display or demonstration, this arrangement creates an atmosphere of easy informality that draws people in and helps them relax. For example, if you are promoting health products, you might invite people to come and relax on a recliner while you massage their back with a vibrating wand. Passersby are likely to stop and watch, and that gives you the perfect opener to talk about your product.

Using a Free Drawing for Prizes

A free drawing for prizes also pulls customers since people are attracted by the chance to get something free. To attract attention, announce the competition on a sign with big bold letters and indicate what the prize will be. A good item is an introductory kit with samples of your product. Or offer a small amount of your most popular product. Some distributors also use drawings to give away slow-moving items in their product line.

One easy way to run a drawing is simply to ask people to leave their business cards for the drawing. Also, have some small business cards or index cards on hand for people to fill out if they don't have their own cards, which may often be the case at a consumer-oriented show. To screen who is entering the drawing for their likely interest in your product or business opportunity, use preprinted cards that

CHART 20.2: INTEREST CARD

NAME _____

ADDRESS _____

CITY _____ STATE _____ ZIP _____

PHONE (day) _____

PHONE (evening/weekends) _____ FAX _____

I am mainly interested in your product as (check one)

   A consumer only (　)   Business opportunity (　)

   Both as a consumer and as a business opportunity (　)

My usual occupation is: _____

Comments: _____

ask a few key questions. Such cards should ask for the person's name, address, and home and business phone numbers; include some questions about the person's interests. A sample card format appears in Chart 20.2.

A 3" by 5" card size is recommended, because you can file these in a standard file container. Also, it is helpful to separate your file into three sections or use a separate file container for each major interest category: consumer only, business opportunity only, or both consumer and business interests. This way you can readily use different follow-up approaches or assign different priorities to following up with these different groups.

Making Sure You Have Everything You Need

Be sure you have all the materials you need to set up your booth. Find out from the show organizers exactly what they are providing in your booth and what you have to bring. For example, most shows provide tables and chairs; in some you have to bring your own. Some shows permit you to tape signs to the wall, others require you to hang everything from a curtain.

Then, make a list of everything you need, noting what is already provided and what you still have to get. (The checklist in Chart 20.3 is designed to help you do this.) Include on your list the product samples and literature you need, as well as any display aids, like easels, posters, signs, hooks, string, wire, or tape. If you need any special equipment such as a projector to show slides, a tape recorder for tapes, or a cash box, list these, too.

Check off all the items you have and whenever you acquire anything else, note this. When you pack for the show, use your list to check off everything you pack. And use your list again after the show when you pack to go home. This way, by using a checklist, you bring everything you need . . . and you take it back with you, too.

Operating Your Booth

You can run a booth yourself, but it's best to have at least one other person and perhaps several sharing your booth, even if they aren't in your own sales group. This way you can relieve each other, have some time to get around the show and enjoy it yourself, and can generally keep up each other's morale.

Another advantage of sharing a booth is that you look more organized and professional when you have a few people in your booth. Also, your booth looks more fun. Then, too, if you are sharing with someone in your own sales group, one of you can be in the booth talking up the program, while the other is in the front of the booth or just outside making comments to those who pass by to get them interested in stopping at your table to learn more. Also, the up-front or outside person can take some literature and go talk to exhibitors in other booths about the program. Additionally, some distributors pass out materials if they talk to people in the aisles who are interested.

However, be careful to check on show policies regarding any promotion outside of your own booth. Sometimes exhibitors are free to circulate to other booths and within

CHART 20.3: SHOW CHECKLIST

ITEMS NEEDED FOR SHOW (CROSS OUT ITEMS NOT NEEDED, AND ADD OTHERS	ITEMS PROVIDED BY SHOW	ALREADY HAVE	STILL NEED	ITEMS REPACKED
Tables				
Chairs				
Company name sign				
Posters				
Easels				
Cash box				
Box for sign-up cards				
Sign-up cards				
Interest sign-up sheet				
Business cards				
Presentation manuals				
Product samples				
Literature				
Miscellaneous supplies				
Tape				
String				
Wire				
Tools				
Hooks				
Pencils/pens				
Other				
_____				
_____				
Video/sound equipment				
TV monitor				
Slide projector				
Tape recorder				
Extension cords				
Lights				
Other items needed				
_____				
_____				
_____				
_____				
_____				
_____				

limits talk to others in the aisles near their own booths. But often the show managers frown on this, rightly arguing that any sales material should be distributed only in one's booth or in a designated literature area, since the booth holders have paid for the sales opportunity. So it is unfair for others to undercut these exhibitors by walking around handing out their materials. Sometimes show managers give this freedom to exhibitors, though not to anyone else who happens to be at the show. Thus, since different shows have different policies, check what is permitted at your show.

Presenting Your Program Effectively

As in any sales presentation, have a general idea in advance of the major points you want to make about your product. You only have a few seconds to capture attention and a minute or so to present the highlights unless the prospect wants to hear more. So focus on a few major benefits.

Opening Lines Some distributors effectively call attention to their product by offering a few friendly and attention-getting comments about it as people walk by, such as

> "I'll bet you'd like to have some more energy right now." (to introduce a health product to someone who looks a little tired from the show)

> "We have our free drawing for dinner going on right now. Here's a pen so you can sign up." (to get someone interested in a new food product)

Many distributors do well by waiting until a person starts looking at their posters or fliers or picks up a sample of their product which shows at least a stirring interest. Then, they pick up on whatever the person seems to be interested in and describe it more fully. For example,

"That trip is just one of the many we offer. You can go anywhere in the world you want." (to promote interest in a new travel club)

"We have a dozen dinner products in the line now." (to someone who has just sampled one of your food items or is looking at food packages)

Generally, you will find more receptivity from people who have at least shown a passing interest in what's in your booth, since many people who are walking by without already looking will keep on and ignore you or politely decline. But if you are willing to spend the extra energy and weather the higher likelihood of rejection, I have found it is an advantage to try to attract these seemingly oblivious passers-by, since some will stop due to your comment, and you may find some additional customers or distributors this way. This approach works because many people at show's put up a kind of better against being overwhelmed by all the variety. But when you say something, this breaks through their screen, and if what you say is inviting enough, they'll be open to listening to hear more. When you do say something to break the ice, avoid the relatively overused opening cliches such as "Can I help . . . ?" or "Can I explain . . . ?" Mostly, people tend to answer no.

Instead, *think of creative openers to get people interested and involved.* Inviting people to try something is always good: "Would you like to sample some of our great new carob drink?" "Would you like to relax and enjoy a massage?"

Other Attention-Getters   Other good attention getters include video presentations on a TV monitor or slide-sound presentations on a self-contained slide projector.

Demonstrations in your booth also help draw a crowd. For example, at one show I attended, the most popular crowd pleaser was a cooking demonstration, in which a man energetically chopped up vegetables, popped them in a blender, handed out free drinks. Meanwhile, as he worked, he gave a running sales pitch, so that when he had finished the demonstration, everyone watching had heard the major benefits of his product. Then, right after the demonstration concluded, he was ready to move quickly into his close, in which he invited people to take advantage of the superdiscounted show special, which many did.

Alternative Approaches Have a few alternative approaches in mind so you can easily vary your style depending on whether a person is more likely to be a consumer, a distributor, or both and whether a person is interested in hearing a detailed presentation now or just wants a quick review and some literature, with any follow-up later.

Sketch out a general outline of what you want to say under varying conditions. Then, practice a few times until you feel comfortable at giving your presentation with ease.

Encourage Sign-up Whatever opening approach you use, try to get everyone who expresses some interest to buy or sign up now if possible or at least write down their name, address, and number on something—whether it's a list or a card for a free drawing. This way, you build up a mailing list for further contact, and you can follow up later to sell your product or talk up the business opportunity of becoming a distributor.

Chapter 21

FIVE TIPS FOR SELLING HEALTH PRODUCTS SUCCESSFULLY

Many MLM organizations sell health products, including vitamins, diet programs, protein supplements, stress reducing tapes, and a whole range of other products and programs which promote wellness. Also, they may offer items that indirectly promote health, such as water purifiers and air filters, that are designed to produce a better environment.

Often the products sold are fairly new or experimental, said to represent some kind of breakthrough in the field. Multilevel marketing is seen as being a good way to spread the news through a personal, hands-on demonstration and testimonial approach. Frequently, too, new products are supported by the endorsements or testimonials of well-known people to help lend their credibility and appeal to marketing the product.

These may all be very good reasons to market the product MLM, and some health products are ideally suited to this approach. However, it is also important to take into consideration some special concerns in working with health products to be sure you have not only chosen good products that really do what they are designed to do to improve health, but that you can also support what you say yourself, so you are effective in marketing these products. This kind of consideration applies to selling any product, but it is even more so in the case of health products, because you have to be very careful about making medical and effectiveness claims for such products which go beyond what has been approved or supported through testing by the appropriate agency, such as the FDA in the case of drugs. Then, too, products of this nature must be appropriately labeled and advertised, not only in advertising, product, and sales literature, but in anything you may create yourself to promote these products, or you can bring on the heavy hand of government regulation. In fact, if enough distributors make misleading claims, this can jeopardize the company itself, and there have been such cases:

Consider the experience of an MLM selling mouthwash. The company had to relabel its packaging and scrap its advertising as well as many of its original distributors to counter the claims of medical and dentist support that the firm or its distributors had made by claiming the mouthwash's effectiveness in fighting cavities and gum disease by eliminating plaque. Eventually, the company was sold and its company logo and product line were renamed.

The following guidelines will help you deal with the special concerns that arise when selling health-related products, so you can do so with more knowledge, confidence, and hence more sales.

HAVE THOROUGH, IN-DEPTH
KNOWLEDGE OF YOUR PRODUCT

Become fully knowledgeable about the claimed benefits for your product, and understand clearly how the features, effects, or uses of the product provide those benefits, and be able to explain why the product can achieve these results.

This kind of in-depth knowledge is especially important with health-related products, because you have to know clearly what you can claim and what you can't, so you don't get into the problems of making misleading or false claims, which can be so damaging to your business and the company's business in this field.

Accordingly, apart from any celebrity endorsements and quality literature, you still need to know for yourself that the product can do what it says. In turn, acquiring this knowledge will both help you in making a commitment to market this product and this company and in being more convincing to consumers, leading to more sales.

How to Be Sure Your Product Can Do What It's *Supposed* to Do

Look beyond the sales literature and brochures to the fact sheets and to any articles about the product which have appeared in well-respected magazines and newspapers. Find out what these materials say about the product's contents, why the product works the way it does, what any tests have shown about its effectiveness, and so forth. Many companies, in fact, will put together their own press kits or sales packets containing this information, and that's a good sign when they do. Otherwise do your own review of what this product or similar products of this type have done. Ask your sponsors and other distributors you are working with what they know about these questions.

Use the product yourself for a while, and observe the results. Do you feel different? Better? And if so, what factors suggest that it is really the results of this product rather than something else you might have done to change to become healthier at the same time. The more you can link the changes for the better to this product and not to something else, the more confident you can feel about this product's effectiveness and in conveying this knowledge and confidence to others.

For example, say the product is a vitamin or nutrient that is supposed to give you more energy and increased mental alertness. If you can, try taking the product for a while without changing anything else in your usual routine, and see if you do in fact experience more energy and mental alert-ness. This way, you can better say it was the product that had this beneficial effect on you, whereas if you make all sorts of changes in your life at the same time (take a vacation, change your diet, get out of a bad relationship, *and* take this vitamin or nutrient), the improvement in your health and mental state could be due to any or all of these things combined.

Ask others to try the product and report the results back to you. As in your own self-monitoring of the results, see if you can separate out the effects that might be due to the product alone from effects due to general changes. With other people, you may not be able to ask them to try not to change anything else, as you do with yourself if you want to conduct a more precise experiment. But at least you might ask after the fact if there was anything else that they did much differently from usual when they started using the product. Then, if they didn't, that helps support the view that the product contributed to the change, but if they did, then consider what influence the product might have had as part of this overall change.

Some good ways to get people to try out a product and report back to you which some distributors use, include the following:

- Give the person a *free sample* to try; then call to follow up a day or two later to ask them for the results, ready to take the order if the person reports good results.

- Suggest the person take a *trial order,* say for about a week, two weeks, or 30 days, perhaps even offering a discount or other incentive such as a free gift, to encourage trying. Then, check back with the person from time to time to see how things are going, and suggest a regular order if things appear to be working well.

- Offer the person a *be satisfied or your money-back* offer if the person will just try the product or program and follow the directions for using it as indicated.

Most people are more willing to take a chance under such conditions, and generally people don't ask for their money back later. Then, again, if the product works well, you are likely to get another order.

RESEARCH ANY REGULATORY TESTS OR ENDORSEMENTS

Check with your sponsor or company on what kind of regulatory approvals or government tests the product has gone through, and what sort of certificates or endorsements it has from well-respected people in the medical or scientific community.

Such information is important to your own credibility and marketing efforts in convincing others about the efficacy of the product. Commonly, companies with health-related products will have such information readily available, and this is another good sign of a good company and good product, which you can use in deciding to represent this product. While the celebrity glitz may be an important selling tool, having this underlying scientific and medical support, along with the necessary approvals by the appropriate agencies, can be crucial in the product's long-term sales success. Then, become very familiar with these credentials and endorsements so you can easily cite them in marketing the product.

LIMIT MARKETING CLAIMS ON EXPERIMENTAL PRODUCTS

If you are marketing a health-related product that is experimental and hasn't gotten the official imprimatur of the government or medical establishment, make sure you know what you can claim for it and that the company and people you are working with are also making the appropriate claims they can make.

Sometimes MLM companies take on products representing unorthodox or not-yet-accepted therapies or health claims—products that may be perfectly effective, and in time, may get acceptance from the mainstream. However, it is very important to limit claims to what you can or to preface your statements by the indication that certain types of certification or approvals are pending. Likewise, the company, your sponsor, and the distributors must be similarly cautious and not try to claim more than is appropriate, because this runs the risk of being put out of business once the regulatory or other interested authorities become aware of this. This has happened to a number of companies.

For example, it may be fine to say that a product will make you feel more alert, give you more energy, help you feel less stressed, or whatever, since you are only stating general personal benefits which many other types of products might do, too, not just health products. But if you start using terms with a medical or therapy slant, such as "curing," "reduces illness and disease," and the like, then your product may need to have approvals. Thus, you and your company have to be extremely careful in marketing such new and breakthrough products. Sure, talk about how good they are, if they are. But do so in a way that is safe from official interference.

Your company may already have guidelines to cover what you can say or can't, and this is good. If so, be sure to follow them, and tell everyone you are working with to do the same. Likewise, such caution should be reflected in company literature, videos, ads, and anything you write or design yourself.

For more information on what you can or can't say about a particular product, check with the appropriate regulatory agencies or professional associations in your area or state, as well as with your own sponsor or company. For example, agencies to contact for a new diet program, high-energy formula, or aloe cream cosmetic to tighten the skin might be the Department of Health or Federal Drug Administration. Also, you might check with some of the professors at your local university or medical school in the appropriate department to see what they might know about such products and claims.

HIGHLIGHT ANY BACKUP SUPPORT

Once you feel fully knowledgeable about your product and how and why it does what it does and know what you can and can't say about it, present your product or program to emphasize the benefits. But also provide some highlights of the backup support you have, and be ready to go into more detail with those who want detailed facts.

Some companies will have already done this for you in their company literature, so you can easily stage what you tell potential customers and new distributors. Or organize your own materials in this way. It's a kind of three-step approach in which you

1. *Feature benefits,* for example you'll feel better, feel less stress, have more energy, and so on, whatever you can claim;

2. *Support your claims with some basic information about how the product works to provide this benefit* and provide some limited backup support to show who is behind the product and its claims (doctors, researchers, scientists, therapists) and why the product works the way it does (e.g., it has this special enzyme or herb formula). Perhaps include your own experience or that of other distributors here.

3. *Have the more detailed factual information ready* to show the prospect you really do know this product well and are convinced by the evidence that this is a good, effective product. This might include having a sheet with endorsements from well-respected people in the field, a brief report of successful tests with the product, a list of testimonials of people who have found the product effective for them and how they used it, and so on.

LEARN ABOUT THE FIELD REPRESENTED
BY YOUR PRODUCT

Learn what you can about the field represented by your product, so you can show you have a general background of knowledge in this area which adds to your credibility.

Anyone who is already a practitioner in this field, such as a doctor, nurse, or dentist, who is marketing a health product on the side already has a leg up on other distributors, because he or she already can speak with authority on the field. So people are more apt to believe what he or she says about a new product. His or her expertise in the field generally carries over to provide a broader endorsement of the product—not only by that distributor who has decided to market the product, but by the field generally of which that person is a representative.

If this isn't your field, you can still compensate for this by getting as knowledgeable as you can by reading about it, going to workshops and seminars, and having discussions and presentations about the subject with other distributors representing this product. For instance, if you are marketing a vitamin or food supplement, learn about nutrition: read books on life extension techniques; join a local health and fitness group.

Also, to give yourself more credibility in this area, perhaps put together a little bio sheet in which you highlight those activities or jobs you have held in the past which relate most strongly to what you are doing. For example, say you are marketing tablets to raise energy and reduce stress, and you at one time worked in the field of recreation. Feature this in your bio to show how you worked with people to reduce stress and help people relax through recreational activities. Then, include your bio as part of your presentation folder or handouts you share with people to help show your knowledge and credibility in marketing this product. With other general-use products, this kind of credibility building is not necessary or less necessary, because the products may speak for themselves and just about anybody can be convincing with a modicum of knowledge about the product. But health products tend to bring out that skeptic and prove it to me quality in people— they want to feel more certain the product will work and be good for them. It's much like the sort of thing that happens when people go to doctors. They want to feel the doctor knows and can tell them what to do; they want to feel a sense of trust and reliance from an authority that knows. Well, much in the same say, when you market a health product, people feel more comfortable buying and using the product if they feel it is coming from a credible, reliable source.

Thus, be willing to spend that extra time it may take to become well-informed and knowledgeable, not only about your specific product and its competitors, as you might for any product, but also about the field of your product generally. You'll be more convincing, more self-assured, and will make more sales that way. In fact, with this extra knowledge, you can better know what people need and help to show them this, which can help you up your sales as well.

Chapter 22

BECOMING A
SPEAKER TO PROMOTE
YOUR PRODUCT

Besides giving the usual sales and opportunity presentations, a good way to get more exposure—and sales—for your product is to become a speaker on a topic related to your product. That opens the door for you to speak to all sorts of groups, as well as get publicity and quotes as an expert on that topic, and then, as part of your presentation or as a plug afterward, you can mention your product, maybe even sell it on the spot.

This chapter deals with how to develop your speaking skills and arrange for speaking engagements. Chapter 24 deals with how to get publicity for the speaking you do as well as publicize your product and organizing promotional events to get publicity too.

FINDING AN AUDIENCE WHO WANTS TO
HEAR ABOUT YOUR PRODUCT

Once you develop an interesting topic that people want to hear about, there are many possible forums. Start locally and be willing to speak for free; then, as you gain experience and build a reputation, you can move onto larger and larger areas, as well as even get some money for your speaking, too.

Groups and other sources that are possible audiences include

- local civic and community service groups, such as the Rotary, Lions Club, and Kiwannis
- community discussion groups that bring in speakers, such as Friends of the Library and City Club
- local radio and TV talk shows
- local school, college, and university groups that have guest speakers
- conferences, conventions, panels, and workshops on your topic

In fact, speaking can become a self-supporting business by itself, and if you get very serious about it, there are groups you can join which help the serious professional speaker, such as the National Speaker's Association. Thus focus here will be on how you can use speaking on a largely local community basis to build interest in your product, though you can always do much, much more.

FINDING A TOPIC TO SPEAK ABOUT

One key to getting booked to speak in the first place is having a topic of general interest to speak about. You can't just go in and give a sales pitch on your product, although you may be able to spend a few minutes doing this or giving out information on this during or at the end of your talk, as well as give out or collect business cards for future follow up. But your initial focus must be on having something of interest to say that people want to hear. Then, your talk serves as a way to build up your credibility as an authority as well as serves as a bridge to your product.

So in choosing a topic, find something related to your product that people will find of interest. For example, if you are promoting a health product, come up with some health talk on something your product does. An example of this might be talking about "How to Extend Your Life," featuring a discussion of new scientific findings on what makes people live longer, if you are marketing vitamin pills or energy supplements. Another might be developing a talk on "How to Better Enjoy Your Camping Experience," if you are selling a food product which comes in a pot in the boiling water bag and is useful in camping. Or if you're marketing a new communications product or system (such as cellular phones or a membership program that offers lower long-distance rates), what about a topic like "How the New Communications Revolution Is Changing Our Lives." In all these talks, remember, you can't treat this like a long commercial—your emphasis must be on being generally informative and entertaining, and then, like in other media, you can work your commercial into a brief pitch during or at the end of your spot.

How do you come up with a topic that's both of interest generally and related to your product? Think about some of the issues in the news or that people are talking about, where the use of your product might be helpful, or at least, the topic is related to your product category. Perhaps ask friends and associates for suggestions on what they might like to hear about in that general product area (health, communications, food, etc.).

Eventually, you want to come up with one or a group of two or more related topics you can talk about (though don't list too many topics—perhaps suggest three or four for variety and up to a maximum of six or seven). Some topics may immediately come to mind. You can also use Chart 22.1 on the following page to help you come up with some ideas.

Preparing Your Talk

Once you have selected your topic, then prepare a talk for about 20–45 minutes, which you can adjust, depending on how long people want you to talk. You might also allow some time at the end for questions (perhaps 10 minutes

CHART 22.1: POSSIBLE TOPICS FOR MY TALK ON HOW TO PROMOTE MY PRODUCT

BENEFITS OF MY PRODUCT	GENERAL TOPICS SUGGESTED BY THESE BENEFITS—LIST AS MANY AS YOU CAN FOR EACH BENEFIT	PRIORITY OF TOPICS BASED ON ESTIMATED INTEREST LEVEL (RATE FROM 1–5)

with a 20-minute talk, about 15 minutes with a 45-minute talk), and a few minutes to talk about your product.

If you have a series of related talks, you can use the same information in different talks. So one title may attract one group to hear that talk, another title may attract another, but it's basically the same program.

If you are not used to public speaking, consider joining a group like Toastmasters to help you learn how to feel more comfortable and prepare a talk. Or try out in front of a small group of friends. Should you decide on the Toastmaster's route, check in your phone book under Toastmasters (or Toastmistress—there used to be a separate group for men and women, but many are combined now).

Once you have some basic skills as a speaker, you might consider joining the National Speaker's Association, which has branches in most major cities; check the local telephone book, or call the national office in Phoenix, Arizona, at (602) 265-1001, or fax (602) 265-7403, to find out the nearest chapter. The group is excellent for helping you refine your presentation skills as well as develop techniques for marketing yourself as a speaker. Besides local meetings, the group also has a national newsletter with tips for speakers, regional and national workshops on speaker skills and marketing tips, and other programs to help you develop as a speaker. It's also a great place for networking—and some of the people in the organization may be interested in your product as well.

As for preparing your talk, here are some basic guidelines:

Research and Collect Information on Your Topic. This includes both gathering data from outside sources and collecting your own anecdotes on the topic. One of the keys that makes a talk interesting and engaging for listeners is personalizing it with your own personal stories, so include some of these, as well as other information that helps to add support and credibility to what you are saying. For example, say you are doing a talk on "Why

One-Third of the American Public Is Always on a Diet, and How to Keep Pounds Off," because you are marketing a weight-control program. You might include some stories about your own struggles in losing weight and your experiences of the differences in people's reactions to you when you were fat and when you were slim. And then, you might include some information on various comments and studies by researchers in the field, describing their findings and opinions. Then, as appropriate, mention your own product here and there or in a special time set aside to do a brief pitch for your product.

To help in organizing your talk, you might use some index cards to write down your ideas, summaries of surveys and comments, and personal stories. Or perhaps use files to accumulate information and stories on different topics. Maybe use other people's stories, too, and when you do, be sure to keep track of who said what, so you can credit them in your talk.

Then, Weave Your Material Together. Start with an introduction in which you give a brief overview of what your talk is going to be about, and perhaps use a personal story or interesting finding as a lead-in to attract attention and the desire to learn more. Then, in your talk, focus on a few key points—usually three or four—and use your stories or information to support these points. Then, close with a wrap up that ties together what you have said before, or perhaps briefly summarizes the main points you have made. Sometimes a closing story that brings together these ideas which have gone before is also good. In the speaking profession, this approach reflects a classic formula—tell them what you are going to tell them, tell them, and then tell them what you have told them. Certainly, other approaches may work fine for you, but this is a common formula, and might be especially good to follow when you are first starting.

Consider Using Graphics, Slides, Overheads, or Demonstrations to Support or Increase Interest in What You Are Saying. Often, just a talk is fine, particularly if you are just giving a brief presentation (say, 20 minutes at luncheon or after dinner). Also, if you are an engaging speaker or use audience participation in conjunction with your·talk, you may not need or want to do this.

But often just about any type of talk can be enhanced by visuals or demonstrations, where you use pictures, graphs, charts, hands-on illustrations, and so on.

Think about Ways to Involve Your Audience Through Questions, Audience Participation, Interaction with You or Others in the Audience, and So On.   This is another way to break up a straight talk by getting the audience to be active. For example, throw out some questions, and ask for audience opinions or experiences (such as "How many people have been on a diet?" or "What are some reasons people have found that their diet doesn't work?" Then, call on a few volunteers, and when people respond, it helps to react by briefly recapping what you heard them say, commenting on their remark to show how it is a good or typical one, or saying something brief like "Yeah, that's a good one." This response or feedback shows people you are really listening and care what they have said and encourages other people to contribute as well.

Another possibility might be to use some exercise (related to your topic of course) in which people in the audience can participate (such as a way to raise energy or reduce stress, if you are talking about life extension techniques).

Then, too, to stimulate audience interaction, you might suggest that people turn to a neighbor and share some experience or get into a small group to do this. Afterward, to bring everyone back together and encourage interaction with you, you can ask a couple of people to share what happened or how they felt about this experience.

Decide How to Best Bring Your Own Product or Company into the Picture.   For this, it's good to consult with the program organizer of the group you are going to be speaking to. Find out what you can say about your own product, and whether you can include a pitch for products during or after your talk. Some may be quite agreeable to having you do this; often, this is a kind of quid pro quo offered to speakers who are talking to a group for free. In return for their free talk, they can get to do a product or company plug. But in other cases, the program organizer may not want you to do this, but may allow you to give out this information as a handout (which can be given to people as they walk in, be left on their chairs or on the table where they will be sitting, or in a pile of handouts, perhaps next to samples of your product). It's important that you establish these guidelines of what you can and can't say, so you don't end up with hard feelings for doing a promotional pitch when you aren't supposed to do this (for instance, some civic and community forum-type groups may be especially sensitive to people doing this, because they don't want to appear to be endorsing some product or service, whereas other groups may be much more receptive, because they are made up of businesspeople who are actively promoting their own businesses as part of being in the group (such as the Rotary Club, at least the ones which I attended).

Then, within the limits of what you can do, decide the best way to do it. For example, assuming you can say what you want during the talk, consider whether you can easily talk about how your product does what you are talking about within the body of your talk. If so, this is a good place to fit it in, because when a commercial pitch is part of a presentation, like an ad contained within editorial copy, it packs more power. Then, at the end, add a reminder or a short product promotion if you can, and if you have been able to put out samples of your product or sell them at the meeting, mention that these are available. Or if you can't appropriately use this pitch in the body of your talk, just do what you can in the end.

Prepare the Material You Need to Promote Your Product within the Approved Guidelines. Once you are clear about what you can do and have decided how to pitch your product, prepare the necessary materials to do this so you can set this up at the meeting. For example, if you can hand out sample kits during or after your talk, put these sample kits together. If you can distribute fliers, prepare the brochures, fliers, or other materials you plan to hand out and perhaps use a special cover letter or flier designed to appeal to the members of this particular organization, such as a personal letter from group members to you about what you have to offer.

Also, consider the possibility of using special offers to induce people to act now, if you are permitted to do this, and if you can and want to make such an offer, include this information on your letter or flier. Or perhaps even make up a special offer card which you can use at this and other speaking engagements (such as 10 percent discount on all purchases at this meeting).

GETTING READY TO CONTACT GROUPS

With your talks or series of topics prepared, you next have to find groups to speak to. With small informal groups and program organizers you already know, you may be able to set this up informally. Just a discussion and a brief written description of what you are going to talk about may be enough.

But once you start to do this seriously, with larger more organized groups and people you don't already know (and even those you do), you will need some kind of promotional material, and even a brochure, to describe your topics and provide some background on you. Then, as you do this more and more and establish a track record, start putting together a list of references and perhaps some sample reference letters to create a little promotional pack that will add to your credibility and help get you more assignments. This kind of backup can also help you get fees for your speaking as well, and as your track record adds up and your promotional package becomes more impressive, so can your fees—while the size of the group you are addressing—and the volume of products you can sell—will increase too.

In the beginning, though, just a sheet with the topics you talk about and a bio about yourself is fine. On the next pages, you'll find some samples of what I have done to promote my own speaking to groups on various topics—including direct selling and MLM techniques. You'll note that each one lists a general theme, and then includes specific topics I can talk about in each area. Another way to do this is to list the general category, and then come up with some snappy titles for each of the topics in this area you want to talk about.

In writing your bio, keep it down to a page, or even a paragraph or two, highlighting what you have done that is most relevant to the topic you are going to talk about. Perhaps even write up your bio as you might want someone to read it in introducing you at one of your presentations. One approach is to use a paragraph narrative style, such as I have done in my own bio which is attached for illustration. Or another approach might be to list in set-off style your major accomplishments, again highlighting those that are most relevant by listing these first.

You can always update your bio, keeping the same basic format. For example, as your organization grows and you get more press coverage or opportunities to speak to groups, you might include some of the most impressive achievements. And even if these achievements may not relate directly to your specific sales activities for your product, you can write about them in a way that they might seem applicable. For example, on my bio sheet, I note that I was on the Phil Donahue, Sally Jessy Raphael, and other shows for some of my books. Actually, these appearances were for earlier books that has nothing to do with the topics I am talking about now. But I can refer to these appearances legitimately.

Also, include any credentials that may give you credibility, even though they are not directly related to your present subject. For instance, I list my Ph.D. and J.D. degrees, even though these are not really relevant when I talk about direct sales techniques. But the degrees add to a general sense of authority and credibility that helps to impress those who might consider having me speak for their group.

INTRODUCING GINI GRAHAM SCOTT

Gini Graham Scott, Ph.D., J.D., is a nationally known writer, game designer, and organizational/business consultant, speaker, and seminar/workshop leader specializing in conflict resolution, problem solving, creativity, lifestyles, and social dynamics. She is the founder and president of Changemakers and Creative Communications and Research, involved in new product development and promotion.

As a writer, she has published over 20 books on diverse subjects. Her books on social dynamics, lifestyles, conflict resolution, problem solving, and creativity include: *The Truth About Lying* (Harbinger House 1991), *Private Eyes* (Citadel 1991, with investigator Sam Brown), *Resolving Conflict* (New Harbinger Press 1990), *Mind Power: Picture Your Way to Success* (Prentice Hall Press 1987, audio version 1989), and *The Creative Traveler* (Tudor 1989).

Scott's books on direct sales, business and law include: *Building A Winning Sales Team* (Probus 1991), *Everything You Need to Know to Be Successful in Multi-Level Marketing* (Prentice Hall 1991), *Get Rich Through Multi-Level Selling* (Self-Counsel Press 1989), *Effective Selling and Sales Management* (Brick House 1987), *Strike It Rich in Personal Selling* (Avon 1985; New World Books 1988), *Positive Cash Flow* (Bob Adams 1989), *Debt Collection* (Oasis Press 1987), *It's Your Money* (Avon 1987), and *Collect Your Court Judgment* (Nolo 1988).

Scott has received national media exposure for some of her books (including appearances on the Phil Donahue and Sally Jessy Raphael shows). She is also launching a series of weekly radio programs called *Changemakers* on KUSF-FM in San Francisco (starting April 1991) featuring interviews on various topics. She received her doctorate in Sociology from the University of California in Berkeley in 1976; did some post-doctoral work with several U.C. Berkeley anthropology professors from 1979 to 1982; and received her J.D. degree from the University of San Francisco Law School in 1990.

INTRODUCING GINI GRAHAM SCOTT . . . BACKGROUND HIGHLIGHTS

Education

- Ph.D. in Sociology—University of California, Berkeley
- Post-doctoral study in Anthropology—University of California, Berkeley
- J.D. in Law—University of San Francisco Law School

BUSINESS AND WORK EXPERIENCE

As an Author and Designer

- Author of over 20 books on various topics, including:
  - Conflict Resolution and Personal Development
  - Increasing Personal Power and Creativity
  - Current Social Issues and Concerns
  - Groups and Organizations
  - Business Success and Sales and Marketing Techniques
- Designer of over 2 dozen games and toys, including:
  - Glasnost: The Game of Soviet-American Peace and Diplomacy (published in the US, and in German and Soviet editions, with the first Soviet run of 100,000 copies; Clio Award in 1989)
  - Screwball, manufactured by Hasbro Industries

- Designer of over 1 dozen children's dolls and character licenses with children's book and product line tie-ins, including *Little Devils, L'il Robots,* and *L'il Impies*

As a Speaker, Media Personality, Teacher, Community Leader, etc.

- Speaker and workshop leader at national and international conferences
- Radio talk show host of the series: *Changemakers,* now featured on an independent radio station in San Francisco and being syndicated nationally
- Teacher at numerous colleges and universities, including West Georgia College, San Francisco State University, and Dominican College in San Rafael
- Investigative researcher for major consumer group and private investigators, including Sam Brown and Dee Moody, with whom co-authored books
- Volunteer panelist and trainer for Community Boards, a neighborhood conflict resolution group in San Francisco
- Award-winning photographer—photos in book, calendar, exhibits
- Member of numerous writing, media, community, business/professional groups

The flier and bio sheet should be enough to introduce you to the smaller and local groups. You may also need to develop a cover letter to accompany them, which basically states in a paragraph or two that you are sending the enclosed materials about your talks and yourself (perhaps in response to a conversation with the program organizer) and briefly highlights what you would like to talk about and how you have the background to do this. Read the letter on the following page as a sample of what you might say. You'll note that this letter also refers to a list of references and reference letters. Include these once you get them, and each time you do a talk, try to get the agreement of the person you gave the talk for to be a reference and to give you a letter on the group's letterhead which you can use in the future (assuming you have done a good job and everyone liked your talk).

Then, as you gain more experience doing this, consider putting together a more developed promotional kit or brochure. The promotional kit will be less expensive, since it basically involves combining the fliers, letters, reference lists, and any press clips or articles that you already have into an organized packet in an attractive folder. Use a leatherette or vinyl or pebbled cover stock folder, which come in various colors and have pockets in each cover where you can place your promotional materials. These are available in office supply and larger stationery stores. Then, insert the following items:

- list of speaking topics (with perhaps brief descriptions of each topic if you think additional information would be useful)

October 26, 1990

Mr. Jack Smith
Program Director
Pines Bluff Community Center
123 Davis Street
Pines Bluff, California 94108

Dear Mr. Smith:

I was pleased to hear of your interest in the possibility of my doing a talk for your group on "Ten Key Steps to a Successful Diet."

Per your request, I am enclosing a copy of my list of topics on the subject of dieting and nutrition generally, along with a bio about myself. A list of references of previous groups I have spoken with on these subjects is also enclosed, along with a few sample letters of reference.

    I will be glad to adapt this subject to the specific interests of your group, and I can leave some time at the end of the talk for audience questions. I can also work in some audience participation exercises if you like.

    I will look forward to hearing from you and discussing when I might do this and the arrangements for the program with you further.

                Sincerely,

                Jennifer Jones
                Director, New Diet America

JJ;aj

- brief bio of yourself (which could be a separate sheet or might be included at the bottom of your list of topics, depending on how long it is)
- list of groups and organizations you have spoken to before
- one to three reference letters from the groups that have given you the most enthusiastic response or which are the most well-known in your area; if possible, choose groups which are of the same type or are in the same field as the group you hope to be speaking to; these will be more convincing, since the program organizer can better relate to such groups because of the common identity)
- one to three press clips, if any, about talks you have given before

    Also, include a business card (some folders have a small inset with corner cuts so you can insert a card) or a label with your name, address, and number. In addition, if you have one, add a picture.

Another approach which some speakers use as their speaking business develops is the brochure, sometimes by itself, or sometimes as an element in a promotional kit such as just described. This can get expensive—about $500 to $2,000, for a professional job. But it's also increasingly necessary for people to have these if they want to speak to large organizations, corporations who use speakers at things like conventions and luncheons, and other major speaking events. You'll also need to have some good photographs and graphics to do this well. To get an idea of what to do, look at some examples of what other professional speakers have and consult with people in the graphics and printing business who create these sorts of things. A group like the National Speaker's Association can also help you with its workshops, local meetings, and how-to cassette program. A detailed discussion on how to put one of these together is beyond the scope of this book.

Creating a Demo Tape or Video

Demo audiotapes and videos can also help you get speaking engagements with some groups. These won't generally be necessary with the smaller and local groups, where you speak for free, and the groups are used to get nonprofessional speakers. However, as you expand to larger and larger groups and to a more regional audience or beyond, these become increasingly important, until finally, on the professional level of public speaking, an audiotape becomes a requirement, and in many cases, the program director who books the speakers will want to see a video, too.

Professional audiotapes and videos can be expensive. However, you can put together a demo audiotape which is sufficient for your needs in the early stages of starting to get speaking engagements with almost no expense. One way is to tape a program you do do. Assuming, it was a good meeting where you gave a good, well-received talk, that's all you need. Perhaps add an opening statement, even some music, and a close, for an extra finishing touch. You can similarly work with a friend who has a home video, or you can get a local video student or small video company to be on the scene, at a cost of anywhere from the cost of the film or $10 to about $100 for an hour or two of shooting and some editing and titles. (For example, I did my first video for $125 when I gave a talk at a local convention, and the organizers arranged for a video unit to be available at discounted prices to shoot the speaker's talk or workshop and provide a single edited tape, with opening titles. It wasn't a true professional job, but it was adequate at the time.

Alternatively, if you don't already have a prearranged speaking engagement you can tape or video, you can set up a session just for taping. A good way to do this is to invite friends or the people in your sales group, and let them know this will be a free program you are planning to tape. Perhaps provide refreshments as an incentive for people to show up to be there. Then, do the best possible talk you can, while you tape or have someone video it.

Whatever kind of early tape you make—at a regular speaking engagement or at one you set up to make your tape—you can always upgrade as you get better. In fact, consider taping all your talks. Then, you can always use the best pieces out of each, should you want to do some kind of collage tape, or substitute a better performance for the tape you are currently using.

Similarly, look into getting a better video if you start off with a home-grown one as your speaking activities expand.

When you first send out inquiry letters, these tapes or video aren't usually necessary when you are contacting the small and local groups, and this can keep down your mailing and inquiry costs if you don't include demos, though you might include these in a follow-up mailing to those groups that express some interest in knowing more. However, as you approach larger and more regional or national groups to speak to them, such tapes or demos may be expected with your initial inquiry. You can get a feel for what to do if you do a premailing call to the groups you are approaching to find out what the program director would like to receive.

FINDING GROUPS TO CONTACT

Now, with the material you need to support what you are doing, you must find and make contact with the appropriate groups. The process is much like seeking out leads and contacting them for your MLM program generally.

First, target your market by figuring out which groups would be most interested in your general topic (if you're talking about diet or health, besides the general interest community and civic groups which book speakers, there might be some specialty groups in your area that might be especially interested—such as a Vegetarian Society chapter, a large health club which has speakers, a women's business group, etc.).

Then, find out what groups of these types exist in the area where you want to speak. You can obtain this information from several sources:

Look in the Yellow Pages of your phone book under the relevant listings. For example, in my own directory, there is a listing for "Associations," which then lists a variety of other organizational categories. Some of these which you might find of special interest for MLM programs might be these, depending on your particular product type:

- Athletic organizations
- Business and trade organizations
- Clubs
- Environmental, conservation, and ecological organizations
- Fraternal Organizations
- Human services organizations
- Political organizations
- Professional organizations

- Religious organizations
- Senior citizens' service organizations
- Social service organizations
- Women's organizations and services
- Youth organizations and centers

Another source of local groups might be a directory of members or local associations and organizations produced by your Chamber of Commerce.

Also, ask friends and business associates if they know of any groups you might contact, particularly if they are members, which can help to give you an in.

If you can get the name of the appropriate contact—the director or program director—use it. If you have a person to connect you with this organization, he or she can tell you. Or if you are using a telephone first approach, find out who to speak to when you call; then briefly describe your ideas for talking to the group with that person, and send your promotional materials or packet to him or her. Otherwise, just direct your materials to the program director and use the organization's address. It will then be directed to the right person, and if there is interest, this person will contact you, and you can thereafter deal with him or her.

Handling Your Initial Contact and Follow-Up

After you have sent out your initial material (either after a preliminary inquiry call or in a direct mailing without a call), then plan to do some follow-up within a week or ten days if you haven't heard from the person to whom you sent your material. The follow-up process is similar to following up after you have sent out information about your product to work toward getting the sale. Find out if your proposed speaking arrangement is being considered, if any other information is needed, how long the consideration process will take, and the like. Perhaps suggest a meeting, if the person seems receptive and the group might be a likely prospect. This might also be a good time to offer to send a sample tape of your talk, if you haven't previously sent this out with the initial mailing.

Then, if there is interest, work out the arrangements, and handle the details much as you would in planning for a presentation on your product. For example, find out how long the talk will be, how many people will be there, what kind of equipment you will need (slide carousels, screens, VCR monitor, etc.). Also, find out a little about the audience, so you can adapt your talk to them. Then, too, learn what you can say about your product, if you can give out handouts or sell product at the end, and so on. And be sure to get directions to the meeting site, if you are not sure where it is, so you avoid any delays due to getting lost. You can use Chart 22.2 to help you plan.

Finally, send the program director for the meeting a confirming letter about the date and any special arrangements for the meeting. Should there be any payment agreement, be sure to note what you understand about this too. Invite the program director to be sure to call you if anything is incorrect, and it's a good idea to call yourself a few days after you send the letter to make sure it has been received, so that you know everything is set.

If the program director is going to be sending out any information about your talk in advance (fliers, newsletter listings, etc.), request a copy for yourself (this helps to reaffirm that the date is set, plus you may be able to use some of this material later, in promoting yourself as a speaker). Also, to be doubly sure, it's a good idea to call a few days before the meeting just to be sure everything is still on, as planned, if the program director hasn't already called you to do this.

GIVING YOUR TALK

Before you leave to give your talk, check over any materials or equipment you will be using, to make sure everything is there and in working order. This is especially important if

CHART 22.2: TALK PLANNING INFORMATION

Date of Talk _____ Address: _____

Program Director/Contact _____ Phone: _____

Directions to Meeting (if needed) _____

Presentation Format
1. Length of talk:
2. Special characteristics of audience to consider:
3. Special interests/points to emphasize in talk:
4. Special presentation considerations (more serious/funny/etc.):

Equipment Needed
1. Slides or slide projector?
1. Screen?
3. VCR or monitor?
4. Overhead projector?
5. Tape recorder?
6. Other?

Product Promotion Possibilities
1. Size of audience?
2. Is it possible to *sell* product? If so, how much shall I bring?
_____
3. Is it possible to *announce* product information?
4. Can I display or give out handouts? Which ones and how many will I need?
    Display _____   Distribute? _____
    Fliers to display or give out?   How Many Needed?
       1. _____   _____
       2. _____   _____
       3. _____   _____
       4. _____   _____
       5. _____   _____

you are going to be bringing audiovisual equipment—make sure the equipment not only has power or bulbs as planned, but that you have backup fuses and bulbs, so that if anything goes off during your presentation, you can quickly replace it.

Then, leave with plenty of time, so you can get to the meeting site about 30 minutes to an hour in advance so you can have everything set up with a little time to relax and get ready before everyone arrives. The amount of time you will need depends on how much material or equipment you are bringing. It's always better to arrive early and allow a little extra time just in case, so you are sure. This way, with plenty of time to spare, you can better deal with any of the unexpected things that can come up before a talk in an unfamiliar setting and to an unfamiliar group (such as taking the wrong road or finding out that the directions you have been given are unclear, learning that you need to change a bulb on your equipment, finding the chairs have not been set up, etc.). Also, arriving early can give you a chance to meet and mingle with some of the early arrivals, so you can warm up the audience a little in advance, and will have made some personal connections, that will help you have more rapport with the audience. And this feeling of support can help you to feel more enthused and confident yourself so you give a better talk.

If possible, have copies of information about you, your company, or your product at the desk as people come in so they can pick it up, or leave it on people's chairs. Another good strategy is to have some kind of handout with useful information on one side related to your talk, and then on the other, feature information on your product and company, perhaps even a form for people to fill out for more information. This kind of approach can even work if you are not supposed to do a direct product presentation, because program directors will usually be willing to let you give out useful information, and then, this information helps to give added authority to the promotional information on the back, and people can contact you for further information.

Another technique which some speakers use when they can't sell directly at the meeting is to offer anyone in the audience interested some free useful information (usually related to their topic), and they ask anyone who would like this sent to them to speak to them after the meeting and give them a business card. This is a good way to get leads of people for future follow-up.

At the end of your talk, indicate that you can stay around to answer any questions or talk to people personally. If you are able to sell product, you can do this by the area where you have your product display set up. Then, ask those who want to have a conversation with you to wait for a moment while you take care of any sales. Be ready to handle any sales first, and as necessary break away from your conversation to do this. Also, ask anyone you have a conversation with while you are still selling to position him or herself to avoid blocking your product display, and stand yourself so you show you are easily open to selling something (about half toward your product display and half toward the person you are speaking to). Then, if someone comes by, excuse yourself from the conversation briefly to make a product sale or give out information to someone who may have interest in either product or becoming a distributor. Collect cards from people who are interested in knowing more.

Or if you can't sell product or do any recruiting on the spot, keep general conversations brief and try to collect cards or give out information for future follow-up to those people who seem like likely prospects.

Through these techniques you can make the most of your informational presentation to either sell on the spot or get leads for future follow-up.

FOLLOWING-UP AFTER THE MEETING

To maximize the power of your speaking engagement, follow-up with the leads you have obtained within a week or ten days after the meeting. Now use the usual follow-up techniques discussed in previous chapters.

In addition, follow-up with the program director to help build your reputation as a speaker. Within a few days, call to thank the program director for inviting you, or send a thank you note for this. Also, ask the program director, either in your call or letter, to provide you with a reference letter about your talk. Explain that you would like to be able to include this in your portfolio, and possibly use the program director's name or the group's name in your list of groups or organizations you have spoken to. Many program directors will be very glad to do this—especially if you have spoken at no charge or for a small honorarium. It's their way of providing you with some compensation for doing the program.

If the program director is busy, offer to draft a letter yourself, for his or her approval. If possible, get the program director to put any correspondence on the organization's own letterhead. But if it is not possible to do this and you do get the director's agreement to use a quote or the name of the group as a reference, just write this up yourself and use it in your list of credits or quotes like this.

These letters and quotes or credits will help to build your reputation as a speaker, and you can use them to help get engagements for larger and larger groups, as well as getting paid or getting more money for what you do.

Chapter 23

DOING YOUR OWN PUBLICITY

If you are able to create or participate in a particularly interesting event, you may be able to get some free publicity in the local, even national, media. Likewise, if you set up a speaking engagement, you may be able to get some publicity for that.

The difference between publicity and advertising is that advertising is promotion you pay for, and you have control over when and where and if it appears. By contrast, publicity is free, but you don't have any control over what you get or if you get it. It's up to the people in the media, based on what they think would be interesting to their readers, listeners, or viewers. However, you can raise your odds of them doing a story or at least listing your event somewhere, if you can put together your publicity materials in an effective, professional way, and if you can turn whatever you are doing into something that has news, educational, or entertainment value, so some media person wants to pick it up.

This chapter will focus on getting local publicity, since it is more realistic to seek this type of publicity for what you are doing, particularly in the early stages of developing your program. However, as you start building up a PR track record, and as your own organization becomes larger and more regional or national in scope, or your talks to groups expand in scope, then by all means think of expanding your PR efforts accordingly. There are all sorts of books on doing your own PR you might consider then, or even hiring your own PR person to do all or most of your PR for you. Here the focus is what you can do yourself locally.

TYPES OF PR POSSIBILITIES

The types of PR possibilities available locally include the following:

- Calendar listings for events in the local newspapers, advertisers, magazines, and so on
- Public service announcements (if you are doing your program for a nonprofit group or there is some other acceptable public service angle) on the local radio or television
- Interviews and appearances on local radio and TV talk and interview shows
- Interviews about you and your company in the local business columns or press
- Feature stories about your product or service, if there is some kind of appealing informational or entertainment hook
- A news story about some event you create or participate in, if it draws enough people, is unique enough, or otherwise might have some special-interest hook
- A general article or program in any media, where you are quoted as an expert, and your company or activities mentioned in connection with your quote

SOME GENERAL GUIDELINES IN DOING PR

Unless you have a personal contact, you'll probably have to do everything initially by mail, using the appropriate sort of PR release. This will give the person who receives it an introduction to your event or news item; then, you or your assistant can follow up within a few days to a week to make sure the release has been received or send a replacement if it hasn't been received or has been discarded.

This mailing-first approach is usual in PR, because media people are very busy, and most don't like to get phone calls. Also, many don't like to get follow-up phone calls either, although generally, PR people do expect to follow-up on press releases soon after these are sent (usually three days to a week), and these follow-up calls are an important part of the process in the case of trying to arrange for interviews, appearances, feature stories, and news stories. However, when you are trying to get calendar listings or public service announcements, it is not usual to follow up, and most people doing these listings or announcements don't want these calls. They will either use the material you have sent as is or not use it, and your call will usually just be seen as an annoyance. Similarly, if you are going to be quoted as an expert by someone, you just need to wait until someone calls you if they are doing a relevant story after you have alerted the media to your background in this field.

Finding Out Whom to Contact

To do your PR outreach, you need current lists of the particular media contacts you want to make and keep your lists updated regularly if you do additional PR, because people move around frequently, especially in radio and television. Also, columns and radio/TV shows and show formats change frequently. So use lists that are no older than a few months old. If you can use the list of someone who is working in the field locally, that would be ideal, since their list may be up to date within weeks of your mailing.

You can obtain lists from several sources:

- A local PR person who makes his or her lists available for sale, though most PR people don't sell their lists. However, contact the Public Relations Society of America (try the White Pages or the Yellow Pages under Public Relations). The head of the local group might have some suggestions about where you can go to contact someone.

- A publisher who puts together lists of media people in your area. This will vary from city to city; generally, you will have better luck in finding such a publisher in a larger city, and there may be organizations of media professionals that put together such a list and sell them. (For example, in San Francisco, an organization called Media Alliance does this, and a local publisher puts together a loose-leaf binder with lists of the local media, updated every three months, which sells for about $100.) To find out if there are specialty publications like this for your city, check with the local Chamber of Commerce or Public Relations Society of America chapter, or call some of the major media sources in town.

- National publishers, available in most large local libraries, which put out media guides for major cities, usually once a year. These will be less up to date than the sources you get through working PR people or PR services in your community; however, they will at least give you the major media, and you can subsequently do some of your own calling (or have someone do this for you, perhaps a student at about $6 to $8 an hour), to find out about current changes in personnel and programming. Some of the major media guides include Bacon's Publicity Check and Standard Rate and Data. Also, check with your local librarian on other suggestions for local media lists.

PREPARING AND SENDING OUT YOUR PRESS MATERIALS

There are certain standard formats that media people are used to receiving for different kinds of press announcements. Also, it's important to take into consideration the lead times for the publications or TV/radio stations you are sending material to, so your material arrives before the deadline, and also provides enough time for appropriate follow-up, and perhaps sending duplicate materials, if necessary. Following are descriptions of the type of materials to send to each of the major sources of PR and general lead-time guidelines. (Recognize, though, that there will be variations from city to city and publication to publication; so check local preferences.)

Calendar Listings

If you are having an event or giving a talk on a specific date, send a calendar listing to your local newspaper, advertiser, or other local publications and magazines which list activities. This listing should include the title of the event, what the event is about, the date, the time, the location, any phone number to call for information, and if there is any charge. You are more likely to get the event listed, if there is no charge.

Such listings can be sent to general events listings, special weekend listings, or sections which list events of a certain type (such as local business activities). Even if these different calendars are in the same publication, send a calendar description to each events listing separately. In this case, it's usually best to simply direct the listing to the Editor, Calendar (listing the specific type of calendar if this is necessary to distinguish it from another calendar listing), unless the name of the calendar editor is actually listed in the publication.

A sample calendar listing which I used for a party to promote a game which I designed is on the following page. The listing can go by itself; or if you have a flier about the event, you might include this. It may be helpful in leading the calendar editor to run your listing, although it is not necessary.

You may also find that if you send in subsequent listings, your event may be more likely to be listed, since you'll get credibility, as long as your event doesn't recur too often. Probably, you can't expect to get a free listing every week or two weeks. But if there are three or four weeks between events or more, that should be fine.

COMMUNITY CALENDAR LISTING
FOR IMMEDIATE RELEASE
DATE: October 10, 1988   Contact: Bobbi Randolph
                                     Elizabeth Reagh

Sponsoring Organization: U.S.-U.S.S.R. Friendship Society, Changemakers

Topic: A gala party celebrating the growing friendship between the U.S. and Soviet Union and the introduction of GLASNOST: THE GAME OF SOVIET-AMERICAN PEACE AND DIPLOMACY

Title: A Gala Party Celebrating the Introduction of Glasnost: The Game of Soviet-American Peace and Diplomacy

Format: A party featuring Russian entertainment, singers, dancers, music, dancing, and a

multi-media USSR slide show at the Red
Square, a Soviet-theme club. From 9–10 P.M.,
and afterward you are welcome to stay on
for the regular program.

No charge with reservation.

Saturday, November 5—9–10 P.M. for
Glasnost Party (then stay on for the
regular club program)

Red Square
1748 Haight Street (near Cole)
San Francisco

For information and reservations, call (415) 931-8725

Plan to send these listings out *each time* you want to
try for a listing for an event. Don't try to send a group of
listings for a series of weeks far in advance.

Generally, for a weekly publication, send out your listing
about two weeks to ten days in advance. If it's a monthly publication, note the publication deadline. You will generally
need about four to six weeks in this case for a publication
printed on newsprint; perhaps a little longer if its published
on slick paper—perhaps six to eight weeks for a local city
magazine.

To maximize the efficiency of your mailings, check on
the deadlines when you call to verify the accuracy of your
listings and do any updates. Then, make a note of this on
your PR list, so you are sure to get your material out at the
optimal time for consideration.

Public Service Announcements on
Local Radio or TV

These are like calendar listings, except on radio or TV.
The one requirement many radio and TV stations may have
in doing these is that the event be not-for-profit or that the
group sponsoring it be not for profit. So if you are doing a

paid engagement for a private commercial group, you are unlikely to get a free PR listing. You will normally be expected to pay for a regular commercial air spot.

But if the nature of your presentation or sponsoring group qualifies, then you can try sending a release. Again, no guarantees, but try. To do so, design your PS announcement into three standard time slots; if your announcement is read, the announcer or show producer will decide how much time is allowed.

Because timing is so important in radio and TV, be sure to read your announcement aloud, using a normal pace of voice, to make sure the announcement is the time stated for that spot. If in doubt about what's "normal," err on the side of reading the spot too slowly, so that your announcement may end up too short rather than too long for the time slot. If the announcement runs too long, it may not be used or your announcement may be cut, with the result that crucial information might be left out.

The usual time slots are 60 seconds, 30 seconds, or 10 seconds. Add an additional 20-second time slot if you wish. As in the calendar listing, you basically want to say what the event is, what will be happening, where, and how to make arrangements to attend. Also, in the longer spot you can go into more detail, and perhaps add an introductory hook to attract interest, and say a little about who is sponsoring the event. In the shorter spots, you won't have time to do much more than describe what's happening, where, and who to call.

Following are some sample announcements I used for the Glasnost party. Note also the usual format used to introduce these spots. The head says "Public Service Announcement," notes that it is for immediate release as of a certain date, indicates a kill date (when the announcement will no longer be useful), and includes the name of a contact or contacts, plus a number to call. Sometimes a flier about the event accompanying this PS announcement might be helpful to attract interest and give you backup credibility. But again it's not necessary.

PUBLIC SERVICE ANNOUNCEMENT
FOR IMMEDIATE RELEASE: 10/10/88
KILL DATE: 11/6/88   Contact: Bobbi Randolph
                                       Elizabeth Reagh

– 60 –

If you are interested in celebrating the growing
friendship between the U.S. and Soviet Union, you're
invited to a gala party on Saturday, November 5th,
celebrating the introduction of GLASNOST: THE
GAME OF SOVIET-AMERICAN PEACE AND
DIPLOMACY. The party will be held at the Red
Square, a Soviet-theme club, at 1748 Haight Street
from 9 to 10 P.M., and then you are welcome to stay
on for the regular club program. There is no charge
for this party. The event will feature Russian
entertainment, singers, dancers, music, dancing,
and a multi-media USSR slide show. The GLASNOST
game which inspired this event has just been
launched by Changemakers, a San Francisco
Company devoted to making a change, and the
John N. Hansen Company, which is publishing and
distributing the game nationally. The celebration on
November 5th is being sponsored by Changemakers
and the U.S.-U.S.S.R. Friendship Society, a non-profit
organization devoted to promoting better U.S.-Soviet
relations through education. Also, representatives
of the Soviet Consulate in San Francisco will attend
this event. For further information and to make
reservations, call (415) 931-8725. That's
(415) 931-8725.

– 30 –

If you are interested in celebrating the growing
friendship between the U.S. and Soviet Union,

you're invited to a gala party on Saturday, November 5th, celebrating the introduction of GLASNOST: THE GAME OF SOVIET-AMERICAN PEACE AND DIPLOMACY. The party will be held at the Red Square, a Soviet-theme club, at 1748 Haight Street from 9 to 10 P.M., and then you are welcome to stay on for the regular club program. There is no charge for this party. The event will feature Russian entertainment, singers, dancers, music, dancing, and a multi-media USSR slide show. For further information and to make reservations, call (415) 931-8725. That's (415) 931-8725.

– 10 –

A gala party celebrating the introduction of GLASNOST: THE GAME OF SOVIET-AMERICAN PEACE AND DIPLOMACY on Saturday, November 5th at the Red Square starting at 9 P.M. For details and reservations, call (415) 931-8725.

• • • • •

Plan to send these out to the stations about two weeks in advance. Address them to the director of public affairs at the radio or TV station you are contacting. In this case, the name of the person isn't necessary. Also, generally, no follow-up is necessary or desired for such announcements. The director of public affairs will use your spots if desired and will take into consideration what other public service announcements he or she has that day or week, as well as the likely interest of your event, in deciding whether to run the announcement or not.

INTERVIEWS AND APPEARANCES ON LOCAL RADIO AND TV TALK AND INTERVIEW SHOWS

Sometimes the organization of a special event can help you get an interview or arrange an appearance on a local radio or TV talk show, but any PR contacts or arrangements can also be made irrespective of this. The key criterion the radio or TV people will be considering is whether you will be an interesting, informative, or entertaining guest with something to say that will be of interest to listeners or viewers. You may be able to plug your event in the course of the interview or appearance if this is scheduled close enough in time before your event for this to make sense. But otherwise, you can just use the interview or appearance to provide a more general plug for your company or product. In some cases, the hosts will permit you to give out specific information over the air about where any event is, how they can buy the product, and your address or phone number. But in other shows, you won't be able to do this. The best you can hope for is a general mention about the name of your company and product and the city where you are located, so people who do some research can obtain your phone number and call you. In some cases, the station will keep your name, address, and sign-up location or ordering information at the station for a day or two to give this out to callers. When you or your assistant sets up the arrangements, check about what you can do, so you can be prepared to do any on-air plugs you can, or have a brief write-up of what the receptionist should take callers, so you can give this to the station.

Thus, your release to talk or interview shows should feature the interest of the topic you want to talk about with a catchy hook or angle to attract attention, rather than focusing on the news value of any promotional event. In fact, you may get more mileage out of linking your press release to the talks you are doing to groups than to product promotional events, which might be perceived as too commercial for these shows.

Some possibilities might be tying what you are talking about or what your product does to interesting events in the current news or current issues of controversy. Some examples might be trends in health, if you are marketing a health product, controversies about nutrition if you are marketing a food product, and so forth.

You'll see an example of such a release which a publicist for one of my books uses to set up speaking engagements for me with radio and TV hosts. At the time, the Donald Trump–Ivana Trump split was big news, and I had just written a book about resolving conflict, so the publicist sought to tie in my book with this issue and show how I might be able to talk as an authority on this topic as well as on conflict generally. The result, from a mailing to about three dozen top shows in San Francisco and Los Angeles, was about a dozen appearances, including one TV interview, and a few half-hour radio interviews, as well as shorter spots.

In this case, some backup material to give you credibility is helpful, including a biography, list of previous radio or TV shows you might have done, suggested questions your host might ask and capsule answers, and also a photo if this is for a TV appearance. In addition, you might also mention the availability of a sample audiotape or videotape, in case the person arranging the show wants to see this. You also might include a brief cover letter, highlighting what's in the press release and what else you are including in the mailing, although the letter is not necessary. It's best not to be your own contact person when you do this. Use an assistant or make up a name; you have more credibility and will be taken more seriously when someone else is setting up your PR for you. It sounds odd and undermines your credibility if you appear to be promoting yourself and "tooting your own horn."

This press material should all be sent to the show's producer—who is not necessarily or usually the host of the show. In fact, in the larger shows, the producer is almost never the host. Since both shows and show producers change quite regularly in this business, make sure your lists are current, and if you don't get your list from someone in the field or a PR service that provides regular updates, call the local radio or TV stations yourself to find out current shows and producers. There will only be a few local stations and a relatively small number of radio stations, so this shouldn't be too difficult.

Then, ask the receptionist for the current information, so you can send a press packet to the appropriate person.

    Contact: Sue Avila   **AVAILABLE May 21–22**
                (916) 444-5130

HOW IVANA TRUMP CAN SAVE HER MARRIAGE— OR AT LEAST HER $2.5 BILLION

    The possibilities for conflict are endless—from husbands and wives like Donald and Ivana Trump, to corporations like Apple Computer and Microsoft, to countries like Russia and Lithuania—whenever human relationships are involved.

    "Almost anything can lead to conflict," says Gini Graham Scott, Ph.D., author of *Resolving Conflict*, "failures to communicate, misunderstandings, lies that get discovered, competition and discussion which escalate into hostile encounters. The key is not to *avoid* conflict, but to manage it."

    Dr. Scott describes five styles of managing conflict: competition, accommodation, compromise, collaboration, and avoidance. "No style is better than another and all are appropriate at different times," she says. "For example, Ivana Trump is effectively using the competitive style to gain public support. Lithuania, on the other hand, needs to compromise or collaborate in order to gain their independence because Gorbachev needs a face-saving, diplomatic way to let them go."

    Let Gini Graham Scott inform your audience about how to resolve the conflicts in their lives.

● ● ●

Additionally, be sure the radio and TV stations you contact do in fact have talk or interview shows. If they don't—say if they just do music or news or are a foreign language station—there's no point wasting your energy and money sending them information. That's why zeroing in on the names of particular shows and producers will help you do this efficiently.

Since these talk and interview shows aren't tied to particular events, you can send these packets out anytime these are ready. However, if you do want to try for scheduling around the time of a particular event, allow two to six weeks lead time for scheduling. Generally, scheduling will be arranged more quickly on radio and at the smaller shows (more like about two to three weeks) and take longer with the larger shows and on TV. Yet the media are always very unpredictable, and you may find, due to a sudden cancellation or hot topic in the news, someone may call you and want you to be on the show within days. On the other hand, you may not hear anything for months, and all of a sudden, someone pulls your packet out of the file and wants you.

In any event, do plan on some follow-up for these packets—about four to seven days after you send them out. When you do, have whoever has been listed as the contact on the press release do so—or use the same fictitious name yourself if you have done this. Just don't sound like you are doing your own PR, though if the producer or assistant producer or host should subsequently want to talk to you, be ready to do so. (And if you are pretending to be your own PR person in doing this, wait a couple of days if you can, or at least a few hours, so whoever is arranging the show with you won't recognize your voice.) In many cases, you may find that the show host or producer will want to do a preinterview with you over the phone to ask you some questions and get your response, to both make sure you will be an interesting guest and (assuming you passed this test) to help prepare for the interview.

As for your interview or appearance itself, be prepared with a general idea of the main points you want to make, so you can work these ideas into the conversation. Also, expect to say whatever you do briefly—commonly, on TV, they like you to be able to talk in 15- to 30-second sound bites, so the conversation flows quickly, and in radio too, there is an emphasis on brevity. Again, the 15- to 30-second reply is a good guideline, although on radio you will commonly have more leeway, particularly on the longer format shows, where the interview will go into more depth. But on many of the most popular shows, you will only have a few minutes between commercials, so you have to pack a few questions and answers into that.

It is also helpful to find out from the producer or host how much time you will have on the program—15 minutes, 20 minutes; two 4-minute segments—so you can plan accordingly.

Then, when you set up the program, see if you can get a copy of the tape or video or make your own arrangements to have someone record it. Commonly, radio stations will be glad to give you a copy, though they may ask you to bring your own blank tape. Some TV stations will be willing, especially the smaller ones, though again, you may need to provide your own cassette. However, the larger shows often will not do this, so you have to make your own arrangements. The cheapest way is to set up your own VCR to record at the time you will do the interview or have a friend do this for you. However, there are also videotaping services which will not only tape your program but give you a copy with the commercials and other interviews on the show edited out, so the focus is on you. (The cost of this will be around $100.) If you plan to do a series of shows, the service can do a series of air clips for you on the same tape, and there may be a slightly reduced price for combining all these clips together.

The advantage of getting these tapes, of course, is you can use them to build credibility and help you get future bookings. Also, as you build up a collection of these, you can combine the highlights from a series of tapes to create a collage of appearances and interviews, which is what many professionals do in making a presentation audio- or videotape.

INTERVIEWS ABOUT YOU AND YOUR COMPANY IN THE LOCAL BUSINESS COLUMNS OR PRESS

In approaching the business press, you, of course, need a business hook. As long as this hook is already there, you can use the same sort of releases you send to radio and TV talk shows or for feature or news story articles. Or if these other press materials don't have this business hook, then you will need to develop a separate release for this market.

The types of things the business press may be interested in are

- new product breakthroughs or marketing approaches to these products (if you are just setting up an ordinary MLM marketing structure for another health, food, or other type of product, this probably won't quality, even if there is some product advantage. Unless this advantage is really dramatic, the difference won't qualify as a news story; the advantage is just too subtle to interest readers).

- a *very* large response to your program (underline "very" here; there's possibly a story if this growth rate is so large that it is unusual, but otherwise, it's just a business-as-usual sort of phenomenon—nothing that's particularly interesting or news).

- a controversy over your product or marketing techniques. However, the caution here is whether you will come out looking good in this controversy story. For example, a breakthrough product that's initially banned but then comes out looking like a rose can be good for you. But if the controversy is over the effectiveness of your product and the dissenters can't be immediately discredited, the article might do more damage than no news at all. Similarly, articles about the legitimacy of MLM can sometimes stir up a hornet's nest. So be sure the controversy or outcome of it is on your side, before you try to highlight this in any press materials.

- something unique or unusual about you in marketing this product (former physics professor decides to promote new diet breakthrough, formerly bankrupt business turns telephones into ready cash, etc.).
- a growing trend in your product category or in your business of which you are a part. Such an article will focus on the overall developments in this area, but then you can be featured as a key authority in the field or your product can be highlighted along with others in this category. (For example, "New protein powdered drinks sweep the diet market; score new gains in creating losses"; or "MLM businesses boom in response to coming recession"; etc.).

Again, the usual approach is to send a press release and then follow up a few days later, although some business editors and columnists may be accessible for a preliminary discussion in which you discuss a few possible article ideas and then send in your press materials, adapted based on this discussion of what the editor wants. (Also, another advantage of this discussion, if you can do this, is you can shape or tailor your material generally and send it to other editors in other areas, who might be interested in stories on this approach too.)

If you can, get the names of the current business editor or columnist for the paper. Or send any press materials to the "business editor" of that publication.

Still another possibility in some papers, most commonly those in smaller cities or towns, is to provide a guest column which you can write under your own byline (assuming you like to write, or maybe someone in your sales group can do this, or hire a ghost writer for about $50 to $100 to do a piece for you which you can then use in a number of publications. Just be sure that you only give the publication first time or one-time rights, permitting you to publish the same article elsewhere).

One business article I was able to arrange appeared as a feature in the San Francisco Chamber of Commerce's monthly business magazine. In this case, I happened to meet the editor who had a "People's Section" on local business-people doing interesting things and gave him some of the press materials we had prepared. He found the idea suffi-ciently interesting; so using my materials, a brief interview with me, and a photo taken by a photographer on assign-ment to the publication, he did the article.

FEATURE STORIES ABOUT YOUR PRODUCT OR SERVICE

The approach here is much like dealing with a busi-ness editor, except now you need a feature or people-oriented hook (which could combine a people orientation with business, as long as the people emphasis is strong). When in doubt, do separate releases so your approach is more targeted to the media section you want to reach. Just keep in mind that these releases will be going to the editors for sections with titles like "People," "Style," "Foods," "Of Women's Interest," and the like, and target your material accordingly.

Think about what may be uniquely appealing and of human interest about your product, company, or you. While some of the unique business angles may work here, too, think about nonbusiness benefits and features of your product that may make an interesting story. For example,

- "Campers lost in the woods survive on algae" (if you are selling diet nutritional tablets made of algae)

- "Peace groups use new program to promote peace" (if you are promoting some sort of product that is used as a fund-raiser by peace groups)
- "80-year old grandmother discovers new career in her backyard" (if you have someone in your sales group who is very old and successful)

Also, sometimes celebrities involved in a program may provide that special newshook that may interest features editors, although usually this works best in a smaller city or town where celebrity involvement is not so common or newsworthy. In big cities like Los Angeles, New York, or San Francisco, celebrity connections may not be newsworthy, unless there's some corporate hoopla coupled with a media blitz—not something you can normally do.

Again, use the press release with follow-up about a week later approach. As usual, note deadlines in sending these out if you want to tie the feature to any dated event. With newspapers, allow a week or two; with weekly papers, about two to three weeks; with monthly publications, about four to eight weeks.

As with business editors, get the names of the current feature editor for a particular section of the press if you can. Or address your press materials to the "Features Editor." Here, too, you may find there are guest columns where you might be able to submit an article, though again, the article must be informative, with any promotional material about you and your product or company at the end of the article. If you are marketing products in the health or foods area, these lend themselves especially to articles by you on this topic, and again, if you can't write it yourself, maybe a person in your sales group or a ghost writer can.

You'll see an example of a release I used for Glasnost on the following page. Note that I included names and phone numbers to contact, used the usual approach of beginning with the notice "For Immediate Release," and then included a headline featuring what I thought was currently most news-worthy. Also, I included a subhead for an added slant.

> Contact: Bobbi Randolph
> Elizabeth Reagh
> (415) 567-2747

FOR IMMEDIATE RELEASE

GLASNOST GAME GATHERS SUPPORT FROM OFFICIALS, GROUPS, AND INDIVIDUALS INVOLVED IN PROMOTING PEACE, CITIZEN DIPLOMACY, AND SOVIET-AMERICAN RELATIONS

"IT'S MORE THAN A GAME: IT'S A WAY OF CHANGING ATTITUDES AND PROMOTING PEACE AND UNDERSTANDING"

"GLASNOST is not only an interesting game, but it's beyond a game, because human relations and war and peace is not a game." Ken Kelley, journalist and interviewer who recently interviewed President-Elect George Bush.

"I think the game is helpful, because . . . this will help to introduce people, both children and adults alike, to the ideas and notions that our leaders have to deal with in their everyday lives and work." Gennady Zolotov, USSR Deputy Consul General, Soviet Consulate.

"We feel that this GLASNOST game is going to be a real breakthrough for the American public, and for the Soviet public, too. I think it is of great value because it encourages the exchange of ideas and debate, and it promotes the issue of peace, which is the issue of our times." John Garb, President, U.S.-U.S.S.R. Friendship Society of San Francisco.

These are just some of the comments made
at a recent press conference held at the Red Square
Night Club in San Francisco to launch GLASNOST:
THE GAME OF SOVIET-AMERICAN PEACE AND
DIPLOMACY. The game, published by the John N.
Hansen Company, Inc. of Millbrae, California, is now
in stores all over the country. It is also now being
used as a fund-raiser by individuals and groups
involved in promoting peace, citizen diplomacy,
and Soviet-American relations. Gennady Alferenko
of the Foundation for Social Inventions in Moscow
is currently arranging for production of the game
in the Soviet Union as a joint venture, and a book
on the Soviet Union by the creator of the game, Gini
Graham Scott of San Francisco, is now scheduled
for publication in 1989 by the New World Library
under the title: A CITIZEN DIPLOMAT IN THE
U.S.S.R.

Additionally, the trademark, art, and logo for
the game are being licensed by TM&C Licensing of
Florham Park, New Jersey. According to company
president Carolyn Caffrey, who has also handled the
licensing for Lionel Trains and Hasbro Industries:
"We see this image on the game box cover of the
Soviet and American hands shaking as a powerful
symbol of the new improved relations between the
two superpowers. This opening up of Soviet society
is something unique and historic, and we have had a
great deal of interest in licensing this image from
national manufacturers, since the American
consumer is responding to this trend to better
relations."

According to publisher John Hansen, who
appeared at the press conference, "Some very
exciting things are being planned for the game. It is
now being handled by our company's 23 showrooms
and 150 salesmen around the country, and a big
advertising promotion with F.A.O. Schwarz in

Washington, D.C. has just run as a national kick-off. Plans are also underway to produce the game in England next year."

The game's creator, Gini Graham Scott, who heads up Changemakers, says there has been a growing response to the company's grassroots marketing campaign, too. According to Scott: "My original idea for this game was to contribute to the growing desire for peace between the world's two great superpowers, and I have been gratified by the acceptance the game has achieved. I'm very, very pleased we have been able to initiate a network of distributors through educational organizations, new age companies, and individuals and groups working for peace and improved Soviet-American relationships. So far some of the individuals and groups involved in distributing the game include Jane Hauser of Beyond War, who is based in Walnut Creek; Chris McCluney of the Washington Research Institute/3220 Gallery in San Francisco; Gordon Fox of the Washington Council of American-Soviet Friendship in Seattle, Washington; Margaret Harlow of the Network of Women in Slavic Studies in Alexandria, Virginia; Victoria Litz of the Citizen Exchange Council in New York, New York; the U.S.-U.S.S.R. Friendship Society in San Francisco; and the No War Toys Coalition in San Francisco. I have also demonstrated the game at numerous conferences and meetings, including an exhibit and presentation at the Silicon Valley Entrepreneurs' Club in Santa Clara."

The advertising and packaging for the game has also been entered in the 1989 prestigious Clio Awards for originality in packaging.

For more details on the game, full transcripts from the kick-off press conference, interviews with the game designer, Gini Graham Scott, or

photographs of the game, press conference, or
Silicon Valley Entrepreneurs' Club exhibit, please
call (415) 567-2747.

• • • • •

A NEWS STORY

This is probably the hardest kind of story to get for a
product promotion. One possibility might be having a big,
special event—but it has to be very special to get any news
coverage, especially if you live in a big city where there is
lots of competing hard news. In a smaller city or town, however, you may have more luck, because there is less competition from local and national news. Another possibility if
there is some news angle about your product or company
itself is to have some kind of press party, to which you invite
the press.

In either case, you never know if you will get news coverage, because coverage depends on what else is going on at
the time. And even if it seems that you will have a good response to your advance reservations to your event or press
party, if something comes up at the last minute, there can go
your news coverage—though you can try to follow-up afterward with the people who expressed some interest initially
but then didn't come. Maybe they'll be willing to do some
special interview or story with you once other things calm
down.

In any case, you will still need a press release with a
headline highlighting the event or the press conference. Put
your details about what, why, how, where, and when in the
first paragraph, so you provide the gist of the event or press
conference and create some interest in being there. Then,
go on with the details and include any backup material
along with your press release, such as a flier or invitation to
the event or press conference. Also, if you've gotten any

previous clips that increase credibility or show interest in what you are doing, especially in the national media, include these.

FOR IMMEDIATE RELEASE   Contact: Bobbi Randolph
Elizabeth Reagh

GAME CELEBRATING GLASNOST GETS NATIONAL PRESS ATTENTION

KICK-OFF CELEBRATION TO BE HELD AT RED SQUARE

IN SAN FRANCISCO NOVEMBER 5 PRE-PARTY PRESS CONFERENCE 8–9 P.M.

A gala San Francisco send-off in the spirit of glasnost will be held to celebrate the new game with a Soviet theme: GLASNOST, which is now getting national attention, on Saturday, November 5th, just two days before the celebration of the Russian Revolution. It will be held appropriately enough at the Red Square, a Soviet-theme club at 1748 Haight Street on the 5th from 9 to 10 P.M.

There will be a press conference before the party from 8 to 9 P.M. It will include a representative from the Soviet Consulate, as well as the GLASNOST game designer, Gini Graham Scott, from San Francisco, and the game's artist and publisher, and officers of the U.S.-U.S.S.R. Friendship Society. Also present will be the editors and publishers from New World Library, which will be publishing Gini Graham Scott's new book on the Soviet Union next year: A CITIZEN DIPLOMAT IN THE U.S.S.R., and Sanford Kellman, owner of the Red Square, which features Russian decor, entertainment, videos, slides, and music every Tuesday and Saturday night.

The game, which has just been launched nationally, has recently been featured in The New York Times in an article on how America is suddenly discovering an interest in things Russian. The game has also gained praise from numerous individuals seeking to improve Soviet-American relations, including the Consul General of the Soviet Consulate in San Francisco, the President of the U.S.-U.S.S.R. Friendship Society of San Francisco, and representatives of the Soviet Peace Committee in Moscow. The game has been produced by Changemakers, a company in San Francisco devoted to making a change, and the John N. Hansen Company, Inc., of Millbrae, California, which is publishing and distributing the game nationally. The celebration on November 5th is being sponsored by Changemakers and the U.S.-U.S.S.R. Friendship Society.

In the GLASNOST game, players are Americans and Soviets involved in negotiating, debating, and engaging in business and cultural exchanges. The object of the game is to work towards peace, and players score by obtaining Peace Chips for themselves and their countries through getting pairs of Soviet and American Chips, that represent a balance of power. The game is designed to not only be fun and exciting, but to be educational and encourage players to think and talk about topics of current Soviet-American interest—everything from how the U.S. and Soviets can encourage more trade and tourism to what American TV programs would do well on Soviet TV.

The designer, Dr. Gini Graham Scott, has been to the Soviet Union twice with GLASNOST, once on a legal studies trip in 1987 which inspired the game, and most recently on a trip this past summer with a citizen diplomacy group, where she played and showed he game to dozens of Soviet citizens. A representative in the Soviet Union is arranging for production of the game in the U.S.S.R.

Besides GLASNOST, Scott has had over 24 games published with major companies, and she is the author of 15 books.

For further details on the game, to make reservations for the party, or to schedule interviews with Gini Graham Scott, please call (415) **387-1771.**

• • • • •

A good example of this approach is the Glasnost press party we set up at a local nightclub which was then featuring a Soviet theme. We also included clips from *The New York Times* and *Newsweek,* and we arranged for a number of prominent people to be at the event and make brief remarks at the press conference to give the event more clout. About a dozen press people showed up, and we even got a TV journalist who did a 2-minute segment for a big Soviet news program broadcast to about 18 million people. Then, that became an item that could be used in subsequent press releases about the game.

Note again the standard release format: "For Immediate Release," "Contact:," and a head, with a subhead explaining a little more about the event, and a subhead announcing the time of the press conference.

In the case of news releases, these should go to the local city editor of the larger papers in your area (on the order of a *San Francisco Chronicle* or *San Jose Mercury*), to the news editor of smaller daily and weekly papers, and to the news assignment editor of your local radio or TV stations. If you know the name of a local news editor, and there is only one news editor for a paper or other media in your area, use this. Otherwise, just sending the release to the editor by title is fine, since there may be different people who handle the news assignments depending upon when your event or press conference is scheduled.

Include any supporting material along with your release to build your credibility, such as clips from other areas or national media, if you have them. If there has been just a brief mention, use a red pen to highlight this with underlining, bracketing, or an arrow. I've included some examples from my own experience in doing this with the Glasnost game.

In the case of news releases, send it to arrive about a week to ten days for the print media and about three to four days in the case of radio and TV news. Again, follow up, in this case a day or two before the event or press conference to check if the media plans to send anyone to cover it. If they have lost or discarded the release, be prepared to give a brief, interesting description to spark their interest in the event, and then send the release again. Finally, do one last follow-up on the day of the event or press conference to reconfirm that people are coming, remind those who may have forgotten or pushed your event or press conference down in priority, and take one last shot at sparking the interest of anyone who may not have gotten your release or may have ignored it before.

A GENERAL ARTICLE OR PROGRAM IN ANY MEDIA QUOTING YOU AS THE EXPERT

Generally, you can get this kind of coverage by sending one of the other types of releases to the media, along with some general biographical information about you and a list of the types of topics where you might be quoted. Then, if the recipient has any interest in this, he or she may file your material for future reference.

*To contact Gini Graham Scott about
speaking, workshops, seminars, consulting, or other books and tapes, call
or write:*

> **Changemakers**
> **715 48th Avenue**
> **San Francisco, CA 94121**
>
> **(415) 387-1771**
> **FAX: (415) 387-1779**

INDEX